PRAISE FOR *A WILDERNESS OF MIRRORS*

The trouble with pessimism is that it isn't dark enough. Nor is optimism bright enough. *A Wilderness of Mirrors* takes us deep into the shadows of our culture of mistrust. With his unsparing look at recent history, Mark Meynell uncovers a relentless litany of examples, from dreamy-eyed hopes for international understanding to intelligence cover-ups, political campaigns based on fear, spin doctors, and the rest, leaving us convinced that things are far bleaker than we had imagined. But then the book follows with hope, a radically different kind of hope, brighter than we'd thought possible. The gospel commends proper suspicion, a Jesus subversive of established order, but especially love, the love of God that enables us to "love your crooked neighbor with your own crooked heart." Just as Ecclesiastes *and* the Gospel accounts belong in the biblical canon, so Meynell's fresh apologetic confronts us with both miserable desolation and great joy.

WILLIAM EDGAR, professor of apologetics at Westminster Theological Seminary

A Wilderness of Mirrors is a really good book — well researched, well written, and well worth reading. Mark Meynell does an excellent job of analyzing the skepticism of our age and showing there are good reasons for cynicism. However, he also shows us why the God of the Bible is utterly different and how we must learn to doubt our doubts if we are going to see God for who he truly is as the promise keeper. We've all struggled with trust, but Mark gives us a solid base from which we can learn to truly trust.

STEVE TIMMIS, executive director of Acts 29 Network

A Wilderness of Mirrors is born out of years of paying attention to the world. Remarkably adept at understanding the cross-Atlantic cultural complexities between the United Kingdom and the United States — and set within the complexity of globalization — Mark Meynell is as perceptive a reader of contemporary politics as he is of modern art. With his richly wrought theological vision and uncanny honesty, he offers a way forward for all who wrestle with how to form a good life in this disorienting time in history, where the more we know, the more cynical we must become. Here we are offered a hard-won, deeply thoughtful reason to believe otherwise.

STEVEN GARBER, The Washington Institute for Faith, Vocation, and Culture and author of *Visions of Vocation: Common Grace for the Common Good*

Leaders, experts, and institutions alike have abused us with their spin and self-serving manipulation so we no longer feel able to trust anyone. A *Wilderness of Mirrors* is a penetrating cultural critique that explains how and why trust has collapsed in our society. This is neither a simplistic nor an easy book, but it is profoundly challenging and will repay careful reading.

JOHN STEVENS, national director of FIEC
(Fellowship of Independent Evangelical Churches, UK)

It is easy to feel waterboarded in cynicism living in Washington, D.C. It is a city that houses leaders and journalists who are superb at crafting lies and deceit for personal gain. A *Wilderness of Mirrors* is a timely resource for anyone who finds life dominated by mistrust and suspicion. Mark Meynell's insights help us better understand not only why such cynicism is warranted, but how the gospel is the only reason for hope.

CHUCK GARRIOTT, the Presbyterian Church in
America's Ministry to State director, Washington, D.C.

In this profound book, Mark Meynell resists the temptation to tell us what to see in this illusory, fallen world. Instead he lays the groundwork that allows us, through faith, to perceive for ourselves. He isn't concerned with telling us *what* to think, but rather with providing insight into *how* to unravel for ourselves life's confusing inconsistencies.

MICHAEL CARD, singer, songwriter, and author

A *Wilderness of Mirrors* is a book that reads like a crime novel. Comprised of fast-turning pages and thorough research into the subject matter, it is a clear and accessible presentation of the argument. Mark Meynell's book comes as a welcome and needed contribution to the discourse about trust and trustworthiness as essential ingredients for the flourishing of society.

DR. KOSTA MILKOV, director of the Balkan Institute
for Faith and Culture in Skopje

A WILDERNESS OF
MIRRORS

A WILDERNESS OF
MIRRORS

TRUSTING AGAIN

IN A CYNICAL

WORLD

MARK MEYNELL

ZONDERVAN®

ZONDERVAN

A Wilderness of Mirrors
Copyright © 2015 by Mark Meynell

This title is also available as a Zondervan ebook. Visit www.zondervan.com/ebooks.

Requests for information should be addressed to:
Zondervan, 3900 *Sparks Dr. SE, Grand Rapids, Michigan 49546*

Library of Congress Cataloging-in-Publication Data

Meynell, Mark.
    A wilderness of mirrors : trusting again in a cynical world / Mark Meynell.
        pages   cm
    Includes bibliographical references.
    ISBN 978-0-310-51526-5 (softcover)
    1. Trust — Religious aspects — Christianity. 2. Integrity — Religious aspects —
Christianity. 3. Honesty. I. Title.
BV4597.53.T78M49   2015
261 — dc23   2014045435

All Scripture quotations, unless otherwise indicated, are taken from The Holy Bible, *New International Version*®, *NIV*®. Copyright © 1973, 1978, 1984, 2011 by Biblica, Inc.® Used by permission. All rights reserved worldwide.

Scripture quotations marked MSG are taken from *The Message*. Copyright © 1993, 1994, 1995, 1996, 2000, 2001, 2002. Used by permission of NavPress Publishing Group.

Cover design: DualIdentity
Cover photos: Shutterstock
Interior illustration: Alex Webb-Peploe
Interior design: Kait Lamphere

Printed in the United States of America

15 16 17 18 19 20 /DCI/ 21 20 19 18 17 16 15 14 13 12 11 10 9 8 7 6 5 4 3 2 1

For
Andrew Fellows
&
Gavin McGrath —
good friends
who get me
as much as they get this stuff

CONTENTS

CONTENTS

FOREWORD

I was once asked to write an article for a magazine in India, during the time we lived there in the 1980s, on the topic "Why I am a Christian." I remember the headings went something like, "Because being a Christian is satisfying, because it is secure, and because it makes sense." I was trying to express how my Christian faith not only gave me personal fulfillment along with the security of eternal salvation, but it also made intellectual and explanatory sense of the world we live in. That third point came back to mind as I read Mark Meynell's intriguing book.

It makes sense to me, I wrote, that this universe is not merely the product of inexplicable chance, but rather the creation of the personal, powerful, and loving God of the Bible. It makes sense to me that the mess the world is in is due not merely to lack of progress, ignorance, or any of the myriad inadequate diagnoses and remedies that humanity has spawned, but rather to a fundamental moral rebellion against the very source of our humanity and our rejection of God's benevolent authority in God's own world—the Bible's radical analysis of sin. Anything less is naive and fails to make sense of reality as we know it. It makes sense to me that the God who created such a wonderful world should, out of love, choose not to destroy but to redeem it through Jesus of Nazareth and his incarnation, death, resurrection, and ascension. And it makes sense to me that the God who promised and accomplished all of that in biblical history would not (will not) leave the whole project unfinished, but will finish the story in the full restoration of creation envisaged by Isaiah, Paul, and John of Patmos.

It is that story that makes sense, because it is the gospel story of the mission of God, and it drives our own mission in the world. That is the story, and the Person, we can trust in a world where trust is crushed under cynicism, abuse, irony, and conspiracy theories.

Mark Meynell's exceptionally perceptive and well-researched critique of our culture exposes how the loss of trust at every level of society reflects the loss of any capacity to "make sense" of "life, the universe, and everything"— which in turn is the result of the deliberate rejection of any story that could offer such universal "sense" after the manifest failure of the modernity "story." It seems we can only trust if we have confidence that both the story on offer and the one who is inviting us to share in that story are themselves trustworthy and hold some guarantee of a good ending. Part 3 of this book compellingly claims that the whole-Bible gospel narrative provides exactly such a confidence, as a hard-won word of hope in a "wilderness of mirrors," a call to trust again, and a motivation for a biblically rooted, authentic, and humbly confident mission by God's people in God's world.

Christopher J.H. Wright,
Langham Partnership,
author of The Mission of God
and The Mission of God's People

PART 1

FRACTURING TRUST:

THE LEGACY FOR OUR AGE

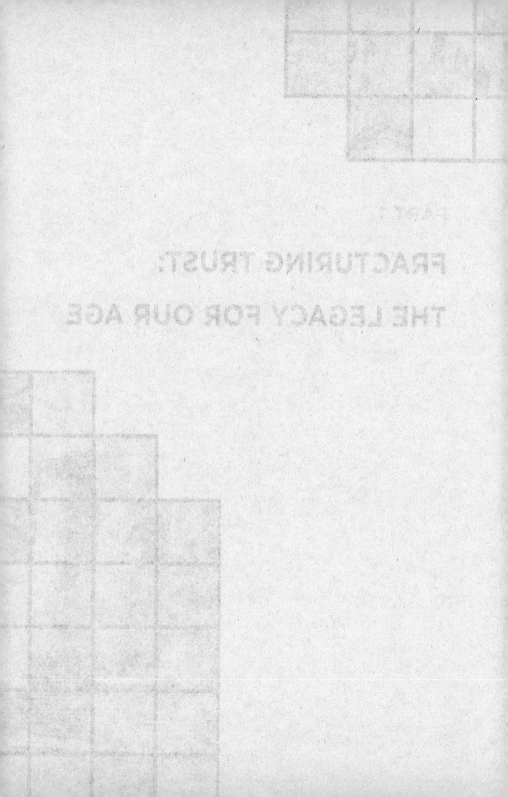

Things fall apart; the centre cannot hold;
Mere anarchy is loosed upon the world,
The blood-dimmed tide is loosed, and everywhere
The ceremony of innocence is drowned;
The best lack all conviction, while the worst
Are full of passionate intensity.
  William Butler Yeats, "The Second Coming"

... if way to the Better there be, it exacts
a full look at the Worst.
  Thomas Hardy, "In Tenebris II"

INTRODUCTION

THE STATE WE'RE IN

Optimists seem thin on the ground these days. Sadly, I am not talking about the temperamentally buoyant; they are, thankfully, in plentiful supply. I mean amongst those with a reasonable grasp of modern cultural trends. Optimism in the face of these challenges seems as ludicrous as the crucifixion chorus in *Monty Python's Life of Brian*, with its singsong tenacity in always looking "on the bright side of life."

Nevertheless, this book is self-consciously optimistic. But only in the end! We must traverse some rugged terrain before that point, exacting, to appropriate Thomas Hardy, "a full look at the Worst." For things do *feel* different now ...

Human beings have always deceived and been deceived; conspirators have always hatched plots; spies have always made others' business their own. Such things have always occurred around centers of power. This gives history its spice—otherwise, what would there be to entice historians to trawl the long-forgotten antics of past generations? So perhaps the only surprise today, as contemporary plots and betrayals are frequently unearthed, is that people are still surprised.

But it *feels* different now. The West in the early years of the twenty-first century seems afflicted by a deeper, more corrosive cultural mood than previously. It affects the street and the academy, the private and the public, politics, the arts, and the media. We no longer seem willing to trust those in power. We no longer instinctively respect the institutions we once revered. We seem inured to betrayals of trust and fear commitments of any kind, whether personal or political.

As part of an Ipsos MORI poll published in February 2013, more than one thousand people in the United Kingdom were asked whom (from a list of various professions) they would trust to tell the truth.[1] The table below shows the results:

Professions	Expected to Tell the Truth
Doctors	89 percent
Teachers	86 percent
Scientists	83 percent
Judges	82 percent
Estate Agents/Realtors	24 percent
Members of Parliament	23 percent
Bankers and journalists	21 percent
Politicians generally	18 percent

An even worse story can be told across the Atlantic. In June 2014, Americans were asked to identify whether they had "a great deal," "quite a lot," "some," or "very little" confidence in named institutions.[2] The only groups with a combined "a great deal" and "quite a lot" score of more than 50 percent were the military, schools, and the police (and even these three only just scraped past the halfway point). At the other end of the spectrum, the picture was dire:

Institutions	A great deal	Quite a lot
Newspapers	12 percent	10 percent
Big business	9 percent	12 percent
Television news	10 percent	8 percent
Congress	4 percent	3 percent

Now, statements to pollsters do not necessarily reflect behavior. People still vote, still buy houses through agents, still save in banks, albeit with varying degrees of reluctance. This is not to deny a problem, however; it matters if people *say* they do not trust. Philosopher Onora O'Neill made this point well in her 2002 BBC Reith Lectures: "We may not have evidence for a crisis of trust; but we have massive evidence of a culture of suspicion."[3] She warns that the "supposed crisis of trust may even, if things go badly, lead to a genuine crisis of trust."[4]

Such festering sores threaten the health of civilized society. How can people live together if they no longer trust one another? Trust takes years to build, but seconds to destroy. Or as the Dalai Lama remarked in 1980 about his interminable Tibet negotiations with Beijing, "Frankly speaking, it is difficult to believe or trust the Chinese. Once bitten by a snake, you feel suspicious even when you see a piece of rope."[5] Perception and memory are everything; logic can have little to do with it.

A Perfect Storm?

Just as reconciliation and renewed trust in postapartheid South Africa were inconceivable without the truth (however grisly), so the inescapable task must be to face the grievances and betrayals behind our current predicament. Of course, attempting to articulate the mood of a society, let alone the whole of the West, is formidable and perhaps futile. I do not presume to undertake it. Instead, I merely seek to sketch conspicuous trends, drawing threads together from my own observations and the scholarship of others.

What does seem apparent is that in the second decade of this twenty-first century, we are still struggling to come to terms with the fraught legacy of the previous one. It has become commonplace to say that 9/11 changed the world forever; it was a sickening turning point. Nevertheless, it arguably only exacerbated rather than transformed the cultural tendencies that preceded it.

As we will see, one of their common features is our expectation of betrayal. Arthur Ponsonby is credited with being the first to observe that "when war is declared, truth is the first casualty."[6] But the greater legacy of the last century is a consequent casualty, namely, *trust*. While the annals of human history are littered with tyrants, wars, and migrations, no period can compare with the last century's industrialization of oppression and brutality. Humanity has never before witnessed such an accumulation of power over so many by so few, nor the sheer scale of its abuses. The combined death toll of the Nazi, Soviet, and Maoist regimes alone is incalculable. Is it surprising if subsequent generations are nervous of political demagoguery?

These anxieties have converged with what might be called a perfect storm of uncertainty. Responding to the horrors perpetrated in the name of strident ideologies, thinkers rejected the very possibility of authoritative frameworks or "metanarratives."[7] This condemned us to, or liberated us for (depending on your perspective), the limitless possibilities of personal choice.

Add to this heady cocktail our heightened guardedness about spin and media manipulation, is it any wonder that conspiracy theories hold an appeal greater than ever before? After the Cold War, Watergate, and, more recently, WikiLeaks, we live in a world of shadows. Shadows are insubstantial yet full of foreboding. The problem is, how do we respond to them? It feels like trying to staple mercury. Yet the greater our sense of unease, the greater our yearning for more substance.

The agony is that we no longer trust the time-honored safe havens. For example, the church seems as tainted as any other institution, and its message as dangerous as any grand narrative. This book is therefore an attempt to probe the shadows, to assess some of the prevailing assumptions and anxieties of our time head-on, and to fumble toward some solid ground. The hope is that in holding to a spirit of orthodoxy, we can take care to throw out the bathwater without inadvertently discarding the proverbial babies.

I should say at the outset that this is no academic conundrum, but a very personal quest. It began with an idle conversation about the moon landings. A friend was convinced the entire Apollo program was history's most elaborate hoax, and nothing would persuade him otherwise. Around that same time, British politicians were making headlines in 2009's parliamentary expenses scandal. This caused the public's respect for politicians to plummet to record depths, which felt to me only partially justified. I knew, for a fact, that at least *some* had integrity. Yet no one seemed to be having that.

However, the most personal aspect of this matter derives from a personal battle with depression dating back to my years working in Uganda. The triggers have been occasions of betrayal by some of the individuals or institutions I relied on the most. So in many ways, this book's journey has been my own. But it is a journey many others have walked as well, as we'll see in the graphic illustration that appears at various points in this book.

The first section analyzes the last century's legacy of mistrust, demonstrating how a culture of suspicion inexorably infects everything in its wake. Opening with the big picture of the trustworthiness of ruling authorities (focusing on the nation-state in the twentieth century), we descend via those who mediate reality to us (through political spin, advertising, and the media) down to the micro level (focusing on betrayals by caregivers, including the church).

The second section considers some of the consequences of untrammeled suspicion. A brief personal digression (reflecting on some of my own experiences of betrayal) is followed by an exploration of two of the most serious social consequences, namely, paranoia and alienation.

The third and longest section considers a Christian theological response, while fully acknowledging some of the controversy in doing so. For the contention in this book is that, despite the general problems with metanarratives, the Christian framework continues to offer our culture a viable escape from what we shall see as a wilderness of mirrors.

Theirs not to make reply,
Theirs not to reason why,
Theirs but to do and die.

*Alfred, Lord Tennyson, "Charge
of the Light Brigade"*

When the president does it, that means it is not illegal.

*Richard Nixon, thirty-seventh president
of the United States*

CHAPTER 1

WHERE THE BUCK STOPS!
Rulers Have Failed Us

If hindsight offers the delusion of historical inevitability, the future offers the mirage of infinite possibility. We easily forget that while the past is now "fixed," it never was while options were weighed and choices made. The world then lives with the consequences. What our generation tends to overlook, whether willfully or not, is that our options are *inevitably* shaped by the past. History matters. Always.

Unfortunately, this gets ignored. Behind the closed doors of deliberations in the run-up to the 2003 Iraq War, a senior Middle East expert, Dr. Michael Williams, was briefing Prime Minister Tony Blair. He explained the generations-old tensions and deep divisions inherent within Iraqi society, as well as why occupying Westerners might not be altogether welcomed. "Blair casually brushed him aside: 'That's all history, Mike. This is about the future.'"[1]

The major flaws in the Iraq War process were perhaps exposed at that very moment. The prime minister revealed not simply an ignorance but a spurning of history, as if an invasion (to bring "Iraqi freedom") could inaugurate a "Year Zero."[2] A decade later, that sounds naive at best, culpably irresponsible at worst. How can we possibly imagine the past is irrelevant to our present or future? Even a cursory glance at foreign involvement in the Middle East suggests that the arrival of Western tanks might have less than propitious resonances.[3] We despise history at our peril.

That is not to deny the appeal, however. The study of history is fraught with difficulty; its lessons are rarely comforting; it rarely serves simplistic sound bites or ideological agendas. So, as the German Hasselbacher says to his English friend Wormold, protagonist of Graham Greene's exquisite satire

Our Man in Havana, "You should dream more, Mr. Wormold. Reality in our century is not something to be faced."[4]

Nevertheless, this chapter's purpose is to deliberately face that reality. Contemporary disillusionment with the powerful has not arisen spontaneously. What follows, then, is an arbitrary trawl of a few episodes from what Walker Percy described as "the most scientifically advanced, democratic, inhuman, sentimental, murderous century in human history."[5]

Intransigent Leadership:
The Officer Class and the Trenches (1914 – 1918)

The last century dawned with many grounds for optimism. Scientific and technological advances, for example, were gaining momentum. Although United States Commissioner of Patents Charles Duell had reportedly claimed that "everything that can be invented has been invented," his opinion in 1902 was, in fact, very different: "All previous advances in the various lines of invention will appear totally insignificant when compared with those which the present century will witness."[6]

Had he lived, he would not have been disappointed. Consider the wonders of eradicating smallpox, the might of microchips, and the triumph of the moon landings, to name but three. However, the ends to which even these technological innovations would be put were not always so benign.

In 1912, August Bebel, leader of Germany's Social Democratic Party (SDP), made a prophetic speech in the Reichstag:

> "There will be a catastrophe … sixteen to eighteen million men, the flower of different nations, will march against each other, equipped with lethal weapons. But I am convinced that this great march will be followed by the great collapse [at this moment many in the chamber began to laugh] — all right, you have laughed about this before; but it will come … What will be the result? After this war we shall have mass bankruptcy, mass misery, mass unemployment, and great famine."
>
> The record states that his words were drowned out by mocking laughter. A right-wing deputy called out, "Herr Bebel, things always get better after every war!"[7]

Bebel died the following year. But as historian Frederick Taylor proceeds to comment, "Another year after that, booming, brilliant Berlin would be a city at war. A city of hunger. A city of despair." Bebel had seen that humanity, not just Germany, would suffer.

The statistics from just three key World War I battles prove the point:

- The First Battle of the Marne (September 1914) offered the bitter firstfruits of the reaping to come. Barbara Tuchman described how it had sucked up lives "at the rate of 5,000 and sometimes 50,000 a day, absorbing munitions, energy, money, brains, and trained men."[8]

- The Battle of the Somme (July–November 1916) caused the "prodigal spending of lives by all the belligerents that was to mount and mount in senseless excess."[9] On the opening day alone, the British army suffered its worst day in its history, with 60,000 casualties. By its conclusion, the Allies had suffered over 650,000 casualties and the Central Powers, 450,000.[10] And the dividend from this exorbitant expense? An advance of roughly seven miles.

- Calculating the statistics for the Battle of Passchendaele (July–November 1917) is even more fraught than for other battles, but recent studies suggest both sides lost roughly a quarter of a million men.[11]

The difficulty with such figures is that they leave us dazed and uncomprehending. More disturbingly, they even seem paltry compared to the horrors of the next world war: six million Jews killed in the Holocaust; perhaps as many as twenty-seven million perished in the Soviet Union (roughly ninety times the number of United States casualties).[12] We might try to imagine the impact on individual families in order to personalize it a little (for example, members from both sides of my own family were cut down in the trenches). But ultimately, how can we ever grasp the colossal scale of this waste? Such is the horrifying legacy of warfare's industrialization. This slaughter could never have been accomplished by ships of the line and siege engines, let alone by arrows or muskets. Technological advances seemed merely to offer military strategists greater scope for carnage.

No wonder survivors spoke so vociferously against it. Any residual Victorian deference lay slain in the sea of Flanders' freshly dug graves. There genuinely was a sense that "lions had been led by donkeys,"[13] no matter how just the war aims might have been or how unfair the criticism.

Despite not leaving school until 1921, George Orwell sensed that the conflict's effect went far wider than on those (like him) on the political left. Because the war had been conducted mainly by "old men ... with supreme incompetence," everyone under forty was consequently "in a bad temper with his elders, and the mood of anti-militarism which followed naturally upon the fighting was extended into a general revolt against orthodoxy and authority

... The dominance of 'old men' was held to be responsible for every evil known to humanity."[14] D. H. Lawrence echoed him: "All the great words were cancelled out for that generation."[15] The halcyon days of pre-1914 (such as they were) could never be retrieved.

Few articulated this disaffection more poignantly than the war poets. Some, like Rupert Brooke and Siegfried Sassoon, had lived privileged lives prior to the war. Sassoon, for instance, had a private income sufficiently large to sustain a charmed lifestyle of hunting, cricket, and writing verse. As its beneficiaries, these were the men most likely to defend the status quo. Trench warfare, mustard gas, and shell shock shattered all that.

Here, Sassoon gazes back in his mind's eye from his trench to the lofty command posts. But he had the moral authority to write like this. He had been awarded the Military Cross for "conspicuous gallantry" in 1916 and then found himself in hospital the following year.

The General
(Denmark Hill Hospital, April 1917)
"Good-morning; good-morning!" the General said
When we met him last week on our way to the line.
  Now the soldiers he smiled at are most of 'em dead,
  And we're cursing his staff for incompetent swine.
"He's a cheery old card," grunted Harry to Jack
  As they slogged up to Arras with rifle and pack
    ...
But he did for them both by his plan of attack.[16]

How had it come to this?

All leaders shoulder formidable burdens. The higher they climb, the weightier they become. Many must rue the day their ambitions propelled them toward high office, and only those who have experienced similar burdens can understand it. A White House staffer for three presidents described the moment when "confident men realize what they've gotten themselves into."

When you get in, you discover nothing is what you expect, or believed, or have been told, or have campaigned on ... It's much more complicated. Your first reaction is: *I've been set up*. Second is: *I have to think differently*. Third is: *Maybe they had it right*. And it isn't long before they ask, who am I gonna talk to about *this*?[17]

What is true of presidents is surely also true of all but the most conceited chief executives. And generals.

The complexity of warfare on a continental scale always makes it unpredictable (a good reason by itself for maintaining war as the last resort). Even Adolf Hitler recognized that. "The beginning of a war is always like opening a door onto a darkened room. You never know what's hiding in there," he apparently declared.[18] Yet complexity hardly even begins to explain such catastrophic loss of life. One factor must surely have been the culture of leadership itself, which could be absurdly blimpish. For example, one World War I German general, Max von Hausen, simply could not comprehend "the hostility of the Belgian people," despite the occupation of their supposedly neutral country! He even assumed that aristocratic etiquette would trump national resentment, harrumphing when the hospitality at the D'Eggremont family château to which he was billeted was less than lavish.[19]

Then, as the war progressed, commanders displayed a stubborn inability to learn from the experiences of 1914. Strategies ossified; the slaughter escalated. Yet still the French marshal Ferdinand Foch stuck rigidly to his tactics, because, "there is only one way of defending ourselves — to attack as soon as we are ready." So, "for *four more years* of relentless, merciless, useless killing the belligerents beat their heads against it."[20] This was even after the Battle of Morhange (August 1914), which had "snuffed out the bright flame of the doctrine of the offensive. It died on a field in Lorraine where at the end of the day nothing was visible but corpses strewn in rows and sprawled in the awkward attitudes of sudden death as if the place had been swept by a malignant hurricane."[21]

Foch was certainly not the only stubborn commander. The Allies eventually won through some tactical advantages, through General Douglas Haig's deliberate policy of conquest by attrition, and through the arrival of the United States. But ultimately, it was because the Central Powers were exhausted and depleted first.

People tried to steer the strategists away, of course. Officers in the field tried to communicate their impressions to senior staff, but if reports did not conform to the prevailing military theories, they were routinely ignored. Even the British prime minister, David Lloyd George, failed to have Haig dismissed. After the Battle of Passchendaele, he remarked that "Haig does not care how many men he loses. He just squanders the lives of these boys."[22] The general survived, largely because he had inveigled the full support of the king, George V.[23] But for many, he personified the intransigence of the old guard.

Tuchman's observation that "the impetus of existing plans is always stronger than the impulse to change" has been rightly applied to many different contexts.[24] But when it results in carnage, it is a tragedy. Yet Flanders' fields would not be the last setting to witness it. The rubbled suburbs of Stalingrad and the sweltering jungles of Vietnam would reverberate with echoes of the same charge.

Popular perceptions were clear: Grand strategists think little of ordinary lives, and even when they do, they are too often reluctant or unable to modify plans to fluctuating circumstances.

You just can't trust them.

Secretive Leadership: Woodrow Wilson and the League of Nations (1918 – 1920)

There is nothing quite like the frisson of being sworn to secrecy. It automatically grants status. In matters of state, the more secrets you know, the more powerful you are. It is also what motivates some to become spies or journalists (or both), with perhaps the primary difference being the size of intended audience. Secrecy is its own intoxicant.

There is no room for naiveté here. Some secrecy is inescapable in leadership. One argument against total transparency is that it renders truth telling about politically toxic questions almost impossible. This was precisely why Tony Blair regretted pushing freedom of information legislation through Parliament. He regarded that as one of his two greatest errors (the other being the ban on fox hunting!). If every position paper or deliberation is subject to subsequent disclosure, Blair concluded that people will "watch what they put in writing and talk without committing to paper. It's a thoroughly bad way of analyzing complex issues."[25]

Yet the drawbacks are obvious. Cynics quickly retort, "Well, he *would* argue that, wouldn't he?" Secrecy *can* become the locked door behind which illegal or immoral plots are hatched, as conspiracy theorists constantly remind us. Isn't this the reason that mature political systems seek to constitute checks and balances, even if these must occasionally be hidden from view?

Furthermore, voters are unnerved by the thought of hidden deals that will have calamitous consequences for them. For example, the details of a nation's foreign policy are rarely the subject of election manifestos (apart from vague commitments), and so they tend to be decided by a precious few. The First World War is again a case in point.

It seemed extraordinary then, and even more so a century later, that the assassination of an Austrian prince by a Serb in a Bosnian city would plunge the *whole world* into war. Yet because of an impenetrable web of international alliances, the various European powers were sucked in one by one — the Triple Entente (the series of agreements between France, Britain, and Russia that ballooned into an alliance incorporating the United States and others) on one side, and the Central Powers (the German, Austro-Hungarian, and Ottoman Empires) on the other. It would entirely deserve the biting satire of this *Horrible Histories* school playground setting:

> And so a Serbian gang known as the Black Hand (honest!) waited till the Emperor [or rather his heir] came to Bosnia ...
>
> The first stone had been thrown. Austria declared war on Serbia, and Germany helped Austria so Russia helped Serbia so France helped Russia. Germany marched through Belgium to get to France so Britain helped Belgium.
>
> The First World War had started. It was expected to last about four months but it lasted for four frightful years.[26]

Having taken the United States into the war in 1917, President Woodrow Wilson felt responsible for fashioning the peace. Even before his 1916 reelection, he was analyzing how Europe had degenerated so fast. A leading cause was the secrecy of these alliances. He argued in May 1916 that this is why the war began "without warning to the world, without discussion, without any of the deliberate movements of counsel with which it would seem natural to approach so stupendous a contest."[27]

It's not hard to sympathize. Surely, talking is better than killing, isn't it? This was what drove Wilson's passionate advocacy for the new League of Nations (for which he won the 1919 Nobel Peace Prize), forerunner of the United Nations. "It will be our wish and purpose," said Wilson, "that the processes of peace, when they are begun, shall be absolutely open and that they shall involve and permit henceforth no secret understandings of any kind."[28] He went on to outline the famous fourteen-point program of peace, of which his first point was this: "Open covenants of peace, openly arrived at, after which there shall be no private international understandings of any kind, but diplomacy shall proceed always frankly and in the public view."[29]

It was a fine aspiration. Indeed, it was central to the founding philosophy of the United States itself. Thomas Jefferson feared that secrecy was detrimental to the republic's political health, because transparency enabled "the contest of opinion" in contrast to the secret mysteries of monarchy.[30] During that same period, English political philosopher Jeremy Bentham argued,

"Secrecy is an instrument of conspiracy ... It ought not, therefore, to be the system of a regular government."[31]

Woodrow Wilson's idealism seems hopelessly naive today. Many might still strive for such goals. But the common perception is that decisions affecting entire populations are made by unaccountable people (with or without political leaders) in secret rooms. Isn't this what fans the flames of conspiracy theories? Without transparency, the likes of the World Economic Forum in Davos, Switzerland, or the Bilderburg Group, or Yale's Skull and Bones society are always going to fall under suspicion.

Unfortunately, an irreversible step was taken on June 18, 1948. President Harry Truman signed NSC 10/2, an executive order that mandated the newly formed CIA to carry out operations in such a way that "if uncovered the U.S. government can plausibly disclaim any responsibility for them."[32] As Timothy Melley notes, this "institutionalized not simply secret warfare but also public deception as a fundamental element of U.S. policy."[33]

Shifting Leadership: Raids over Berlin (1945–1949)

In the immediate aftermath of Nazi Germany's defeat, the country was divided into four sectors by the victorious Allies—the United States, United Kingdom, France, and USSR. But it did not take long for the alliance to teeter. Tensions and quibbles swiftly degenerated into the old prewar suspicion and second-guessing. Less than a year after Victory in Europe (VE) Day, Winston Churchill gave his famous "Iron Curtain" speech in Fulton, Missouri. While being careful to acknowledge the valiant efforts of the Russians during the war, he warned of impending Communist control throughout the East, and especially in Germany. "This is certainly not the Liberated Europe we fought to build up," he declared.[34]

The problem was Berlin. The capital was itself divided into the same four sectors, but the whole city was situated deep inside the Russian zone and was thus surrounded. As relations deteriorated, West Berlin became a flashpoint. The Soviet Union blockaded all land and river access in 1948, in advance of seizing control over the whole city. Against all odds, the Allies managed to keep West Berlin supplied from the air, with more than 275,000 flights in one year.[35] The blockade was thwarted, and so the USSR lifted it the following year. The now inevitable path to two Germanys was paved.

Within the blink of an eye, enemies were to be defended at all costs and allies thwarted at every turn. But many must have found the sudden volte-face hard to reconcile with their grief after the war. Novelist John le Carré suggests that the about-face even felt like a betrayal to some:

> It's quite amazing the betrayals which historical reversal thrusts upon us, and so very many of my characters are the victims of an accelerated history that we live through. They are left-over men, the no-man of no-man's land, who have tried and simply become exhausted; have tried to toe the line and been defeated.[36]

The only defense against these twists and turns is often a resigned, dark humor. Just shrug at the absurdity of events beyond our control, like this unnamed drinker in an East Berlin bar, days after the wall fell in 1989. "So … they built the Wall to stop people leaving, and now they're tearing it down to stop people leaving. There's logic for you."[37]

Of course, it is unfair to blame governments for changing policies. Circumstances inevitably change. History reminds us never to hold too unswervingly to old allegiances and to be wary of the hasty demonization of an enemy. The great Victorian British prime minister Viscount Palmerston acknowledged this in the House of Commons: "We have no eternal allies, and we have no perpetual enemies. Our interests are eternal and perpetual, and those interests it is our duty to follow."[38]

Consider Afghanistan. Not too long ago, CIA operatives were training and supplying Mujahideen fighters in their struggle against Soviet occupation, as highlighted by the 2007 Tom Hanks film, *Charlie Wilson's War*.[39] They even distributed ten thousand Qur'ans in Central Asia, using religion to "undermine the godless Soviets."[40] Geopolitical priorities might have changed drastically in 1989, but Afghans still had enemies to fight. Their own targets shifted as many coalesced into the Taliban, funded and trained by none other than Al Qaeda. But Al Qaeda would not reach global consciousness until that bright, terrible September day in 2001. Even more recently, politicians were rapidly changing their tunes about President Assad of Syria, once the realpolitik of contending with ISIL (the Islamic State of Iraq and the Levant) presented a far greater threat.[41]

Yesterday my enemy's enemy was my friend. But when my enemy ceases to be my enemy, my old friends may cease to be strategic. My old enemy's enemy might then become my own enemy. That is confusing, to say the least. But then, even a modicum of historical awareness always leaves one disoriented. No wonder propagandists are so selective in their use of history.

Conspiring Leadership:
The Paris Summit and the Spy Plane (1959–1960)

The Cold War was an espionage war, which perhaps was precisely what prevented it from becoming hot.[42] Despite the contrived shock when moles were unearthed, the CIA and KGB (together with their cobelligerents) were stalking each other across the world in great numbers. In 1959, the Soviets calculated that West Berlin was the home of forty-eight espionage, "terror," and propaganda organizations. The generally accepted estimate of Communist agents working from East Germany at the same time was sixty thousand.[43]

Central to America's espionage arsenal was its most costly gadget — the U-2 spy plane. It required nerve and skill to fly, especially at its operational altitude of over seventy thousand feet. It was crucial, however, to the U.S.'s desire in the 1950s to chart Soviet weapons capabilities. The problem was that President Dwight Eisenhower prided himself on not having "to stoop to Soviet-style practices like espionage."[44]

Then the unthinkable happened: A U-2 was shot down — on (of all days) May Day 1960, the celebration of all things Communist. Soviet Premier Nikita Khrushchev was informed while the Red Square parade was actually in progress. Assumed to be secure because it flew far higher than combat aircraft, pilot Francis Gary Powers's aircraft was brought down by a flukily accurate surface-to-air missile. Engineers had assumed that survival from such heights was impossible, but Powers was caught and taken to the KGB's infamous Lubyanka prison.

Subsequent developments played further into Soviet hands. Unaware of the pilot's fate, Washington attempted to preempt political discomfort with official statements. So on May 3, NASA released a cover story approved by Eisenhower, announcing that a plane "making high-altitude weather studies" in Turkey had experienced difficulties.[45] It could then be spun as a fatal accident. They even issued a photograph of another U-2 hastily repainted in NASA livery.

Khrushchev relished the spectacle of Washington digging deeper into the deception. At precisely the right moment, he produced the evidence with a conjurer's flourish — not just the plane's wreckage 1,300 miles *inside* USSR airspace, but the pilot himself, alive and well. Eisenhower was forced to come clean. He later recalled, "I didn't realize how high a price we were going to have to pay for that lie. And if I had to do it over again, we would have kept our mouths shut."[46] This time, the operation's deniability was not plausible at all.

The absurdities were many. Both sides were spying on the other. Both sides *knew* they were spying on each other. That was implicit in the deal less than two years later to swap Powers for notorious Russian spy Rudolf Abel on Berlin's Glienicke Bridge. But even more bizarrely, Russia had been fully aware of every one of the U-2 overflights.[47] Diplomatic etiquette demanded that such things never be acknowledged, however, which led to Washington's string of deceits. The point is not that they were worse than Moscow's. The shock for many Westerners was that they were *not better.* "The idea that their leaders might lie was new to the American people. There were no serious consequences for Eisenhower, however: he would soon be leaving office."[48]

The consequences for the wider world were quite a different matter. The much-heralded Four Powers Paris Summit, scheduled to start on May 15, 1960, was now completely undermined. It was to be the first time the U.S., USSR, UK, and France had met at this level for five years. It could have led to significant détente and arms reduction. Instead, ostensibly because Eisenhower refused to apologize for the U-2 mission, Khrushchev left after only a day.

There could be no escaping the facts. The world now knew for certain what previously had only been assumed: Despite assurances to the contrary, states conspire in secret.

Manipulative Leadership:
Kennedy versus Nixon (1960)

The intelligence community is easy to disparage, but that is perhaps unwise. At its best, it forms a crucial component of a nation's defense. Winston Churchill, for one, put great store by it; he can claim high credit for encouraging the quirky genius of British wartime espionage. Without the cracking of the Nazi Enigma codes at Bletchley Park, history would have been very different. Since then, we will never know the number of plots foiled by the FBI or CIA, MI5 or SIS. The cliché that secret services enable ordinary citizens to sleep safely in their beds at night contains more than a grain of grim truth.

The U-2 program is a case in point. It was invaluable, because "the U-2 photographs quickly confirmed the limited size and inferior capabilities of the Soviet long-range bomber force."[49] But its discontinuation after the Powers debacle did not just have military importance.

The year 1960 was the year of the Nixon/Kennedy presidential race.

The catchy formula "missile gap" (the U.S. government's perception that the Soviet Union had more missles than the U.S.) was politically potent, and Kennedy exploited it to the full.[50] For the West's worst fears had been aroused in 1957 by the Soviets' launch of Sputnik 1, Earth's first artificial satellite. Then, within six months of Kennedy's election, Colonel Yuri Gagarin would become the first man in space. The "missile gap" appeared to fit the facts.

The truth was that the imbalance lay in the opposite direction, namely, that the USSR lagged *far behind*. Had the U-2 overflights been completed, there would have been ample evidence for this, which could then have been used to refute the Democrats' rhetoric. This matters because of the closeness of the popular vote in the 1960 election. Kennedy defeated Nixon by only 0.17 percent (or just over one hundred thousand votes).[51] Counterfactual history is fraught, but it is not hard to imagine the balance tipping in Nixon's favor had Kennedy been forced to withdraw his "missile gap" rhetoric. One historian certainly thinks that "Kennedy owed Powers," and that "a journeyman American pilot and a dutiful Russian antiaircraft gunner [had] unfashionably large roles in world affairs."[52]

Nevertheless, Kennedy had made a shrewd political calculation (as all candidates must), sensing the value in portraying incumbent Republicans as weak on defense in the nuclear age. Fear is a powerful motivator. When people subsequently discover it was aroused needlessly and falsely, is it any wonder that cynicism grows? And it is a phenomenon that is not exactly unknown in our day.

This is one reason that the preparations for the Iraq War are now viewed with such fury. On September 24, 2002, British prime minister Tony Blair presented findings from the UK's intelligence service's "September dossier" to the House of Commons,[53] asserting there was clear evidence of Saddam Hussein's weapons of mass destruction:

> [The dossier] concludes that Iraq has chemical and biological weapons, that Saddam has continued to produce them, that he has existing and active military plans for the use of chemical and biological weapons, which could be activated within 45 minutes, including against his own Shia population, and that he is actively trying to acquire nuclear weapons capability.[54]

This influenced President George W. Bush and led to characteristically punchy headlines in Rupert Murdoch's *The Sun*: "He's got 'em ... let's get him" and "Brits 45 mins from doom: Cyprus [site of a major British base] within missile range." The extent to which the government knew these claims to be false at the time is highly contentious. It was certainly later regretted by many.[55] It rendered the situation far more alarming than it was and fueled claims that Blair used this dossier to bolster public support for an unpopular war.

The common perception was thus that war with Saddam was the goal regardless of the evidence, and that what little intelligence they did have was manipulated to foster fear and justify action.

Steven Garber has spent many years working in Washington, DC, and witnessed countless volunteers, employees, and administrations come and go. He has known many who arrived with high hopes of making valuable contributions to the nation's political life. Yet, even the most optimistic and visionary get afflicted by the epidemic of "Potomac fever," whereby "cynicism is the atmosphere breathed."[56] If this happens to those who are laboring at the heart of things, what hope is there for a population that knows little of the dilemmas and compromises that are the norms of political life?

Glimmers of Light

Thankfully, the human capacity for inspiring integrity and ethical self-sacrifice is rarely snuffed out entirely, even in the bleakest times. Whistleblowers risk everything to bring corruption or criminality to light. Not all leaders desperately cling to power, because institutional or national health must take precedence over egos (from George Washington to Nelson Mandela).[57] Even in the darkest hours, people still have a choice.

This was poignantly described by Timothy Garton Ash in his memoir, *The File*. Soon after the Berlin Wall fell, he revisited the Berlin of his student days in the 1980s to examine his Stasi (the East German secret police) files. This inspired him to write a profound reflection on the horrors and dilemmas of life under totalitarianism. But he could not escape from the fact that everyone still has a choice, however unpalatable — to be either a Claus von Stauffenberg (who plotted Hitler's assassination) or an Albert Speer (who colluded with Adolf Hitler).[58]

Power is an unavoidable reality and *some* people must wield it if society is to function. This is why some enter public, and specifically political, life, despite the dangers or cost. Many are motivated by genuine altruism. The great Václav Havel, playwright and first president of post-Communist Czechoslovakia, held that the only politics worthy of the name concerned "serving the community and serving those who will come after us."[59]

For all their flaws, errors, and even crimes, many leaders have done this. Which is why, strangely, many are proudest of what *did not happen* during their terms of office. "Eisenhower the general was honored for winning a Great War. But Eisenhower the president was proudest of not fighting one."[60] Or consider Kennedy during the Cuban missile crisis. Deeply affected by Barbara Tuchman's recently published *The Guns of August*, he wanted "every officer in the Army" to read it. One of the most haunting passages for him depicts two German statesmen analyzing the conflict:

> "How did it all happen?" the younger man wanted to know.
> "Ah, if only one knew."[61]

Kennedy was desperate to avoid circumstances that might occasion a similar conversation post–nuclear holocaust (as if such a conversation would even be possible).[62] Fortunately, Khrushchev felt the same, as Jackie Kennedy movingly acknowledged in a handwritten note after her husband's funeral:

> You and he were adversaries, but you were allied in a determination that the world should not be blown up. The danger, which troubled my husband, was that war might be started not so much by the big men as by the little ones. While big men know the need for self-control and restraint, little men are sometimes moved more by fear and pride.[63]

This is true leadership by people who understand history's precedents, echoes, and shifts. President Harry Truman, the first and (hopefully) only leader to order a nuclear strike, noted in 1948 that the bomb is "destructive beyond anything we have ever had," with the result that "we have got to treat this differently from rifles and cannon and ordinary things like that."[64]

The problem is that even when people have integrity and leadership competence, we cannot escape the nagging fear that those qualities are not enough. The world is more complex and interconnected than ever before, but it has been accompanied by disillusionment with ideologies and one-size-fits-all solutions. Political revolutions have been tried and found wanting. Consequently, no single group, government, corporation, or alliance is sufficiently powerful or long-termist to make necessary changes.

The best intentions are not enough, a point Graham Greene masterfully articulated in *The Quiet American*. As the protagonist says of the eponymous Thomas Pyle, "I never knew a man who had better motives for all the trouble he caused."[65]

Conclusion

There are many grounds for legitimate suspicion of those in power:

- Leaders are too often resistant to new realities.
- Too much is veiled in secrecy (for good or ill), especially in a world of plausible deniability.
- Consistency is hard to maintain in an ever-changing world.
- Hypocrisy is inevitable when leaders operate at the secret level.
- Leaders have immense power to manipulate public perceptions of reality.

> We hate the truth, and people hide it from us; we
> want to be flattered, and people flatter us; we like
> being deceived, and we are deceived.
> *Pascal,* Pensées

"Pay no attention to that man behind the curtain."
The Wizard in The Wizard of Oz *(1939)*

> Any fool can commit a murder; but it takes
> an artist to commit a good natural death.
> *KGB saying*

CHAPTER 2

LEND ME YOUR EARS!
Informers Have Failed Us

For several years after 2001, I was a lecturer at a small interdenomina-
tional seminary in Kampala, Uganda. One of my annual responsibilities
was to offer a short, first-year course in study skills. Higher education was
a new experience for many, so this was a vital, if inadequate, introduction.
Many came from a rote-learning culture in which the teacher (especially
if Caucasian) was "always right." Therefore, it was essential to find ways to
give permission for critical thinking. One method was to express progres-
sively countercultural viewpoints as the term went on. Of course, strong
relationships of trust between us were key; otherwise, this approach could
have seriously backfired. My aim, though, was to goad them into public
disagreement with me. The teacher could be wrong—and it was acceptable
to say so.

Even more revealing was another exercise in which I would photocopy
pages from two "reliable" commentaries on a significant Bible text. Both were
written by respected scholars who articulated contrasting, or even contradictory, viewpoints. I would pass these around and sit back and watch. A few
might have felt panic, but the majority simply sat in befuddled silence. This
was no reflection on their intelligence, merely on the inadequacies of the
education they had received. The exercise's predicament (if it should be called
that) demanded a response. There are questions to be asked, arguments to be
weighed, and implications to be assessed. It might take some getting used to,
but it was nevertheless an essential step in their educational development.

The point is that these are skills that must, and can, be learned. Few would dispute they are essential tools for life. The appreciation of differing perspectives is beneficial for our own learning and vital in a pluralistic society.

Debates between the "Experts"

Rejecting rote learning for more provocative educational methods, however, is not without its problems. How do we deal with a bombardment of disparate viewpoints, especially when decisions must be made (such as at election time)? We have surely all known a sense of confused passivity after an argument between experts on a serious current affairs program. The debate may be about evidence for and against climate change, or between a Keynesian and a monetarist solution to national debt, or how to tackle narcotics smuggling, but the result is often the same. Each debater seems to make valid points, so we struggle to decide. Invariably, the presenter will close the discussion down with an anodyne "this debate will no doubt run and run, but that is all we have time for." This is partly a ruse. Television thrives on debate, not agreement, and depends on us returning for more. But we are left none the wiser. The joy of inquiry has become a misery, akin to "the twelfth hour of Monopoly on a rainy afternoon."[1] So if a conclusion needs to be drawn at all, we will probably plump for the one who puts his or her case more sympathetically or plausibly. In other words, we are unwittingly following the person who made the better "effect" rather than the better case.

The problem of "experts" is compounded by three other factors. First is the increasing specialization of knowledge and scholarship. The sum of human knowledge seems to grow exponentially in every sphere, as illustrated by the sheer volume of books still being printed or published online. There is just too much to know. In the Victorian era, Thomas Henry Huxley (nicknamed "Darwin's bulldog" because he deliberately pitted evolutionary theory against organized religion) loved to advise, "Try to learn something about everything and everything about something." Yet such an aspiration is probably futile now, on both counts.

How different things were in the Middle Ages, when universities became the focal points for discovering how everything coheres. Quite apart from their theological foundations,[2] the assumption was that everything *could* be connected and integrated. The central quadrangle of Oxford University's Bodleian Library illustrates this vividly. Several doors open onto the courtyard, each labeled in Latin with the subjects taught there. In the same building (completed in 1619) are rooms dedicated to the likes of Greek and

Hebrew, geometry and arithmetic, music and moral philosophy. The point is not that these were the only places to be taught these subjects, but its striking symbolism: All learning *could* be treasured under one roof and was built on the same (in this case, theistic) foundations.

This would be inconceivable today. Not only are those theistic foundations casually dismissed, but knowledge is now too fragmented to be unified. This occurs even within single departments. Historians become familiar with a few decades in one region; biblical scholars concentrate on one literary genre; surgeons must specialize in a small part of the body or in a particular disease. In fact, in 1923, 11 percent of American physicians were specialists; by 1989, more than 70 percent were.[3] It is unlikely that this trend will reverse, since specialties increase prestige and income. Complicating matters still further, individual disciplines themselves house competing and conflicting schools of thought. Knowledge, therefore, constantly becomes siloed. Universities may share a name and location, but in practice, we might better call them "multiversities." Faced with such divergence, how can anyone come to conclusions about what is true?

The second complication is the way experts often function in the public square. Edward Bernays is widely credited with being the pioneer of the modern public relations industry, with his seminal *Propaganda* (published in 1928) still regarded as something of a primer. He was, in fact, Sigmund Freud's nephew and was clearly influenced by his uncle's thought. In the business of what he and columnist Walter Lippmann called "the manufacture of consent,"[4] Bernays was the first deliberately to exploit the social capital of experts.

In *Propaganda*, he imagines a test case of a bacon marketing campaign. In what he calls "the old salesmanship," the process was simply a matter of shouting louder than your competitors. But in the newer salesmanship, the task is to search out those in society who most influence the market in question and then exploit their expertise to market the product. Thus, to sell bacon, you want the physicians who influence eating habits. The sales director knows "as a mathematical certainty, that large numbers of persons will follow the advice of their doctors, because he understands the psychological relation of dependence of men upon their physicians."[5]

This kind of advertising is not product specific but generic in that it seeks "to create circumstances which will modify" people's habits.[6] Bernays did this by introducing committees of professionals to endorse products on the basis of their expertise. This is still commonplace. Whether for toothpaste, detergents, or weight-loss products, the "men in white coats" loom large because they instill consumer confidence.

Perhaps we have become sufficiently alert to this that we easily see through it. However, the phenomenon is less identifiable when the process takes place behind our screens and not on them. A 2007 survey in the *New England Journal of Medicine* found that 94 percent of U.S. physicians had what was termed "a relationship" with pharmaceutical or medically related industries.[7] Of course, this may be as innocent as receiving pads of branded Post-it Notes and ballpoint pens. But it does at least prompt questions about the objectivity of doctors' prescribing habits. Can we always be sure that clinical decisions are untainted by personal influence or financial incentive? This will tie in with the topic of the next chapter, but for now, it is clear why experts' persuasive power is diminished, even while many rightly bring genuine authority and influence. Matters are hardly improved when politicians clamber aboard this bandwagon. Perhaps out of recognition that they are trusted less, they appeal to experts to make the case for a course of action on their behalf. But the downward spiral continues: the more politicized experts become, the less they are trusted.

The most alarming problem is the third, however. A 2009 report from Edinburgh University found that a third of scientific medical researchers admitted anonymously to scientific fraud, with nearly three-fourths saying they had witnessed deliberate warping of data to achieve desired results.[8] Daniele Fanelli, the report's author, wrote, "I had naively assumed that scientists would be principled [but scientists] are human beings driven by their interests, hopes, and beliefs. Given opportunities to cut corners by falsifying data, they may well do so."[9] Furthermore, the science journal *Nature* estimates that around a thousand incidents of falsification or plagiarism go unreported in the U.S. every year.[10]

Some of the circumstances that lead to such incidents make them perfectly understandable: publication deadlines, funding stresses, overwork. These do not place them far along the corruption spectrum. Nevertheless, the trend does little to instill confidence in the growing body of scientific knowledge, especially because its sheer scale makes detection of these frauds all but impossible.

So the "currency of expertise" has been devalued. When experts from diverse fields (or even the same field) debate and disagree, or when their areas of study seem incompatible, we are left without any moorings. When we suspect that those who inform us are concealing corporate, political, or ideological interests, thus rendering their expert assessments less than objective, the effect is corrosive.

Of course, the word *propaganda* today carries none of the positive connotations it had when Edward Bernays popularized it. Even the merest hint that a statement might be "propaganda" arouses intense suspicion about its veracity. Far from simply being a matter of "getting one's message out," it is assumed to be disinformation. What has brought this shift about? To discover, we must now cast light on another set of informers who dominate contemporary life — the mediators between the rulers and those ruled. We must infiltrate the netherworld of the spin doctors' "dark arts."

Distracted from Reality

Barry Levinson's 1997 movie *Wag the Dog* was released with uncanny timing. Conrad Brean, a White House spin doctor (Robert De Niro), hires Stanley Motss, a top Hollywood producer (Dustin Hoffman), to create an election campaign distraction from a presidential sex scandal. As Brean says in David Mamet's taut screenplay, "We aren't going to have a war. We're going to have the 'appearance' of a war."[11] It would be the ultimate "pseudo-event," to adopt historian Daniel Boorstin's potent term for events manufactured solely in order for them to be reported.[12]

It was topical (to say the least), because it came out just *before* the Monica Lewinsky scandal broke. While President Bill Clinton was being investigated by Kenneth Starr, NATO forces actually were being deployed in a conflict in the Balkans, and the United States was bombing terrorist targets in Afghanistan and Sudan.

So Brean explains how it would all work.

> BREAN: You watched the Gulf War. What did you see? Day after day, the one "Smart Bomb" falling into a building. The truth, I was in the building when they shot that shot. They shot it in a studio, Falls Church, Virginia, 1/10th scale model of a building.
>
> MOTSS: Is that true?
>
> BREAN: How the f*** do *we* know. You take my point?[13]

The film's biting satire only barely exceeds the bounds of plausibility. The mention of the 1991 Gulf War is telling since that was the first fully broadcast war. Viewers could watch live-action footage from the comfort of their sofas as they ate their TV dinners. It was extreme reality TV. But who could be sure it *wasn't* fabricated? The footage was below cinematic quality, but that merely substantiated its plausibility. It could so easily have been shot in Virginia.

The fact that it was mediated provoked renowned sociologist Jean Baudrillard to suggest that the First Gulf War "did not take place." His theory caused great offense, because of its apparent denial of the conflict's human cost. But that is to miss his point. He denied it was a war (primarily because Western troops were not engaged on the ground), but termed it a "media event." In his introduction to Baudrillard's essays on the subject, philosopher Paul Patton distills this key idea. It was "not a war, but a simulacrum of war, a virtual event which is less the representation of real war than a spectacle which serves a wide variety of political and strategic purposes on all sides."[14]

Baudrillard's position is evidently extreme, but it is hard to deny his main point. Cinematic special effects are so finely tuned now that when a tenth-scale model of the White House is blown up (as in the film *Independence Day*) or a tsunami strikes the Asian coast (as in *The Impossible*), the untrained eye is unable to detect the fakery. It is interesting, therefore, that filmmakers, in their quest for greater realism, eschew techniques that enable "perfect" video capture in favor of the "edgier," apparently homemade aesthetic of a handheld camera. But then that is itself a ruse to convey authenticity!

So is what we see reality, or a distraction from reality? It is no wonder that many are cynical about leaders' exploitation of distraction. After all, a British government press officer was eventually forced to resign for callously suggesting in an email that 9/11 would be a "very good day to get out anything we want to bury," since the world's focus would be inexorably drawn to Manhattan.[15]

Politicians aren't the only contestants in this particular game. The practice is pervasive. Whether through a product's subliminal association with beautiful, semiclothed women (sex sells) or the listing of a shampoo's scientific-sounding but meaningless ingredients (science sells), distraction is everywhere. Once exposed, it is easy to spot.

Totalitarian regimes are often incongruously obsessed with presenting a good impression. When the Berlin Wall went up, it embodied for many Westerners (not to mention Easterners) the total failure of the Communist system. If Soviet-inspired socialism was so wonderful, why was a defection barrier necessary? The official explanations nevertheless claimed the opposite. It was, apparently, an "anti-Fascist protection wall" (*antifaschistischer Schutzwall*), and those who tried to escape were invariably described as Western agents or criminals.[16] All the wall's intricacies (it was, in fact, a complex of several walls, ditches, booby traps, and border patrols) were deemed "defensive."

Western democracies are not immune from the same temptations. The UK Parliament passed the Regulation of Investigatory Powers Act in 2000, a title that suggests a welcome curtailment of the surveillance state. In fact, the opposite is the case,[17] with opponents dubbing it "the snoopers' charter" because it empowers a very large list of public bodies to eavesdrop on citizens. On a similar theme, the George W. Bush administration introduced the Patriot Act after 9/11, which mandated wide-ranging powers for domestic and secret surveillance. After such a national tragedy, what politician would dare oppose legislation with a title like that?

George Orwell warned of this precise phenomenon in his seminal 1945 essay, "Politics and the English Language." He pulled no punches. Much political language of the time was "largely the defense of the indefensible" because it served policies that "are too brutal for most people to face." This explains the prevalence of "euphemism, question-begging and sheer cloudy vagueness," like "pacification" and "the elimination of unreliable elements."[18] Still, the practice continues apace.

Military leaders speak of collateral damages (noncombatant casualties) as opposed to clean (accurate) bombing, friendly fire (casualties caused by one's own side), or coercive interrogation (torture). "Such phraseology is needed," Orwell observed, "if one wants to name things without calling up mental pictures of them."[19] So his unwavering appeal was for straight talking to serve genuine debate, rather than the wooliness that so often masks insincerity. How different things would be if all public speakers (preachers included) insisted on closing what Orwell calls the "gap between one's real and one's declared aims."[20]

It is easy to see why many people now routinely probe public statements for the agendas they obscure (or bury) rather than take them at face value. But this instinct is fatal for building trust. Senior journalist Jeremy Paxman could have been speaking for many spheres of public life when he said in his 2007 MacTaggart lecture that trust "is the defining problem of contemporary television."[21] For sometimes, distraction is the least of our concerns.

Deluged by Disinformation

We expect the notorious or infamous to deceive. We expect our enemies to indulge in self-aggrandizement. That gives our own propagandists something to work with. So it would not surprise his adversaries that Napoleon's Arc de Triomphe in Paris bears the names of some battles that France actually lost

(Corunna, Oporto, and Toulouse)![22] But it takes a well-informed historian to spot such disinformation.

There are countless fairly harmless examples. Hollywood is a case in point. Movies offer the most accessible window into history for many. As the twentieth century's greatest artistic innovation, they have immense communicative power. Yet, audiences can forget that a film is always a representation of reality rather than reality itself. Even films purporting to be historical are creating a fiction. Artistic license is *always* involved.

What is more disturbing is when artistic license creeps into journalism, politics, or marketing. When respected journalists are discovered plagiarizing or fabricating, there is an appropriate outcry. People were rightly shocked when *New York Times* journalist Jayson Blair was exposed in 2003 or when Jonah Lehrer's 2012 book *Imagine* was found to contain invented quotes from Bob Dylan, which led to publishers recalling the book and to Lehrer's resignation from *The New Yorker*. Of course, many reporters have high degrees of integrity, motivated by values of truth and justice; such high-profile resignations are, thankfully, few and far between. But all face the pressures of a dwindling market share, copy deadlines, and professional rivalries (as in any other sphere). The potential is huge for the unscrupulous to exploit these pressures for ignoble ends.

One controversial newsman in 1960s London, Hugh Cudlipp, is perhaps indicative. He used journalism deliberately to campaign against social taboos and bring down the hypocritical. His methodology, though, hardly instills confidence in the industry. His motto was, "Say it first, get away with it first, and others will follow. At all events, say it first." He regarded the only way for a newspaper to succeed was for it to "be alarmingly provocative in every issue and abundantly confident of its own importance."[23] How often have we witnessed serious allegations being made against the innocent (who, in Western justice, are presumed innocent until proven guilty) in papers on the front pages, only to be retracted weeks or months later in tiny concealed paragraphs? This type of journalism is motivated not by truth but by power and profit. Disinformation is merely a tool.

Let us return for a moment to the Iraq War. Respected journalist Andrew Rawnsley writes of the UK's official 2002 report on Iraq's weapons of mass destruction that "within a year of publication, it became apparent that the majority of the claims in the dossier, especially the most frightening ones, were distortions, exaggerations or *downright false*."[24] Yet, on its basis, the UK joined the "coalition of the willing" in a highly contentious war. Even if there were legitimate justifications for deposing Saddam Hussein, public confidence is destroyed when it is discovered the case was built on falsehood.

This is manifestly not the first time that such things have occurred. But something *has* shifted. English professor Marilyn Chandler McEntyre suggests "it is both the scale of such offenses and the attitude of the public toward them. Tolerance may not be the right term. It may simply be passivity."[25] Could this be the result of the cumulative effect of propaganda over the last century? We have been dulled by the tidal wave of lies. As a government official in the BBC's timeless satire *Yes, Prime Minister* says, "The first rule of politics: never believe anything until it's been officially denied." Remember: plausible deniability is official government policy!

There is moral ambiguity here, of course. Disinformation has arguably played a vital, if delicate, role in righteous causes since time immemorial. Around three millennia ago, the Hebrew midwives lied to Pharaoh to shield newborn Jewish boys from the king's genocidal commands. The textual comment is intriguing: "God was kind to the midwives and the people increased and became even more numerous. And because the midwives feared God, he gave them families of their own" (Exodus 1:20–21). The women's allegiance to Yahweh prompts their deception. They were in the business of protecting life, a greater good that demands a dangerous, messy, and even ambiguous obedience to God.

It was Winston Churchill who famously declared, "In wartime, truth is so precious that she should always be accompanied by a bodyguard of lies,"[26] and he was a master of the art. The contribution of disinformation to the Allies' victory in the Second World War is incalculable. The success of D-Day in June 1944 depended largely on the brilliance of Operation Fortitude, which was itself a key component in Operation Bodyguard. Operation Fortitude was the astonishingly elaborate ruse to convince the enemy that the Allies' inevitable offensive would strike both France (at Calais) and Norway. It was vital to keep Nazi forces out of Normandy until a secure foothold had been established. The subterfuge was sometimes surreal. Whole tank divisions were stationed in East Anglia, but they were made of plywood; a dead pilot was left floating in the Mediterranean carrying fake battle plans; a lookalike of Field Marshall Montgomery flew into Gibraltar. But the trickery worked. Hitler himself was duped, considering the Normandy landings a feint even after they had begun.[27] So in war's complexities or under totalitarianism's dark clouds, deception has its place in the battle for truth and moral good. Fighting a just war may even demand it.

But what of peacetime? Surely there is a fundamental difference between defending a just cause through deception, and using lies to conceal a politician's venality or a product's deficiencies? We are clearly in the realms of moral grayness, but the further we move along the spectrum from honorable altruism, the more questionable the deceptions become.

Consider social media. It is frequently heralded as a great democratizing force. It offers everyone a public voice. Communications professor Clay Shirky puts it well. "The future presented by the Internet is the mass amateurization of publishing and a switch from 'Why publish this?' to 'Why not?'"[28] As a means of rapid dissemination of information, it is unprecedented. However, like all media, it is open to abuse.

Take, for example, "Astroturf campaigns." A campaign might be termed "grassroots" if it has emerged spontaneously from ordinary people and goes on to demand attention by sheer force of numbers. An Astroturf campaign, however, only pretends to have been generated from the bottom up while all the time being another weapon in the PR armory. As a tactic, it predates social media, having been developed in the 1990s by tobacco firms to give the "impression of widespread resistance to [the government's] tobacco plans."[29] But it has come into its own in the Internet era. Light the Astroturf touchpaper, and the dynamics of social media take over, with tweets, Facebook Likes and online polls spreading exponentially. To be fair, many participants may genuinely agree with the campaign's cause. But its origins are a deception, to suit the ends of the powerful.

There is a deeper concern, though. How did those participants come to agree with the cause in the first place? Is there not a blur between information and manipulation? Marketing directors may claim they are solely concerned with broadcasting their product's details as widely as possible. But as that remarkable monastic Thomas Merton put it, this propaganda works *"because we want it to."*[30] It *"makes up our mind for us, but in such a way that it leaves us the sense of pride and satisfaction of men who have made up their own minds."*[31] A modern person has the "illusion that he is thinking for himself when, in fact, someone else is doing his thinking for him."[32] As with Astroturf campaigns, the intention, wrote Eliane Glaser, is to provide "false promises of empowerment."[33]

In this smoke-and-mirrors world, reality becomes malleable and, more disquietingly, artificial. Glaser describes an alarming encounter that suggests this is precisely the aim of contemporary politics, and her vignette is worth quoting in full:

In an influential article in the *New York Times*, published just before the 2004 presidential election, the veteran reporter Ron Suskind recounted an extraordinary encounter with a senior adviser to George W. Bush, widely thought to be Karl Rove. The adviser was telling how much he disliked an article Suskind had written for *Esquire* magazine about the enormous influence exerted on the president by his former communications director Karen Hughes. "The aide said that guys like me were 'in what we call the reality-based community,'" Suskind wrote, "which he defined as people who 'believe that solutions emerge from your judicious study of discernible reality.' I nodded and murmured something about Enlightenment principles and empiricism. He cut me off. 'That's not the way the world works anymore,' he continued. 'We're an empire now, and when we act, we create our own reality.'"

This is what we're up against now: not just spin, not just Machiavellian realpolitik, but the creation of powerful new fictional realities. And the problem is even worse post-Bush, I'd argue, because at least Dubya's regime was widely regarded as playing fast and loose with the facts. Now we have the apparent authenticity of Barack "Honest Tea" Obama.[34]

This is rather a shock for the many of us who naively assume that a "reality-based community" was a positive thing, however difficult or uncomfortable reality might be.

Authenticity seems to be the political obsession currently in vogue. Perhaps it is because so many have been exposed as inauthentic frauds. Yet herein lies the problem. In an effort to convey authenticity, we cannot help having a sneaking suspicion that this, too, is faked. Neil Postman anticipated this back in 1985, in his searing analysis of what constituted a person's credibility. It was not a matter of having a track record for truth telling. "It refers only to the impression of sincerity," wrote Postman. Thus Richard Nixon's problem during Watergate was not so much that "he lied but that on television he looked like a liar." This is alarming, even for Nixon haters, he suggests, because "the alternative possibilities are that one may look like a liar but be telling the truth; or even worse, look like a truth-teller but in fact be lying."[35]

We might assume we are immune to propaganda, but as renowned French sociologist Jacques Ellul warned, it is the educated who are most vulnerable to its effects. Because they absorb more secondhand and unverified information than others, they like to have opinions about everything while at the same time entertaining a high view of their own ability to make judgments.[36] What Ellul grasped, and what countless others have exploited, is that when reality is mediated (as it must be in a world of mass communication), the potential for deception is great. Of course, some argue we are more sensitive to this now, but even that is problematic. The greater our sensitivity becomes, the greater our anxiety about being able to discern the "really" real.

How can we avoid skepticism when electioneering politicians vie to seize the best photo opportunities or to avoid making gaffe-laden juxtapositions? When a leader gives a broadcast speech at a scene of tragedy, we instinctively assume the primary audience is not in the room, but is made up of consumers of news media. The leader needs to convey the broader impression of empathy as, say, "mourner-in-chief." Or in another context, he or she might seek to give a sense of dynamic leadership or a job well done (as in President George W. Bush's notorious 2003 "mission accomplished" photo op on the USS *Abraham Lincoln*). Or take the famous image of President Obama and his team tensely following the SEALs raid on Osama bin Laden's compound. There is little doubt everyone in the photograph was present (despite some insisting otherwise). But they are not (as the image suggests) watching a live video feed, because there wasn't one.[37] The tension was undoubtedly real. But the picture fails to give the complete picture.

There is a final irony in all this, because propaganda does not just affect its victims; propagandists begin to believe their own fabricated reality. This certainly happened to Germany's Adolf Hitler and Joseph Goebbels, despite the former's attempts to be what Edward Bernays described as "the unmoved mover."[38]

Goebbels, the Nazi propaganda minister, is reported to have said, "We do not talk to say something, but to obtain a certain effect."[39] That effect was easy to discern: Germany's total submission to the will of the führer and his regime. The underlying motivation was never truth, but power. Thus Hitler was relentlessly presented as the fulfillment of a quasi-messianic hope, the selfless and steady statesman of genius. And it hit the target. Many trusted Hitler with passionate intensity, even if they simultaneously despised the Nazi Party. This confidence persisted in a few even *after* the end of the war.

The flaw, however, was basic. *None of it was true.* Not one word. In reality, Hitler was chaotic, impulsive, irrational, and megalomaniacal. But that was irrelevant for Goebbels. He merely sought his "effect" by means of a manufactured image that had little resemblance to the reality. Thus a whole nation was conned.

The art of publicity management is a fact of life for everyone in public life. But that makes discernment for those "mediated to" so much harder. It is

of grave concern, therefore, that political commentators on both s.
Atlantic have taken to speaking of a "post-truth political environmen.
British Peter Oborne borrowing the phrase from American Eric Altern.
Oborne goes on to write, "Public statements are no longer fact based, bu.
operational. Realities and political narratives are constructed to serve a purpose, dismantled, and the show moves on."[40] We have only "the effect" on
which to base our decisions, beliefs, or votes, and thus we've gone full circle
to the confusion that comes from watching TV experts.

But the Truth Will Out

History suggests that the grossest deceptions do eventually get exposed.
Terrible tragedies may occur before it happens, of course, but when an authority's legitimacy is established on falsehood, it cannot last. Reality always gets
in the way. Ian Kershaw argues that the popular tide turned against Hitler,
not because of the Stalingrad debacle, but because the führer was evidently
unable to end the war. No longer could he plausibly claim to be "the far-
sighted, infallible, and well-intentioned führer"; silent criticism now broke
the surface, even of the führer himself.[41] Soon, even senior Nazis wanted
Joseph Goebbels to stop churning out propaganda in the face of the regime's
"credibility gap."[42] The yawning chasm between the real and the artificial
had grown too wide.

The powerless are not without weapons of their own in the face of disinformation and deceit by the powerful. Two of the most potent are satire and
the best of investigative journalism. The former has a noble pedigree, especially in English, after the likes of Jonathan Swift's *Gulliver's Travels*. It has a
vital role in exposing what contemporary British satirist Ian Hislop frequently
summarizes as "vice, folly, and humbug." Humor is a useful tool in the pursuit
of truth. But when that truth is concealed by a mountain of falsity, it can only
emerge after active and persistent scrutiny. At its noblest and most impartial,
therefore, investigative journalism has a vital role in preserving a society's
health. So in a suspicious world, Watergate crusaders Carl Bernstein and Bob
Woodward are the knights in armor, role models for aspiring reporters.

We know the powerful sometimes deceive—sometimes for the best of motives, sometimes not. We know the modern media avails the powerful with a mind-boggling range of tools to communicate their message. So why wouldn't they use them? We need to be vigilant, so that we are not duped ourselves. That is why we need, among other things, satirists and investigative journalists. A degree of suspicion is vital.

Yet a solid diet of disinformation scrutinized by satire and journalism will only aggravate the vicious circle of cynicism and suspicion. The more we fear that manipulation is taking place, the more we suspect it needs investigating, which in turn reinforces the fear. Where will it leave us then?

> Our sense of power is more vivid when we break a
> man's spirit than when we win his heart.
> *Eric Hoffer,* The Passionate State of Mind *(1954)*

When you think of the long and gloomy history of man, you will
find far more hideous crimes have been committed in the name
of obedience than have been committed in the name of rebellion.
C. P. Snow (1961)

> I left the Church. I never went back again.
> *Frank Taylor (father of a Boston priest's abuse victim)*

CHAPTER 3

SHOULDERS TO CRY ON?
Professional Caregivers Have Failed Us

For most of us, a visit to the local doctor or church is not generally a cause for trepidation. Yet perhaps it should be! The evidence for malpractice in the caring professions is mounting, and the institutions recognized for generations as trustworthy are no longer exempt from the culture of suspicion. Tabloids thrive on scandals and crimes, and it is always unfair to tar the majority with the brush of extreme cases. But the stories of abuse and exploitation on both sides of the Atlantic are hard to ignore.

- *Educators.* In 2013, evidence emerged of abusive teachers having worked in *all five* of the UK's specialist music schools.[1] Another schoolteacher, Jeremy Forrest, was jailed in June 2013 for abducting the fifteen-year-old schoolgirl with whom he had been having a sexual relationship. This was even after concerns had been raised repeatedly for several months previously.

- *Physicians.* In Chicago in 1997, Patricia Burgus received compensation of $10.6 million for "years of psychological torture" from highly controversial recovered-memory therapy. She had become falsely convinced that she had cannibalized hundreds of children in a satanic cult, sexually abusing her own sons, and being a victim of sexual abuse.[2] Around the same time, a Swedish man, Sture Bergwall (also known as Thomas Quick) was convicted of eight murders on the basis of his own confessions while undergoing recovered-memory therapy. However, by the end of 2013, all of these convictions had been quashed after he recanted his confessions. Then, take one of the most prolific serial killers in history. Dr. Harold Shipman was a local doctor who murdered perhaps as many as 250 of his patients.[3]

Of course, these are extreme examples, and it is unwise to draw conclusions from worst-case scenarios. Yet these examples point to the power imbalance at the heart of *every* professional care relationship. And that is precisely why many have come to fear them.

Suspicious: Because of the Complexities of Care

The vast majority of professional caregivers have a sincere concern for those in need. They invest years to study their discipline and gain sufficient practical experience, for which they are rightly commended. Nevertheless, good motives cannot always be relied on when it comes to negotiating the relational power that comes from professional care.

Power and Individuals

One definition of power is "the capacity to influence others, to cause or prevent change."[4] This does not imply that power is intrinsically negative. In a therapeutic context, a professional's power may be exactly what is needed to save a life. The influence may be such that a patient is willing to accept painful or harmful consequences that accompany professional advice (such as with chemotherapy). The assumption is that the doctor is better trained to deal with the patient's problem. Trust is the crucial ingredient. As one doctor says, "Our patients trust us with confidence and information. They trust us to apply up-to-date and effective technical skills to their problems. They trust us to care for them, medically and emotionally. Above all, they trust us to place their interests first."[5]

Yet other factors skew the power dynamic. These might be age difference (as for school teachers), health vulnerabilities (like physical weakness or mental instability), or institutional disparities (such as managers with control over career prospects). This imbalance may actually need to be exploited for the weaker person's own good. In such circumstances, a person's wish might actually *need* to be disregarded. A disruptive child may need to face disciplinary action; a suicidal patient may need to be taken into protective care. Teachers or social workers are entrusted with the authority to make these decisions, with the ideal outcome being that the recipient of such action eventually recognizes its benefits.

Tabloid journalists are too quick to demonize "doctors who play god," showing little sympathy for the distressing ethical dilemmas doctors constantly face. Their pressures are compounded by their patients' unhealthy expectations. These might be driven by a host of insecurities on a patient's part, but the most painful is surely the sense that this doctor is the last hope. The ability of even the simplest treatments to bring about remarkable transformations lends grounds for such hope. The medical profession has enjoyed wonderful successes that even fifty years ago were inconceivable.

Still, it should be obvious immediately where danger lies. This is why clear boundaries and ethical codes of practice are vital. The oldest such code is probably the fifth-century-BC Hippocratic Oath. The World Medical Assembly updated it in its *Declaration of Geneva*, so that doctors now pledge to "maintain the utmost respect for human life" and that "the health of my patient will be my first consideration."[6] Countless other professions have followed suit.

But if awareness of the need for such codes has grown, why has the credibility gap simultaneously widened? Renowned Swiss physician Paul Tournier described the problem in his 1978 book *The Violence Within*: "To be looked upon as a savior leaves none of us indifferent."[7] He observes that "there is in us, especially those whose intentions are of the purest, an excessive and destructive will to power which eludes even the most sincere and honest self-examination."[8] Few enter caring professions in order to wield such authority, but none remain unaffected by patients' expectations and willing deference. If this is true of the medical world, how much more is it the case in the opaque relational realms of talking therapies and church ministry?

Power abuses do not tend to leave physical scars. But when authority is wielded for purposes other than an individual's flourishing, the effects can be devastating.

Power and Institutions

Unlike many independent counselors, most in caring professions work in institutions. These can bring specific challenges, even after protective boundaries have been put in place. To prove this, psychologist Philip Zimbardo conducted the controversial Stanford prison experiment in 1971, in which a number of carefully selected volunteers participated in a prison role-playing exercise scheduled to last two weeks.[9] The twenty-four students were each assigned roles as guards or prisoners, but within six days the project had to be terminated. Some of the "guards" inhabited their roles so fully that they initiated a highly authoritarian regime (to which most of the "prisoners" meekly acquiesced). Matters soon degenerated into psychological torture and sexual humiliation. Zimbardo himself was not faultless. As "prison superintendent," he allowed the situation to continue for several days.

How could this have happened, and within such a short time span? Zimbardo is clear:

> The power of this situation ran swiftly and deeply through most of those on this exploratory ship of human nature. Only a few were able to resist the situational temptations to yield to power and dominance while maintaining some semblance of morality and decency. Obviously, I was not among that noble class.[10]

Zimbardo was startled into revisiting this painful episode by the horrors of Baghdad's Abu Ghraib prison after the Iraq War. He saw chilling parallels with his experiment and thus discerned that the problem was hardly a question of "a few bad apples" (the official explanation), but as much (if not more) an issue of systemic flaws within a dangerous command culture. He wrote up his conclusions from both Stanford and Abu Ghraib in his disturbing book titled *The Lucifer Effect*. His shocking, though plausible, suggestion is that similar conditions can be found in far more benign settings.

Hospitals are hardly military incarceration centers. Yet, could there be more similarities than we might care to imagine? Patients are not exactly inmates, but they do surrender much of their autonomy (albeit voluntarily) over such matters as diet, visiting times, or lights-out. Some may even require restraining or be encouraged to endure excruciating treatments. Then, from professionals' perspective, hospitals tend to be strongly hierarchical. Doctors wield extraordinary power by virtue of their training, even though nurses often have a better understanding of patient care (as my wife well remembers from her nursing days) and are often more alert to potential mistakes. So it takes considerable courage to speak up in these situations.

Zimbardo cites an unnerving experiment in which an unknown but authoritative-sounding doctor instructed nurses to administer a lethal dose of medication to a patient (a placebo was used). *Only one* out of twenty-two nurses refused.[11] We must not infer from this that hospitals are inherently dangerous or that hierarchies are necessarily detrimental. I, for one, would far prefer to have any complex conditions treated by a highly trained and experienced specialist, even if she was overbearing or arrogant. Mixed motives are always a danger, and the right therapy may well be administered by experts with power issues.

But as Zimbardo notes, half the battle is being conscious of how social influences operate in extreme circumstances, because people are then in a position to become "wise and wily" instead of being "easily influenced by authorities, group dynamics, persuasive appeals, and compliance strategies."[12]

The difficulties involved in standing up for what is right in these contexts are no consolation for those who have suffered. Victims are unsurprisingly reluctant to be exposed to such vulnerabilities again. The relevance of Zimbardo's research will become obvious as we shift our focus to church contexts, but there is one final, tangential factor to consider first.

Power and Ideologies

It can be as hard to resist prevailing schools of thought as it is to withstand the pressures of hierarchies. It is often forgotten that science is no monolithic body of knowledge immune to fad or fashion. Thomas Kuhn exposed the myth of scientific objectivity with his groundbreaking 1962 work on paradigm shifts—revolutionary moments when prevailing assumptions are completely overturned.[13] It is easy to illustrate this phenomenon in the realms of therapy. Swiss Jungian therapist Adolf Guggenbühl-Craig cites the Byzantine stylites who served God by sitting or standing on pillars for years on end. These ascetic hermits were not very well-adjusted or socially integrated by modern standards. However, in the fifth century AD, their strange sacrifices inspired immense respect such that disciples would flock to them for wisdom and guidance. This might not be considered out of place in India today, but it would be a very different matter in the West. Because of contemporary assumptions about "normalcy and adjustment, the ascetics who fasted and mortified themselves appear at best as unfortunate eccentrics, and at worst as mentally ill people in need of treatment."[14]

A paradigm shift has clearly taken place, no doubt brought about by psychological advances. But the trend can be seen again and again. Dominant worldviews inevitably shape what is regarded as healthy. Thus when Communism held sway, its ideology created psychiatric blind spots. The Soviet Union was supposedly the "happiest country in the world," but this meant there was never the public recognition or discussion of depression, to the great detriment and suffering of many of its people.[15] Or take the golden age of ancient Athens, renowned for the high esteem in which it held pederasty (sexual relationships between adult men and boys). Today, it is almost universally judged as illegal in the West, punishable by severe jail terms. Conversely, consider the radical shift in attitudes to adult male homosexuality in the last fifty years. It used to be regarded as a condition for which "sufferers" were encouraged, if not forced, to receive medical or psychiatric treatment. Advocating this today is itself now deemed worthy of psychiatric treatment in some circles.[16]

Shifts in cultural taboos are disorienting. Who is to say that what is considered beneficial or healthy today will not be dismissed as dangerous tomorrow? If fundamentalist religion is deemed a curable mental illness by some today, what will prevent the definition of fundamentalist religion from being stretched to embrace *all* forms of religious conviction tomorrow?[17] After all, Soviet Communists considered psychiatric treatment for the religious, and even for the capitalist, to be entirely legitimate. Prevailing paradigms are never set in stone.

Furthermore, these paradigms might supersede other commitments, as, for example, happened at the now notorious Tuskegee Institute. For almost forty years, medical researchers conducted studies into African Americans infected with syphilis. Quite apart from the profound ethical dilemmas surrounding human scientific experimentation, it was deeply controversial because it took place in the racially segregated world of rural Alabama. Treatment was deliberately withheld from some patients so researchers could observe the disease's progress. In many cases, patients did not even know they were infected. Prevailing racial prejudices outweighed other ethical considerations, to the extent that in 1997, President Bill Clinton had to apologize for a government-orchestrated study that was so clearly racist.[18] There is not the space here to consider the various accounts of "the testing of nuclear radiation, LSD, and Agent Orange on unsuspecting army personnel and civilians."[19]

Power is neutral. The ends to which it is applied rarely are. Medics and therapists have inordinate potential for good … and evil. As examples of the darker side of this power are brought to light, no wonder some are afraid.

Suspicious: Because of the Appeal to God

The notorious nineteenth-century showman Phineas T. Barnum built his reputation (and even a political career) on circuses, freak shows, and scams. Less known today are his religious views. The fact that he grew up in Connecticut during the Second Great Awakening—that extraordinary period of national religious revival—meant he would never forget his childhood terrors of impending wrath evoked by itinerant preachers. He claimed this turned him off to Christianity for life, and he dedicated considerable efforts (such as publishing a newspaper, *The Herald of Freedom*) against the so-called blue laws, legislation that mandated religious practice on a wider population.[20]

So it is no surprise that he loved to tell the story of a grocer who was a deacon at his local church.

> One morning, before breakfast, he called down to his clerk:
> "John, have you watered the rum?"
> "Yes, sir."
> "And sanded the sugar?"
> "Yes, sir."
> "And dusted the pepper?"
> "Yes, sir."
> "And chicoried the coffee?"
> "Yes, sir."
> "Then come up to prayers."[21]

This grocer was no less a trickster than Barnum, but he had the nerve to conceal his deceitful business practices behind the respectability of religion. Religion merely covers up human nature, it seems; it does not transform it. Hypocrisy will thus always be a reliably easy charge to level at the religious. Of course, Israel's ancient prophets were on to this from the start. Amos, for one, blasted those religious people who trampled the needy by "skimping on the measure, boosting the price and cheating with dishonest scales" (Amos 8:5).

So hypocrisy has probably been a factor in dissenters' skepticism since time immemorial. It is not, therefore, a sufficient explanation for the widespread suspicion about religion in the West.

In 1988, the celebrated German theologian Jürgen Moltmann identified some key challenges facing contemporary Christian theology in the West. They have relevance for all ideologies, however. He noted that for most of the twentieth century, the common critique of religion tended to focus on the content of faith. However, recently, it is much more likely to pursue "a purely functional critique of the psychological, political, and social effects of this faith." The question is not about "whether it is true or false, but only whether it has the function of oppression or liberation, alienation or humanization."[22]

Power and the Center of Truth

The fact is that churches, mosques, and temples are not immune from the dangers associated with other caregivers. They might not have the authority to administer medications or have the backing of state legislation to control others, but they have a far more formidable asset, namely, God. And char-latans have claimed divine authority for centuries. With a celestial endorse-ment, almost anything is possible for the unscrupulous.

So under what circumstances can people drift into committing unwit-ting spiritual abuses? When religious leaders tightly control the interpretative boundaries of that truth, or if they claim unique access to it, the stage is set for spiritual abuse. A community's center of power and truth has become indistinguishable and personified in one individual or cabal. Thus, its author-ity becomes absolute. The spiritual abuse of members of that community can follow all too easily.

Power and the Savior Complex

It has been said that in church life, every congregation's temptation is to place their leader on a pedestal, and every leader's temptation is to want to be there. So here is an extreme example of both, taken from a denominational magazine:

> To say that K. is a talented man is an understatement and does not do justice to him. K. is an incredible balance of talent and is leading us because of his example in so many areas. There are brothers among us who are known for their humility, or their passion, or their creativity or their faith. K. is leading us because he is known for all of these virtues and many more. In fact, I cannot think of any virtue that K. is not known for. There is no greater discipler, disciple, brother, husband, father, leader, and friend than K ... K., we love you, we need you, and we will continue to follow you as you follow Christ.[23]

Anyone with even a modicum of pastoral wisdom might be expected to terminate such sycophantic rhetoric immediately, for everyone's sake. How can such delusions of perfection benefit anyone? More to the point, how long can anyone, however devout or well-intentioned, resist before starting to believe the propaganda?

Ken Blue notes how often spiritual abusers are curiously naive about what is happening: "They rarely intend to hurt their victims. They are usually so narcissistic or so focused on some great thing they are doing for God that they don't notice the wounds they are inflicting on their followers."[24] Or as a clergy friend put it after several years under a very difficult boss, "He was like a drunk driver who never looked in the rearview mirror."

Power and the Cultic

By definition, cults tend to be formed around an individual or an idea and are sustained by "unethically manipulative techniques of persuasion and control … to the actual or possible detriment of members, their families or the community."[25] These tendencies can be found in all kinds of contexts, including mainline churches, even those with the most respectable pedigrees and traditions.

In his excellent book *When a Church Becomes a Cult,* Steve Wookey outlines several common features of cults. While each feature is detrimental, when you look at each individually, none has greater significance. A church might be led by an embezzler, for example, but that doesn't make it a cult. What matters is the convergence of these features.

- authoritarianism (strong and controlling leadership)
- elitism (an "us versus them" mentality, perhaps to the point of total social withdrawal)
- the ends justifying the means (for example, dubious recruitment and fund-raising methods)
- financial dishonesty (perhaps to mask the lifestyle indulgences of the leader)
- psychological manipulation (for example, exploiting communal pressures to control the more independent minded)[26]

These are all symptoms of the same fundamental problem, namely, that each feature is driven, at its root, by the abuse of spiritual power. As we so often do with crime stories, we must ask that ancient, noble question: *Cui bono?* For whose good or benefit? In such situations, it is never that of the vulnerable or needy.

In her 1998 analysis of clergy misconduct cases, Candace Benyei noted how each was an exploitation of the power imbalance inherent in pastoral situations. Thus, pastors could manipulate through the threat of abandonment, the assertion of authority, and the use of "animal force," depending on which was most effective in the circumstances.[27] So for "a hungry, empty individual, that special attention [from an abusive leader] is hard to turn down, even when it is inappropriately sexualized."[28] The authority of priest or pastor may then be almost impossible to disobey because it is supposedly divinely mandated. It is as if the will of God has been conflated with the will of the pastor.

Less extreme but still potentially manipulative is the more common manifestation of spiritual abuse sometimes termed "heavy shepherding." Trying to establish when good intentions and honorable motives subtly slide into dangerous territory is difficult, for as we have already seen, the power imbalance in pastoral relationships is unavoidable and not inherently negative.

I first encountered the phenomenon when a friend related an encounter that occurred after he took on a church leadership position in southern England. A young family joined the fellowship, and the father wanted to meet up with his new pastor. There was nothing out of the ordinary in that, until the man put a very strange question to my friend. "What car should I buy?" he asked. Being ignorant of most matters automotive, my friend flippantly replied something along the lines of "a blue one." The real reason for the question soon emerged. This family had recently left a church with such a rigorous mentoring structure that leaders were institutionally responsible for all key decisions in members' lives. The healthy practice of mentoring had been exploited (however unwittingly) into a mechanism of control. As one cult victim discovered to his horror, "I woke up one morning and realized I had not thought my own thoughts for three years."[29]

The mentor here has usurped a person's conscience and will. There may well be seasons in life when this is necessary (such as infancy, crisis, or sickness), but such dependency should never be the norm. This is not to deny the value, and indeed virtue, in submitting to leadership in certain circumstances, a subject to which we will return. The issue is that such leadership can be easily exploited and not just in cults. Mainstream churches can be just as prone to foster abuses of power.

Power and Particular Theologies

Some theological positions may actually exacerbate these problems. For example, legalistic theologies are derived from the premise that divine acceptance is based on an individual's moral achievement. These can provide a fast track to controlling leadership, for invariably it is the leaders who determine which particular moral standards are expected. Often, the list is as arbitrary as it is unattainable. As David Miller puts it when describing the impact on families in such churches, "Legalism inevitably turns children into church mice and Christian leaders into authoritarian monsters."[30]

Or consider the so-called prosperity gospel, which, tragically, thrives in some of the world's poorest regions, despite its deep and cruel flaws. It is a grim exploitation of the generosity that is rightly encouraged as a Christian virtue. Adherents are urged to give extravagantly to their church (in "faith offerings") in the hope of receiving "a hundredfold blessings," often using the analogy of sowing seeds to reap a harvest. After I encountered some appalling cases in Uganda, it seemed this "gospel" is effectively a spiritualizing of the American Dream for the rest of the world in the guise of the promises of God. Quite apart from being a terrible distortion of theological orthodoxy, it is, in practice, a Ponzi scheme for impoverished pastors.[31]

One Ugandan friend spent time in a church planted in a Kampala slum. The pastors appealed for generous giving. My friend went along with it for a few years, not least because he was inspired by sermons to dream of one day being able to park his newly acquired Mercedes Benz in the church's parking lot. Then one day it suddenly struck him. The *only* people who could afford to drive a car to this particular church were the pastors.

Is it any wonder that some are nervous of being sucked into such communities? They fear a loss of autonomy, the control of overbearing leaders, the agendas of the powerful but unscrupulous. Religious organizations do not remain unscathed from the prevalent culture of suspicion.

Perhaps out of the desire to hold on to the spiritual reality that they have previously discerned, some have fled the newer, unaffiliated churches for mainline denominations in the hope of finding a greater security and protection derived from years of tradition and institutional experience. However, recent scandals have indicated that even these places are not safe.

Suspicion: When Institutions Protect Their Own

The epicenter of the recent clergy abuse scandal was Boston's Roman Catholic archdiocese. However, the horrors were by no means restricted to the United States or to Catholicism. Repercussions were felt across the Catholic world, with what was described as "a raging bushfire" spreading to Ireland, the UK, Belgium, Australia, and Latin America.[32] In 2013, the Church of England had to issue its own "unreserved apologies" for a catalogue of sexual abuse and negligence in Chichester diocese (including serious allegations against one of their retired suffragan bishops).[33]

Some have been quick to point to a perfect storm of contributory factors: celibacy (mandatory for Catholic priests), the power imbalances inherent in spiritual care (exacerbated by a strong theological emphasis on clergy/laity distinctions), and the heavy burdens and pressures on priests working in deprived and secularized environments. It is certainly true there are invariably tales of tragedy and heartbreak that lie behind even the most bestial of sexual predators. Yet the reality is clear: "Sexual misconduct is a rupture of the covenant of trust between clergyperson and congregant."[34] Always.

The Boston Globe was at the forefront of exposing the terrible story,[35] and one of the clergy the team focused on was Father Gale Leifeld, rector of a Catholic boys' boarding school between 1977 and 1982. He died in 1994, taking the truth of countless abuses to the grave. What could possibly have gone through his mind to justify his actions? Peter Isely, one of the Leifeld victims, is now a psychotherapist. He has speculated that the priest considered himself to be initiating the boys into "a special experience of love ... I was a boy who needed love and this was what love was to him. But it was really all coercion, force, and terror for me."[36] That Leifeld and many others were free to carry out these appalling crimes is sobering enough. But that was not the only scandal.

A document that came to light in June 2001 proved to be "a turning point: a story about a priest who was accused of molesting children was now a story about a bishop who protected that priest."[37] For it soon became clear that many in the archdiocese's hierarchy, including the cardinal archbishop Bernard F. Law himself, had covered it up over many years. One of the most notorious beneficiaries was Father John Geoghan. He was eventually defrocked and imprisoned, but he became a "potent symbol of the compassion and gentle treatment the Church afforded its own rogue priests at the expense of the victims."[38] Almost two hundred people filed claims against Geoghan and his supervisors.

It is not only the scale of the claims against John Geoghan that is chilling, but the length of time during which he was allowed to be active—more than two decades. The organization's culture of secrecy was a gift for a "calculating predator" of such "deceptive charm."[39] Because of its scale, history, and wealth, the Roman Catholic Church wields unique power. No wonder its victims feel helpless when seeking truth and justice from behind the locked gates of ecclesial privilege. Its ability to conceal criminal behavior might even seem worthy of a corrupt state.

It is now clear that in the United States alone, "between 1950 and 2002, 10,667 victims/survivors came forward and 4,392 priests had allegations of abuse against them. Named were 4.2 percent of diocesan priests and 2.7 percent of [other] priests ... One recent estimate places the total cost of settlements at over $3 billion."[40]

Two final moments from the grim tale are telling. At one point, a bishop, who is also a lawyer, is alleged to have recommended exploiting the Vatican's diplomatic status (and thus immunity) in order to conceal documents that were considered to be dangerous. This could be done by sending the incriminating documents to the Apostolic Delegate in Washington.[41] Are there any comparable organizations in the world (of any description) that can take advantage of that kind of power?

The second came at the funeral of a priest, Father Joseph E. Birmingham. One of his victims, Tom Blanchette, had actually confronted Birmingham before his death and then decided to attend the funeral. Meeting Cardinal Law at the reception after the service, he seized the opportunity to discreetly present his experiences to the archbishop. Law looked shocked as he listened, invited him to return to the church, and then asked if he could pray for him. After laying his hands on Blanchette's head for several minutes, he then said, "I bind you by the power of the confessional never to speak about this to anyone else." Blanchette was appalled. As he said later, "I didn't ask him to hear my confession. I went there to inform him."[42]

Here institutional power and spiritual power converge. A victim of physical abuse then becomes the victim of spiritual abuse. It is the worst possible combination, but Tom Blanchette was hardly unique. Just one feature of this brief exchange demonstrates a brutal distortion of confessional confidentiality. The *priest* is the one sworn to secrecy in the confessional, not the one making confession. Blanchette was not seeking forgiveness at that moment; he was seeking justice. When the archdiocese's publicity department subsequently insisted that Cardinal Law was continuing to meet with victims, it is revealing that he would not meet with Blanchette.[43]

Of course, countless pastors, therapists, and priests serve honestly and genuinely help those in pain and confusion. Even if the figures quoted above are a conservative estimate, it means that well over 90 percent of Catholic priests had no abuse allegations made against them in that period. But that is no solace for victims. When thousands of lives are blighted by abusers, and when scores of senior clerics try to conceal (and thereby aggravate) the problem, of course observers and victims will despair.

Churches then seem no better than other institutions with too much power. Instead, they seem worse—because of their hypocritical claim to be different, to be the community Jesus described as a "town built on a hill" whose good deeds shine light into the world (see Matthew 5:14–16). Denominational or theological distinctions do not concern most onlookers, so everyone is tarred with the same brush. The church seems more akin to a bunkered secret society that goes to extraordinary lengths to ensure its evil deeds never see the light of day. If Jürgen Moltmann is correct about the criteria by which matters of faith are now judged—that the touchstones are no longer matters of truth and falsehood but oppression and liberation—then the church will seem to have failed abysmally.

Learning from the Survivors

Most of us can sympathize with Frank Taylor, seventy-seven-year-old father of one of Father Joseph Birmingham's young victims, who said, "I left the Church. I never went back again."[44] The conspiracy of abuse and concealment was too great for him to regain his trust in the institution or its message. Likewise, victims of spiritual abuse and cultic practices in unaffiliated or newer churches are wary of anything remotely resembling organized religion. The attractiveness of a spirituality (whether or not it is shaped by Christianity) that is not bound by any structures, orthodoxy, or hierarchy is self-evident. Of course, it also appeals to a Western individualistic mind-set, but to dismiss the whole trend on that basis is to ignore the genuine grievances that underlie it.

The surprise, however, is how many resisted that path. After an evidently long and painful journey, some recover and even thrive within more wholesome Christian communities. Some, like Tom Blanchette, turned to another denomination; others sought justice and transformation within their denomination. This has led some to create pressure groups and victim support groups. One such is Voice of the Faithful, whose tagline is telling: "Keep the faith, change the church."[45]

Social media offered such groups revolutionary opportunities for information sharing and collective action, to the extent that the ability of a grassroots protest to take on a global institution like the Catholic Church has become the subject of sociological study. Clay Shirky noted that there *had* been protests and allegations in the early 1990s, but these were quickly silenced, in part because they were not coordinated. By 2002, the Internet facilitated effortless coordination and instantaneous dissemination. The authorities had no means of containing it. Shirky writes, "Social tools don't create collective action—they merely remove obstacles to it."[46]

No wonder the bushfire of suspicion spread so far and fast.

Conclusion

The appeal of healers, therapists, and pastors is obvious—their expertise, training, wisdom. But the inevitable power imbalance offers grim potential for the exploitation of the vulnerable. While very few enter these professions with that as their specific aim, the nature of institutions and systems that are not properly structured is that they can compound the problems rather than prevent them. When this phenomenon is exposed in churches, at both local and global levels, suspicion and mistrust are natural responses.

Thankfully, we are seeing a growing awareness of the corruptibility of caregivers and institutions, of the dangers deriving from the inevitable power imbalances of pastoral relationships, of the need for codes of professional conduct and means of accountability. This is all positive. It can never undo past harms, but it can prevent future abuse (which is often the deep desire of victims). The challenge for pastoral professionals and institutions to have integrity has never been greater.

PART 2

MOURNING TRUST:

LIFE AFTER LOSING IT

Jesus can you take the time to throw a drowning man a line?
"Peace on Earth" (All That You Can't Leave Behind, 2000)*

Midnight is where the day begins.
"Lemon" (Zooropa, 1993)*

You're packing for ... a place that has to be believed to be seen.
"Walk On" (All That You Can't Leave Behind, 2000)*

INTRODUCTION

DISORIENTED FURY:
A Personal Coda

Some of you will no doubt have considered my preoccupation with suspicion curious for a pastor. Yet despite my ranging far and wide through
the history and culture of the twentieth century in the previous section,
the central question has always been an intensely personal one. I, too, have
had my fingers burned. Is trust possible again? For while I have never been
particularly drawn to a conspiracy theory view of the world, I do understand
what motivates it.

A Long Way from Home

Attending two boarding schools from ages eight to eighteen was an
extraordinary privilege, for which my parents had the best of motives and
sacrificed much. Their unconditional love has never been in doubt; they were
implicitly trustworthy. The same cannot be said of one or two caregivers at
my second school, however. This is not to say such people were untrustworthy
in the corrupt or culpable sense. Rather, they were untrustworthy pastorally.
There is an important difference, and yet the repercussions are comparable.

I did not quite fit the mold of the athletic extroverts who thrive in such
places. Though my first boarding school experience had been largely positive,
my second was particularly difficult. I was one of fifty boys living cheek by
jowl, cooped up in a boardinghouse for two-thirds of the year. An inability
to blend and mix could be dire. Thus, for about three years, I lived with low
levels of permanent dread and on high alert for the next humiliation or insult.
I never did master the art of keeping my upper lip stiff (a skill for which these
ancient institutions were supposed to be renowned)!

---

* All lyrics by Bono & The Edge

What I did learn, however, was a profound reluctance to trust. For example, one time, in desperation, I sought out a staff member. He seemed sympathetic, but rather ominously (in retrospect) said, "I'll see what I can do." He then sought out one of my peers. Unfortunately, this chap happened to be one of my tormentors. So naturally, my problems were exacerbated. This was not the only time something like this occurred. Consequently, I felt a huge sense of isolation and helplessness. I had never had that feeling at home, but home was a couple of hundred miles away. The only resort was to construct a psychological shell and develop total self-reliance. Trust was impossible; trust was too risky.

Years later, after reading Nick Duffell's *The Making of Them: The British Attitude to Children and the Boarding School System*, I discovered how common my experience had been. He identifies in such people what he terms the "strategic survival personality"[1] — that was me in a nutshell. I never endured the worst of what had once gone on in these places (the Dickensian horrors of old are thankfully long gone), but I had been through enough to have scars.

My life was turned around just months before leaving school and going to university by hearing (seemingly for the first time) the message of Jesus Christ accessibly explained. I did not realize it at the time, but in retrospect, it is clear I was drawn to him by precisely the fact of his trustworthiness. When I have battled with doubts — a constant as an adult — my anxiety has nearly always focused on doubting God's goodness, not his existence (although that trifling conundrum crops up from time to time). C. S. Lewis (as he does so often) nailed the issue for me. In *A Grief Observed* — his brutally frank memoir of bereavement, only published under his name posthumously — he confesses that his greatest fear was for God to turn out to be a "cosmic sadist":

> Not that I am (I think) in much danger of ceasing to believe in God. The real danger is of coming to believe such dreadful things about Him. The conclusion I dread is not "So there's no God after all," but "So this is what God's really like. Deceive yourself no longer."[2]

Strangers in a Strange Land

The period when this fear became most acute was about halfway through my time in Kampala. I was teaching in a small Ugandan-founded seminary and particularly loved spending time with the students. It was such a privilege and a huge learning experience.

A number of our students were refugees from the surrounding

countries—Rwanda, Burundi, Sudan (as it then was), Democratic Republic of the Congo, and even Ethiopia. To say that their stories were eye-opening is an understatement. The hardship and injustices they faced constantly challenged the complacent securities of home. The experiences of two Congolese men in particular have stayed with me.

M. had been a banker in President Mobutu's Zaire (as the Congo was then called). The term *kleptocracy* ("rule by thieves") was coined for the regime, because the president of that uniquely resource-rich land regarded the central bank as his personal reserves. His lackeys naturally followed suit. This made it a country where working as a banker could prove fatal. But when the Cold War ended and the West no longer needed its African bulwark against Communism, Mobutu fell, and the country was plunged into even greater chaos. In the late 1990s, war became constant, with the country suffering its highest death toll since 1945. While the rest of the world seemed oblivious, the loss of perhaps five million lives provoked the conflict's bitterly ironic nickname "Africa's World War."

M. had to flee his home in Kisangani, eventually reaching Kampala with his wife and three daughters. They had seen close family members hacked to death with machetes. They had lost everything except the clothes they escaped in. They were refugees in an English-speaking country and so had to learn a fourth language. Before enrolling in our college, the family could only afford one room without power or water and one meal every two days with their refugees' allowance.

I will never forget the day M. and I found ourselves alone, chatting in the college library. He smiled bravely as tears streamed down his cheeks. I had been told that African men don't cry. Eventually, he said, "Mark, I could never trust in God if it wasn't for judgment. For I know there will not, and cannot be, justice for us in this world. But this is key for making the Christian message *good* news for me." That was a jolt. Could one reason we rarely hear such sentiments in the West be that we do not suffer as much? We still tend to think that some sort of justice, however flawed, can be found in this world. But for how much longer will we be able to maintain this optimism?

D. was a church pastor who had also escaped with his wife and three children. He, too, had seen family killed during the anarchy, mainly by those with eyes on his family land. After trying to settle in two other countries, he came to Kampala, where he joined our college to complete his training. Soon he was invited to become the first African pastor of a slum church planted by missionaries. D. is a gifted man who became a good friend. He is passionate about truth and integrity. He encountered a local "big man" who had built his property illegally close to the church. This was now causing some structural problems. As D. investigated, he discovered a host of other illicit activities. D. became a threat. Then D. disappeared. He stepped outside in the early evening, dressed for bed and not for going out, and didn't return.

He was gone for a week. It was desperate. It was clear things were not right. Soon we realized that some police officers were complicit — the missing person's report was "lost" only a day after it was filed. I could not understand why others were treating his absence so lightly. Few colleagues seemed especially alarmed. The missionaries were keeping their heads down. His wife was too distraught and her English too weak to enable her to do much.

Who else was going to look out for a refugee? So it seemed left to those of us who had become his friends. We discovered that a mercenary gang of army veterans had been hired to abduct and torture D., and perhaps kill him. It just so happened that a senior Ugandan friend had links with influential people who had links (etc.), and so word got to the gang that, among other things, a *muzungu* (white man) was taking an interest, and they should desist. D. was dumped naked in a forest two hours north of Kampala in the early hours of the next morning and warned that if he ever took further action, he and his family would be killed. He was also told to get out of Uganda.

I sought wisdom from old Uganda hands, and it quickly became clear the only safe way to help D. and his family was to find a country that would grant them asylum via the UN Refugee Agency. But to do that would take ages. In the end, it took nearly twenty months. In the meantime, I fund-raised among friends back home for their rent. D. lived in terror of being seen outdoors. We had to help find his family a new home every few months. It became apparent that those watching D. knew about my family's involvement. Despite the improbability that anything would be done to us, the nervous tension this caused never completely subsided.

The stress of those two years never eclipsed one particular memory, though. As part of his evidence for the United Nations case officer, D. asked me on the very day of his release to take photographs of his torture wounds. The images are as vivid today as when I took them.

I had never encountered real-life horror before. I had never encountered acute and protracted danger before. I had never encountered such brutal malice or cruelty before. I trust I never will again.

Both M. and D. ended up being granted asylum in different Western countries, together with their families. I'll never forget the euphoric relief of D.'s text message after touching down in a wintry foreign airport. His uncertainties had come to an end. But my doubts never have. At times, it felt as if I was drowning in rage and betrayal. Whom could I trust? I had always struggled to trust authority figures anyway. But now:

- I was furious with the world for ignoring the Zaire/Congo conflict and the avalanche of misery it caused (and still causes).

- I was furious with that Kampala "big man" for his blind selfishness and savagery.

- I was furious with the local police officers for their corrupt complicity.

- I was furious with those missionaries for their apparent faintheartedness.

- I was furious with the mercenaries for their rank inhumanity.

- Above all, I was furious with God. What could he have been thinking?

If there was ever a time when I have felt righteous anger, it was surely then. But it was only after returning to London in 2005 that the aftershocks of almost two years of stress, rage, and doubt caught up with me. I was diagnosed with a form of post-traumatic stress disorder, and have battled with varying degrees of depression ever since.

In my more rational moments, it has helped to know I was right to be angry about what happened. I soon came to appreciate that God was also appalled by it. I began to appreciate what M. had taught me. And I rediscovered the solace that comes from the collection of psalms. Yet the enduring legacy was my even greater trepidation about trusting others, especially if they wielded authority. I had witnessed and sometimes experienced the shattering betrayal of abused power. This was not just a psychological problem for me; it was a profoundly spiritual problem.

The past is not dead. It's not even past.
William Faulkner, writer

> I did everything they told me to, in order to be successful.
> I got straight A's and a scholarship. I went to University
>   and got a degree.
> Now I'm sinking in student debt, unable to get a job.
> I have an eviction notice on my door, and nowhere to go.
> I have only $42 in the bank. I am the 99 percent.
>   *Protestor at Occupy New York*

CHAPTER 4

LONELY IN A CROWD:
Alienated and Adrift

The aftermath is usually the forgotten story of conflict and warfare. Trust is impossible and dangerous. Suspicion converts its objects into "them," gouging an unbridgeable chasm. It alienates and fragments.

But what happens when a whole culture is infected by suspicion? What if that sense of the "them-ness" of others dominates? Isn't a decay of social cohesion inescapable?

Learning from the Extremes

Behind the Iron Curtain, the state was suspicious of its citizens. And the feeling was mutual. Anyone could be an informer, so cold reticence was inevitable. Suspicion generated habits that were extremely hard to break. Under totalitarian regimes, everyone is blighted.

Anna Funder tells the story of Miriam, an East German friend from Leipzig. At only sixteen, she attempted an escape over the Berlin Wall and, against all the odds, got within just a few yards of the Western side before capture. Her Stasi interrogators simply could not believe she had done this without help. So after ten days of sleep-deprived questioning, she finally surrendered by inventing an underground escape organization, replete with descriptions of contacts and plans. For a while, her story was believed, a fact that now causes her great amusement. The reason for that amusement is telling. Her "escape plan" entailed asking a complete stranger in a Leipzig bar whether he lived near the wall and could offer some handy escape tips. This was "inconceivable," she said.

Relations between people were conditioned by the fact that one or other of you could be one of *them*. Everyone suspected everyone else, and the mistrust this bred was the foundation of social existence. Miriam could have been denounced by the man for having asked a question about the border and admitting she was thinking of going over, and she could have denounced him in turn for offering to show her how.[1]

Timothy Garton Ash recorded similar thoughts in his East Berlin diary: "Suspicion is everywhere ... It strikes in the bar, it lurks in the telephone, it travels with you in the train. Wherever two or three are gathered together, there suspicion will be."[2]

The world is thus teeming with "them," who surround the ever-diminishing circle of "us." Despite describing a very different context as we have seen, Nick Duffell's identification of the "strategic survival personality" is surprisingly apt. People with this are "oriented for safety ... continually on the look out for danger, seeking fresh ways of out-manoeuvring any perceived threats." The result is that the person "becomes over attuned to defence."[3]

But what has this to do with the West? We have not suffered under totalitarian regimes. There are clearly different degrees of suspicion and its effects. Nevertheless, some of the East's most significant prophetic voices had few illusions about the West. Nobel Literature laureate Aleksandr Solzhenitsyn had been a tireless critic of the Soviet system and was eventually expelled in 1974. In 1983, he gave the Templeton Lecture in which he analyzed the deeper parallels between East and West. Both have "forgotten God," he said. How else, he asked, could the horrors of the Russian Revolution and two World Wars have taken place? More significantly, it was this "mental eclipse" that "allowed the West to accept calmly, after World War I, the protracted agony of Russia as she was being torn apart by a band of cannibals."[4] Controversially, it was, to his mind, post-Enlightenment secularism that bound East and West together.

Like Solzhenitsyn, Václav Havel suffered greatly for his vocal criticism of Communist regimes. But more pertinently, he made a similar, if less theological, diagnosis. In his inspirational 1978 essay *The Power of the Powerless*, he pinpoints this as the "general ability of modern humanity to be the master of its own situation." The East's system is merely an "extreme version of this problem," just "one variant of the general failure of modern humanity."[5] Or as he wrote some years before, totalitarian systems are "a convex mirror of all modern civilization."[6] Western democracy, he argued, did not offer any genuine solutions to the crisis and was actually in greater danger because it concealed the fact better, making people more deeply immersed in it. In other words, in the brutality of the East, it was obvious something was wrong. In the materially comfortable West, it was possible to assume all was well.

Both Havel and Solzhenitsyn pointed to an intrinsic problem shared by East and West—one that touches on the very nature of modern society—despite radically contrasting politics. While Communism might have fallen, capitalism continues, and so does its shared inheritance with other, totalitarian forms of government, which helps to explain today's widespread sense of alienation. Even apart from blatant forms of government deceit, alienation and social fragmentation are the products of a common, inherited outlook on the world.

In the Wake of the Masters of Suspicion

This is not the place to chart the development of the whole course of Western philosophy. Others have done this with far greater authority, Luc Ferry's recent *A Brief History of Thought* being one of the most accessible and lucid attempts.[7] We can, however, identify a few key ideas from those with the greatest impact on our age. It is no accident that they are sometimes called "the masters of suspicion."[8]

- Charles Darwin (1809–1882) dispensed with the need for a divine Creator to explain life's origins, replacing him with the mindless processes of natural selection. Any suggestion that human beings are qualitatively different from other animals must therefore be treated with suspicion, a yearning for a significance we do not deserve. For, at best, that can only be wishful thinking.

- Karl Marx (1818–1883) argued that economic forces lie at the root of all social behavior. Since history is relentlessly progressing toward a classless, egalitarian society, any conflicting ideology that obstructs this progress must be concealing some form of exploitation by its beneficiaries. It, too, is therefore suspect.

- Sigmund Freud (1856–1939) delved deep within the human psyche to detect darker psychological motivations for our behavior, such as sexuality or mortality. Thus, all *conscious* motivations must be treated with skepticism if we are to discover our true motivations.

In their different ways, each thinker bequeathed an increasingly skeptical attitude.

The true master of the art was Friedrich Nietzsche (1844–1900). He was hardly the only thinker to assume that God was a mere superstitious projection of our imagination, but he pursued the consequences of deicide to their logical extreme. The only thing left after the collapse of the sense of an intrinsic, created meaning was "the will to power," which he found "grimly exhilarating." "Truth was not discovered," he asserted. "It was invented."[9]

Nietzsche's thought probably influenced the twentieth century more than anyone else's. His influence on fascism is notorious, despite regarding nationalism and anti-Semitism as abhorrent.[10] Yet he continues to resonate because he recognized that *all* knowledge is now suspect. As he declared in *Beyond Good and Evil*, "Every philosophy *conceals* a philosophy too: every opinion is also a hiding place, every word is also a mask."[11] All that remains is a hermeneutic—an interpretative principle—of suspicion.

Thinkers have since systematically unpicked reality. The intellectual foundations of the whole Enlightenment project of modernity have consequently crumbled. God was not the only casualty of this project of deconstruction; *everything* was—all political ideologies, all social interactions, and eventually what it means to be an individual person. Opinions, especially if advocated by those historically privileged with power, required vigorous scrutiny to expose hidden agendas. The status quo could not stand, because who knows what inequalities and injustices it masked?

This critical spirit derived from the original Enlightenment thinkers themselves, "like the sorcerer's apprentice who unleashes forces which soon escape his control."[12] They cast off the shackles of religion, monarchy, and tradition, challenging their rights to authority—only to themselves become the victims of suspicion. We might relish the seemingly limitless possibilities offered by this newfound freedom, but it is also terrifying. We are left with what Jean Baudrillard termed "a vertigo of interpretations."[13] When it comes to principles for understanding the world, all around us is sinking sand. Nothing is solid. Nothing can defy such scrutiny. At least the philosopher Alfred Ayer was candid enough about his own reluctance to follow this through: "I wish I had been more consistent. Any iconoclast who brandishes a debunker's sword should be required to demonstrate it publicly on his own cherished beliefs."[14]

By the start of the new millennium, most of the deconstructing work was done. In reflecting on the impact of his atheistic Jewish mother and gently Anglican father, the novelist Will Self wrote in 1999 that he entered adulthood in a world "where ethics, so far from inhering in the very structure of the cosmos, was a matter of personal taste akin to a designer label, sewn into the inside lining of conscience."[15] In a closed universe without transcendence or revelation, this is the only option. And for Self, that is fine. All that matters is a choice, a personal preference.

But many cannot share this blithe acceptance. The closing words of Michel Houellebecq's disturbing, at times grotesque, but compelling novel *Atomised* perfectly captured the trepidation of the end of December 1999: "All across the surface of the globe, a weary, exhausted humanity, filled with self-doubt and uncertain of its history, prepared itself as best it could to enter a new millennium."[16]

This uncertainty has shown itself in four perceptions: that society is dislocated, fragmented, dehumanized, and adrift. Each is the product of suspicion, or the cause of suspicion, or both.

Dislocated Generations: A Yearning for Place

To be dislocated is to be uprooted, exiled, lost. It is disorienting and seems inescapable. Suspicion has corroded the routes by which to recover old certainties.

The Past Deconstructed

Houellebecq's phrase "uncertain of its history" is telling. The hermeneutic of suspicion revises all accepted norms and assumptions about the past, on the assumption that history is usually written by the victors. Instead, we must give profile to the stories of those marginalized and oppressed by the "great men" of old. Let us hear the worker, the foot soldier, the peasant; let us hear the anonymous pawns in imperial power games. In turn, these heroes of old must be reevaluated with what author Joyce Carol Oates described as "pathography"—the excavation of their real motivations.[17] Failure to do that will lead to biographers being charged with not really doing their homework. Indeed, if heroes' motivations are deemed admirable, then, as Dick Keyes writes, "the biographer's job was not done with any thoroughness, courage, or honesty."[18]

It is entirely reasonable to allow previously unheard voices to be heard. It is right to be exposed to "readings" of the past not often heard. But how does this avoid the vertigo of interpretations? As David Aaronovitch has rightly pointed out, "Revisionist history did something else. It was (and is) less an alternative way of studying than an adoption of deliberately alternative opinions about the past."[19]

The result is that history is relegated to the status of a resource from which to plunder, rather like the items in gift shops at historical tourist traps. So from the comfort of one's own home, it is now possible to enjoy recordings of monastic plainsong in a room scented with the fragrances of a medieval herb garden while playing an ancient Chinese board game with friends and drinking a Georgian recipe for mulled wine. The past is not so much a foreign country in which they do things differently; it is an Aladdin's cave from which to customize and embellish a lifestyle.

This would be trivial if it merely concerned matters of taste. The challenge comes when historical figures or moments are commandeered to lend a veneer of substance or precedent to contemporary controversies. Because if *everything* is a matter of interpretation, *nothing* can be refuted. No interpretation is more valid than another. In extreme circumstances, history becomes too controversial even to be broached. In the Balkans, for example, an agreed shared narrative to describe the breakup of Yugoslavia has proved dangerously elusive. A similar problem haunts Sino-Japanese relations because of Japan's 1930s occupation of Manchuria and its denials of the alleged atrocities from that period.[20] But even in less controversial situations, the past is no longer a reliable guide to understanding our present, if it ever was. Skepticism has dislocated us from our history. Perhaps Tony Blair was right to ignore history after all?

This is as true on the personal level as it is on the national level. Even for healthy adults in the prime of life, memory plays tricks on us. For example, I have no way of telling how many of my early memories of growing up in Malaysia are the result of genuine recall or of leafing through family photographs. When Timothy Garton Ash returned to Berlin to read his Stasi file, he found himself in a unique situation. He could effectively triangulate his life, comparing his memories with his own diary and his official file. It made him realize how fluid memory is. Our perspectives are in constant flux, reshaped by subsequent experience or interpretations, what psychologists refer to as "the malleability of memory." So his recollections of one friend were irrevocably altered when he learned she had informed on him. But then, if the full story behind why she did it becomes known, his view may change again. So he takes the illustration of a bad divorce, where "today's bitterness transforms all the shared past, completely, miserably, seemingly forever. Except that this bitter memory, too, will fade and change with the further passage of time."[21]

There is perhaps one exception to this rule, namely, suspicion. Suspicion lingers long after the dangers have subsided, especially for those who endured totalitarian surveillance culture. Anna Funder describes the lingering mentality in former East Germans who talk of "*Mauer im Kopf* or the Wall in the Head."[22] The Berlin Wall is long gone, but it still haunts and terrifies those who remember it.

So it would seem the past is not fully knowable even by those who lived through it. And our experience of the present can be scarred by lingering memories of the past, however safe our current situation is. Suspicion robs us of a stable sense of reality.

The Present Deconstructed

Survival in a world of concealed agendas demands a high degree of wariness, a "strategic survival personality."[23] So for all our sakes, we have a duty to expose them. What *really* is the intention behind this statement or that initiative? The oppressed have few defenses, but at least they have the hermeneutic of suspicion to wield against the privileged. That will expose the unacknowledged sexism, racism, homophobia, Islamophobia, or anti-Semitism (take your pick). History seethes with accounts of power abuse. Why should the present be any different?

A further complicating factor is that past injustices reverberate long after they are committed. Just how there can be redress is contentious, to say the least. The legacy of slavery is a case in point. The point here is simply that history must give pause to any who, like myself, are the beneficiaries of past power imbalances. I am, after all, male, white, privately educated to postgraduate level, and from a European country that still profits from centuries of global domination. My privileges are many and great. It is only honest that, at a bare minimum, these are acknowledged. I have a duty to listen to those who, in past generations, would have been ignored and exploited by "my sort."

But here is the problem: This mentality, this hermeneutic of suspicion, tends to presume guilt before it is proven or a defense is raised. It is almost a case of postcolonial guilt by virtue of birth. Is that any less oppressive than the discrimination on account of birth that caused countless executions amid the revolutionary fervor of both Paris (in 1789) and Moscow (in 1917)? Old aristocrats were eliminated simply because of their titles, regardless of actual complicity. That they had benefited from the former inequalities and injustices was never in doubt. But for all the zeal and idealism, one cruel regime simply replaced another. Suspicion created its own narrative, blinding the revolutionaries to nuances that failed to fit with their binary interpretation of reality. It was as dehumanizing as the regimes it overthrew. Suspicion banishes the possibility of generosity or grace.

Social fragmentation is inevitable after this social blindness. Communities oriented around a shared sense of past victimhood will always be defensive. This is understandable in the wake of injustice. But unchecked, it inevitably leads to antipathy and alienation. Others' motives will always be condemned as evil, even as "ours" are presumed righteous. But if one of "us" challenges the interpretations we give, we immediately become one of "them."

This is, of course, a deeply flawed starting point for building any sense of community in the present. The hermeneutic of suspicion actually falls into the old fallacy of the ad hominem argument. Quite apart from the audacity of claiming the ability to read someone else's mind and motivation, an opponent's personal characteristics are deemed sufficient grounds for rejecting his or her case. He says "X" because he's sexist; she says "Y" because she's racist; they say "Z" because they're homophobic. The individuals concerned may indeed be prejudiced, but surely what should matter is the validity of the arguments, shouldn't it? Their prejudice can, and perhaps should, be tackled, but separately. Yet, the hermeneutic has too often subtly morphed from a defense of victims into a weapon for silencing opposition. It achieves this not by invalidating arguments but by invalidating the individuals making them. That, of course, has always been the strategy for dealing with dissenters in the world's most brutal regimes.

What is true individually is true globally. Not surprisingly, Timothy Garton Ash describes our twenty-first-century context as "not a new world order but a new world disorder. An unstable kaleidoscope world—fractured, overheated, germinating future conflicts."[24] It is a world of "us" versus "them," where each group has competing grievances, agendas, and ideals.

The Future Deconstructed

It is easy to overlook how compelling Karl Marx's vision of a truly equal society was. The fairness of his famous mantra—"From each according to his ability; to each according to his needs"—is hard to contest. The flaw was to assume the inevitability of progress toward this utopia. Thus his comrade Friedrich Engels declared at Marx's burial, "Just as Darwin discovered the law of development of organic nature, so Marx discovered the law of development of human history."[25]

The twentieth century exposed the absurdity of such confidence. It is no accident that the period witnessed the rise in popularity of dystopian fiction. Grand visions seem to do more harm than good. A cynicism about *all* utopian fantasies is now only natural. Just after the Berlin Wall fell, graffiti was spotted on a nearby factory wall. It was long overdue. "To the workers of the world: I am sorry."[26] The twentieth century killed off optimism. Utopia really is "no place" after all.[27]

There have, of course, been momentary hiccups to this cynicism. Perhaps this is the result of our dislocation from history, so that we have short memories. When Tony Blair swept his UK Labour Party to victory in 1997 (accompanied by an anthemic Britpop mantra, "Things can only get better"), and when Barack Obama won the White House for the first time in 2008, suspicions were widely suspended. These victories were certainly impressive, especially Obama's with all its remarkable civil rights resonance. Yet, few of even their most avid supporters would agree that the hysteria was legitimate. The messianic triumphalism was short-lived, despite both going on to win further elections.

In our post-ideological age, we have given up on ideological solutions for a better future. So we are dislocated from the future. Many are not pessimists, exactly; they are as likely to respond with a shrug and a "whatever" approach to future visions. Since nothing is inevitable, we take each day as it comes.

Without toeholds in the past, future, or present, we are dislocated, homeless. We yearn for that sense of locatedness that religion and ideology once offered. But they have been snatched away. We can no longer trust the credibility of their advocates or the veracity of their claims. They have been deconstructed as power plays and discarded.

Fragmented Selves: A Yearning for Integration

In *The Power of the Powerless*, Václav Havel describes life under Communism as the years of living "as if." Nobody he knew actually believed in Communism, even high up in the system, but everyone pretended they did. This experience was echoed by a number of my own friends who grew up behind the Iron Curtain, including one who does not recall *anyone* being a convinced Communist.

Timothy Garton Ash called this the "double life," whereby there was a "split between the public and the private self, official and unofficial language, outward conformity and inward dissent."[28] For him, it meant applauding the type of conduct by the state he would never endorse in private life. When buttressed by the force of state control, the culture of suspicion then creates a kind of mass schizophrenia.

Again, these conditions are extreme. However, for different reasons, a comparable split is taking place in the West. Describing the world of spin and distraction (considered in chapter 2), Eliane Glaser observed that "we have sleepwalked into a world where nothing is as it seems; where reality, in fact, is the very opposite of appearance."[29] This coincidence suggests something deeper is going on, perhaps related more to modernity's shared foundations than its different ideological manifestations. Is this what Václav Havel detected in 1978, when he charged Western consumerism with being built on a similar lie?

> The profound crisis of human identity brought on by living within a lie, a crisis which in turn makes such a life possible, certainly possesses a moral dimension as well; it appears, among other things, as a *deep moral crisis in society*. A person who has been seduced by the consumer value system, whose identity is dissolved in an amalgam of the accoutrements of mass civilization, and who has no roots in the order of being, no sense of responsibility for anything higher than his or her own personal survival, is a *demoralized* person.[30]

In other words, the image I project from my belongings matters more than the person I actually am. Sociologist Anthony Giddens agrees. After losing religion, family commitments, and work as the means to personal significance, people resort to having to "construct the self upon all that seems to remain solid and tangible: their physical bodies."[31]

Perhaps this is merely a fact of human nature. We are all complex, full of jockeying hormones, drives, and temperaments. Graham Greene went so far as to suggest that "we each contain several characters—I don't fight them. I accept them. To find an 'integrated' person one would have to look in a lunatic asylum."[32] Contemporary culture offers little consolation. "I don't know who I really am anymore" is no longer the cry of the angst-ridden teenager. As David Lyon has suggested, the big existential question facing individuals is no longer "how do I conform?" but "how do I choose?"[33] But Lyon is not referring to material goods. Choices of clothing and taste are paltry by comparison. The real choice is one of personality and identity.

Many factors will influence that choice. For example, early ambition to hold high political office these days requires the careful crafting of an image as well as a résumé. So many noted how withdrawn, and even lonely, John F. Kennedy could seem, even when with friends. But this was hardly surprising given that his father reputedly said, "Can't you get it into your head that it's not important what you really are? The only important thing is what people *think* you are!"[34]

The Internet offers the perfect testing ground for identity selection. On different browser tabs, it is possible to "be" an Amazon customer of foreign-language novels, a contributor to a current affairs blog, a porn addict, an Internet troll, an experienced warrior panda on *World of Warcraft*—all while simultaneously being remotely logged into the office intranet. Which of these is "authentic"? One churchgoing friend became deeply distressed by his addiction to a sex chatroom as the persona of a member of the opposite sex. That predicament felt as inexplicable as it felt inescapable.

Perhaps Graham Greene was right: true integration really is impossible. Must we resign ourselves to the potential disintegration of personality? If we yearn for some means of integration, we seem to have nowhere to turn.

Dehumanizing Systems: A Yearning for Significance

Despite the West's claims to moral superiority, capitalism ironically tends to be as dehumanizing as Communism ever was. In both systems, individuals are just statistics without significance. However, the power of capitalism is such that it persists in treating people like this, despite promises to the contrary. Its influence persists globally because of its formidable institutions, economic successes, and material comforts.

Since the late Industrial Revolution, corporate power has grown inexorably. Annual turnover and supposed worth now defy imagination. Many corporations, like Amazon, Ford, and Apple, have revenues that exceed some countries' gross domestic product (GDP). Governments might have the power to affect the business climate in their territories, but they must tread the tightrope between attracting and discouraging global business. In fact, some commentators, such as George Monbiot, attribute the prevalent disaffection with modern politics to the power of big business to set the agenda.[35]

The image of all-powerful executives sitting in boardrooms discussing ways to implement their global strategies (to the detriment of ordinary citizens) is hard to shake off. At least politicians are (theoretically) accountable to voters. Accountability to shareholders brings a very different mentality. The only value is the bottom line. Of course, many businesses do take corporate responsibility seriously, not least because it looks good. But some of the horror stories that have come to light in recent years cause grave concern about ingrained corporate cultures. It is because they are so often complex and unintelligible to outsiders that they do not cause the opprobrium that is their due.

It took the collapse of energy giant Enron in 2001 to bring such scams down to earth. Through the systematic use of false accounting, financial smoke and mirrors, and energy price manipulation, the company's power grew inexorably. The culture at the top filtered down to individual traders. Evidence subsequently presented to federal investigators revealed recordings of calls between traders and power plant staff. One requests a "creative" reason for the plant "to go down."[36] This was at the height of the 2000 California energy crisis (the state suffered thirty-eight blackouts during that period). Some of these recordings were used in the 2005 documentary film *Enron: The Smartest Guys in the Room*. The most chilling had to be the boisterous exchange between two traders cackling about all the money they had stolen from "those poor grandmothers in California," juxtaposed with footage of firefighters rescuing people trapped in elevators by the power outage.

Unsurprisingly, many fear that the bigger the institution, the less concerned it will be for "the little people." When profits creep into the billions, what possible bearing can the livelihoods of small towns and families really have on decision making?

Regardless of whether such perceptions are fair or not, the 2011 Occupy movement rippled out from New York's Zuccotti Park to more than eighty countries because of the widespread feeling of being disenfranchised by capitalism. A year later, a senior Bank of England official even declared in a speech that Occupy's protests were taken seriously for a simple reason. "They are right," he declared. "I do not just mean right in a moral sense ... For the hard-headed facts suggest that, at the heart of the global financial crisis, were — and are — problems of deep and rising inequality."[37]

The Global Underclass

Globalization may well have brought untold wealth and mobility, but at what cost? According to 2010 World Bank figures, 2.2 billion people were still living on less than two dollars a day, in what is termed "extreme poverty" or "below the poverty line."[38] That is around one-third of the world's population. Westerners can, by and large, live remotely and obliviously to the hardships caused by this. Yet how differently we would feel and act if those statistics somehow included our own offspring.

The Lost Middle

George Packer movingly recounts the stories of ordinary individuals who suffered in the wake of the 2008 financial crisis. He cites Matt Weidner, a blogger who started posting regularly about Occupy. The subprime crisis resulted from thousands of bank loans deliberately targeted at those who were always going to struggle with repayment (the expectation of defaults was all part of the cynical calculation). But the repercussions were catastrophic and are ongoing. So Weidner insists that Western capitalism as currently arranged is unsustainable for the simple reason that it is built on lies and fraud: "Truth and consequences no longer matter. Lies and greed drive all."[39]

Millions lost their jobs, their homes, and their hope.

This does not make those still in work necessarily content. Too often, their worth has been reduced to mere financial significance or productivity statistics. A former airline reservations clerk described the effect of the introduction of computers at her work:

> You were allowed no more than three minutes on the telephone. You had twenty seconds, "busy-out" time it was called, to put the information into [the computer]. Then you had to be available for another phone call. It was like a production line. We adjusted to the machine. The casualness, the informality that had been there previously was no longer there ...
>
> They monitored you and listened to your conversations. If you were a minute late for work, it went on your file ... You took thirty minutes for lunch, not thirty-one! If you got a break, you took ten minutes, not eleven!
>
> When I was with the airlines, I was on eight tranquillizers a day ... With the airline I had no free will. I was just part of that stupid computer.[40]

Has much changed since Studs Terkel first recounted this woman's experience back in the early 1970s? Just ask the millions who work in call centers around the world or the product pickers in Amazon warehouses who have only thirty-three seconds to collect each order.

The Burned-Out Masters

It is important to recognize it is not just the galley slaves of the ship of capitalism that suffer. As multinationals shift from trumpeting their roles as "engines of job growth" to being engines of "economic growth" (a distinction that, as Naomi Klein pointed out, is only subtle if you're *not* looking for work[41]), even those at the top suffer. They are materially opulent but time impoverished. A U.S. Chamber of Commerce chair once defined a well-adjusted executive as "one whose intake of pep pills overbalances his consumption of tranquilizers just enough to leave him sufficient energy for the weekly visit to his psychiatrist."[42] He was probably only half joking.

The system ignores individuals. F. S. Michaels argues in her provocative but compelling book *Monoculture* that we are all now utility-maximizing consumers for whom the greatest deprivation is the inability to consume.[43] Zygmunt Bauman is right, then, that at its heart, the gross inadequacy of reducing a person to being a mere consumer is precisely what leads to "social degradation and 'internal exile.' "[44] But this is where the culture of suspicion leaves us once it has demolished the possibility of any overarching truth and reality.

Homeless Drifters: A Yearning for Community

London is my home. I was born here and am writing this just yards from a square in which all four of my grandparents lived at different times. Even though London is Europe's largest city, I belong here and feel at home. Yet, for many—the majority?—modern urban life is far from secure or positive. Henri Nouwen put it this way: "Probably no better word summarizes the suffering of our time than the word 'homeless.' It reveals one of our deepest and most painful conditions, the condition of not having a sense of belonging, of not having a place where we can feel safe, cared for, protected, and loved."[45]

Community life in the West is deteriorating rapidly. Carne Ross has shown that studies on both sides of the Atlantic tell the same story. One useful indicator is the number of people living alone in homes rented for less than a year. In Britain, comparisons between the 1971 national census and recent statistics thus show that levels of "rootlessness" are substantially higher. One researcher has observed that "even the weakest communities in 1971 were stronger than any community now" because 97 percent of communities studied "had become more fragmented over the last three decades." The number of Americans who said they had no close confidants tripled. The 2010 United States Census found that more than 31 million Americans live alone, which is over 30 percent more than in 1980.[46]

The reasons are complex. George Packer takes a broad cultural perspective, describing it as the consequence of greater social mobility and the pursuit of personal goals: "This much freedom leaves you on your own."[47] F. S. Michaels goes further, arguing that the economic monoculture has turned mobility into a virtue. People ideally need to relocate at the first gust of changing economic winds. They must "learn to shun long-term commitments, no longer obligated to anyone past the transaction at hand."[48] She quotes philosopher Robert Solomon, who has noted that "we have come to see isolation and loneliness as akin to 'the human condition,' instead of by-products of a certain kind of social arrangement."[49]

Yet another factor is the impact of the culture of suspicion. If I cannot trust those in authority, if I cannot trust those who are different from me, if I cannot trust the agendas of the institutions that govern my life, if I cannot even trust myself, how is a sense of alienation a surprise?

German thinker Peter Sloterdijk has defined this mass cynicism as "the universally widespread way in which enlightened people see to it that they are not taken for suckers."[50] We refuse to let anything surprise us, and to protect ourselves, we expect the least from others and prepare for the worst. Thus we resemble singer-songwriter Paul Simon's "rock" that disdains all friendship, laughter, and loving.[51]

Our lifestyles, aspirations, beliefs, and values are individualistic. So not only has the news we follow (through cable networks or websites) narrowed, so has religion. To appropriate Nicholas Negroponte's witty phrase, it is all about *The Daily Me*.[52] We are all becoming socially, intellectually, culturally, and ethically fragmented. We are rootless and drifting.

The Human Spirit Breaks Through

This has been a relentless journey. It has also been one-sided. For nothing is as bad as it could be. The reason is simple. People are never as bad as they could be. Human beings possess an extraordinary resilience in the most horrendous circumstances. The vestiges of goodness lurk even in the darkest shadows.

People have found ways to subvert the culture of suspicion. Anna Funder writes of a factory worker in East Germany who was approached to inform for the Stasi. The next day, she took delight in telling her colleagues in the canteen, "Guess what! You wouldn't credit it, but they think me so reliable that I've been asked to inform!"[53] This brilliant strategy paid off. She was no longer usable by the secret police, and so she was left alone. Or take the person who was asked to inform on a close friend. He immediately told his friend, and together they planned what he should say. Of course, if this friend had died before the wall came down, nobody would have believed this explanation.[54] But that was hardly a concern at the time. This was trusting friendship thwarting the state's control.

But before we can find constructive ways of encouraging this breakthrough, there is one further consequence of suspicion we will need to come to terms with: paranoia.

In Vegas, everybody's gotta watch everybody else. Since the players are looking to beat the casino, the dealers are watching the players. The boxmen are watching the dealers. The floormen are watching the boxmen. The pit bosses are watching the floormen. The shift bosses are watching the pit bosses. The casino manager is watching the shift bosses. I'm watching the casino manager. And the eye-in-the-sky is watching us all. Plus we had a dozen guys up there, most of them ex-cheats, who knew every trick in the house.

Ace Rothstein (played by Robert De Niro), in the opening narration of Casino *(1995)*

The Rosicrucians were everywhere, aided by the fact that they didn't exist.

Umberto Eco, Foucault's Pendulum

Kennedy slain by CIA, Mafia, Castro, LBJ, Teamsters, Freemasons: President Shot 129 times from 43 Different Angles

Headline from satirical news journal, The Onion

CHAPTER 5

LOST IN THE WILDERNESS OF MIRRORS:
Betrayal and Paranoia

The end of the Cold War did not put spies out of a job. Journalists reporting on espionage did not struggle to find stories, nor did scriptwriters struggle for material. Recent television series show that spy stories are flourishing. The BBC's *Spooks* (called *MI-5* in the United States) thrived for ten years, specializing in highly stylized and melodramatic tales about the war on terrorism. More recently, the FX spy drama *The Americans*, set during the Reagan era, centers on an all-American family that is no such thing. Philip and Elizabeth Jennings are a husband-and-wife team of KGB illegals (undercover agents). It is gloriously subversive. The audience instinctively roots for the Jennings, and yet they represent everything the average Western viewer would be expected to fear most. Then, as a crossover between crime and conspiracy dramas came *Person of Interest*, which focused on "the Machine," a mass surveillance computer system with an increasingly sinister role in wider government conspiracies.

These shows seem to tap into a cultural mood (whether because of terrorism, the KGB world that Russia's Vladimir Putin worked in, or the power of modern technology). Almost as if on cue, in 2013, former National Security Agency contractor Edward Snowden began to disclose thousands of classified documents. The world discovered that dystopian nightmares were far closer to reality than we feared. If knowledge is power, then government agencies wield astonishing power, as do the likes of Google. So we apparently have good reason to be concerned. Suspicion here is reasonable—but what happens when it becomes endemic rather than simply a personal affliction? As campaigning journalist Glenn Greenwald rightly observes, "A citizenry that is aware of always being watched quickly becomes a compliant and fearful one."[1]

The Agony of Trust Betrayed

C. S. Lewis once noted that "everyone says forgiveness is a lovely idea, until they have something to forgive."[2] Betrayal has to be the hardest offense to forgive. It presupposes trust, and trust always entails expectations. When they are not met, wounds run deep and long. Take marital affairs. Even if someone can find it within themselves to forgive a spouse's breach, reestablishing trust is rarely instinctive. Perhaps this is why playwright Arthur Miller observed that betrayal is "the only truth that sticks."[3] Where once we might have given the benefit of the doubt, experience now suggests to do so is folly. We know this on the personal level; we give it less thought on the public level.

We see this in all kinds of ways, of course. It is rare today to find new music that expresses unalloyed joy, movies that evoke unbridled hope, or novels without a jaundiced temper. There are notable exceptions, but if creative artists are the people best positioned to reflect back what is really going on, this is a worrisome sign. As Bertolt Brecht once said of life under totalitarianism, you can't write poems about trees if the forest is filled with policemen.[4]

The problem is that the widespread sense of betrayal has become far more than a matter of perceived shared experience. Is this not a unique moment in human history? Are we not reaching a critical mass of suspicion because of a confluence of historical, philosophical, cultural, and experiential causes? Because of the hermeneutic of suspicion, we now *never* interpret anything at face value. The thinker is thus cast as the jilted lover. Never again can assertions or arguments be granted the benefit of the doubt. Politics, religion, and even science are all suspect. Some even describe this as the era of "credicide."[5] Belief in a reality beyond ourselves, whether in grand stories or great leaders, is being killed off. As literary critic Peter Knight puts it, "Certainty has given way to doubt, and conspiracy has become *the default assumption* in an age which has learned to distrust everything and everyone."[6]

Many of spy novelist John le Carré's characters suffer betrayal, and so he is depressingly frank about the subject. "We have to be enormously cautious with our commitments," he says.[7] This affects every aspect of life, including our families. "We hardly know ourselves—nine-tenths of ourselves are below the level of the water." This is why le Carré sees an intersection between the clandestine world and that of ordinary life. A culture of secrecy models all human interactions because to him it is "a microcosm of all institutional behavior, and of the ever-repeated dilemma which overcomes individuals when they submit their talent for institutional exploitation."[8] It is not just spies who must guard against betrayals; it is all of us.

More in Common with Cold War Spies Than We Care to Admit?

It is impossible to know how a credicidal culture will play out. But where better to grapple with the problem than the Cold War, that era of shadows and double bluffs? Its abiding hallmark was suspicion. Its nadir was the 1970s, the "strange days indeed" that Francis Wheen describes as "the golden age of paranoia."[9]

The Cold War was never a traditional conflict. Rather than platoons battling for terrain, spies competed for intelligence. Timothy Melley catalogues the period's watchwords as "irrationalism, secrecy, uncertainty, and suspicion."[10] Thus the period's "them" and "us" axis between East and West was not the only one. A deep fissure had opened up between the overt and covert, between appearances and substance.

"US": Covert	**"THEM":** Covert
"US": Overt	**"THEM":** Overt

This makes discerning reality almost impossible. It also makes it very hard to know precisely who the enemy, the "them," actually is. The "covert sphere" (to adopt Timothy Melley's term) profoundly disorients its inhabitants, so their experience of life tumbles into the hermeneutical free fall advocated by postmodern thinkers. One of the most influential CIA agents of the period, James Jesus Angleton, vividly described espionage as a "wilderness of mirrors."[11] We *all* arguably live in a wilderness of mirrors now.

Flannery O'Connor once said, "I'm always highly irritated by people who imply that writing fiction is an escape from reality. It is a plunge into reality."[12] Not all fiction aims for that, of course, but the best invariably does. Thus, the best espionage writers can help us plunge into this wilderness. While some wrote escapist capers, others took it more seriously because of their own experience of the secret world: John Buchan (such as in *The Thirty-Nine Steps*), W. Somerset Maugham in *Ashenden*, Graham Greene (several novels including *The Quiet American*), and Ian Fleming (with his James Bond). They described, to varying degrees, the experience of life in the wilderness of mirrors.

Ian Fleming is especially intriguing. He nonchalantly brushed his Bond books aside as "the pillow fantasies of an adolescent mind," but he knew precisely what he was doing. Despite his outlandish plots, two-dimensional characters, and reactionary fantasies, he maintained that everything he wrote had "a precedent in truth."[13] And the more one delves into the annals of Cold War history, the more one realizes the truth of his claim. Much of what we now know *did* happen would stretch fictional plausibility. One retired CIA inspector general has said, "The reality of current-day espionage far outpaces the efforts [of spy novelists] to keep up with it."[14] Consider Ben Macintyre's observation that "Osama bin Laden is far closer a Bond villain than more conventional state enemies: the lone billionaire with a megalomaniac plan. It is surely no coincidence that military targets in Iraq have been codenamed Goldfinger, Blofeld, and Connery."[15]

The best evidence for truth being stranger than fiction must be Kim Philby. The most charmingly plausible of the KGB's Cambridge spy ring, he rose through the ranks of MI6 (SIS), even being tipped as a possible chief. He was eventually sent to Washington as the UK's chief CIA liaison. In his subsequent memoir, he recorded his delight in the delicious irony of his appointment.[16] For in Philby, a Soviet mole had risen to become Britain's most senior Soviet mole hunter.

Spying is "a shadowy trade between truth and untruth, a complex interweaving of imagination, deception, and reality."[17] What can possibly be the connection with modern life? It seems as far removed from the monotonies of grocery shopping and daily commutes as it is possible to get. Of course, we all have a civic duty to be aware of what governments do in our name. Yet, there are more unsettling reasons for probing this world.

Walter Lippmann declared in 1920 that "there can be no liberty for a community that lacks the information by which to detect lies."[18] Or rather, if it is freedom, it is a Ryan Stone–like freedom. Stone is the space-walking astronaut (played by Sandra Bullock in the 2013 film *Gravity*) who finds herself floating freely in the void after her life-support tether is ripped in a collision. There are no moorings, no landmarks, no escape routes.

Such is the corrosive effect of suspicion. The dread is that contemporary Western society, *as a whole*, appears no less adrift than the undercover Cold Warriors of a previous generation. Perhaps this is why the French-American man of letters Jacques Barzun suggests that "the soul of the spy is somehow the model of our own; his actions and his trappings fulfill our unsatisfied desires."[19]

From Suspicion to Paranoia

The *Call of Duty* video game franchise is one of the most successful of all time. The *Modern Warfare 3* version alone has logged more than 1.6 billion hours of online gaming since its 2011 release. Timothy Melley comments, "The result is not merely a fantasy of masculine agency but also a *fantasy of citizenship*," granting the illusion of serving "a grateful nation" from the cosseted comfort of a living room or bedroom.[20] The *Black Ops* edition of *Call of Duty*, set during the Cold War, was marketed with a sophisticated campaign that traded on the culture of suspicion. The 2010 trailer intones, "A lie is a lie. Just because they write it down and call it history doesn't make it the truth. We live in a world where seeing isn't believing, where only a few know what really happened. We live in a world where everything we know is wrong."[21]

The game lures us into the covert sphere. Like the best advertising copy, it taps into a prevailing mood. Gaming is not the only manifestation of this. Consider the global sensation of shows like *The X-Files*, with its mantra "the truth is out there," or the deliberately confusing layers of conflicting reality in *24* or *Lost*. The covert sphere is now a popular cultural phenomenon.

The reason is obvious. We sense we are being kept in the dark about what is really going on. In fact, because of plausible deniability, we *know* we are being kept in the dark. We must then exercise "something like 'the suspension of disbelief' — a simultaneous knowing and not knowing that is … the form of attention sought by fiction makers since time immemorial."[22] The difference is that now we are expected to exercise it, not in a cinema, but at a press conference. How can this not begin to arouse a sense of paranoia? As a protagonist in *The X-Files* put it, "No matter how paranoid you are, you can never be paranoid enough."[23] *The X-Files* is fiction, of course, but *Rolling Stone* critic Ralph Gleason suggested to his readers that after Watergate, no matter how paranoid you are, what the government is really doing is "worse than you could possibly imagine."[24]

Historian Richard Hofstadter famously discerned what he called the "paranoid style" in American politics in 1964. This is not clinical paranoia, which afflicts a victim with the sense of the conspiratorial being directed specifically *against him*. In contrast, the paranoid style assumes hostile forces "directed against a nation, a culture, a way of life whose fate affects not himself alone but millions of others."[25]

The rise of the surveillance society merely compounds matters. During the first decade of the new millennium, surveillance cameras spread like wildfire. For a time at least, the United Kingdom, the world's twenty-second-largest country with less than 1 percent of the world's population, accounted for one-fifth of the world's CCTV (closed-circuit television) cameras. Britain became "the most watched society on the planet."[26] Other industrialized nations followed in hot pursuit. A 2005 survey discovered more than four thousand cameras south of 14th Street in Manhattan alone. We are informed that cameras are installed for our security, and there is perhaps some comfort in that. However, they are surely more an expression of our *lack* of trust than anything else. Some even come with "loudspeakers to broadcast their correctional message to the 'antisocial.'"[27] So it is no longer the clinically paranoid experiencing that eerie sense of being watched; now we *all* do — except we *know* we are being watched; we just don't know by whom.

After chairing a 1976 United States Senate investigation into illegal intelligence gathering, Senator Frank Church declared, "Too many people have been spied on by too many government agencies, and too much information has been collected."[28] This statement hasn't exactly passed its sell-by date. In 2013, some of the true capabilities of intelligence agencies came to light, as the Bradley/Chelsea Manning and Edward Snowden scandals unfolded. The National Security Agency (NSA) in the United States, and its UK counterpart, Government Communications Headquarters (GCHQ), can routinely eavesdrop on billions of phone conversations, emails, and online interactions.

This is not the place to debate the ethics of these capabilities; it is enough merely to point to their effect. It is irrefutable that the just pursuit of international criminals and terrorists can be helped. MI5 director general Andrew Parker explained: "Being on our radar does not necessarily mean being under our microscope."[29] Yet the state clearly has the capability of knowing much more about us than we realize. For the vast majority of citizens, this is unlikely ever to cause problems. Nevertheless, many of us are sensitive about things that are not illegal or unethical. Privacy in matters of physical or mental health and sexuality is highly valued, as it is in discussing untested ideas or even learning a new skill from scratch. It is different for those in power who need checks and balances. "Transparency is for those who carry out public duties and exercise public powers," writes Glenn Greenwald. "Privacy is for everyone else."[30] However, raise a head above the parapet as an opinion former or agitator, and interest is likely—even if you are the leader of a foreign ally, as German chancellor Angela Merkel discovered in 2013. She went so far as to confront President Obama with the accusation that the tapping of her phone was "like the Stasi."[31] She knows better than most of us what that is like; she grew up a pastor's daughter in East Germany.

So can we talk about privacy in a meaningful way? Intelligence agencies aren't the only ones in on the game. Corporations and crime syndicates play too. Coupled with the increased willingness of more and more people to volunteer very personal details on social networks, we seem more exposed than ever before. This would never be a problem within trusting relationships. It is less reassuring in a world of unaccountable bureaucrats, determined hackers, and organized criminals. Is paranoia so unreasonable? Is it not telling that Google personnel refused to speak to CNET reporters after the technology news site published personal information freely available online about executive chairman Eric Schmidt in 2005? Or that Mark Zuckerberg spent millions to buy four properties adjacent to his home?[32] Is this because he has something to hide, or because he simply values his privacy?

The root of 1970s paranoia lay not simply in passive surveillance of citizens, however. The greater concern was the concealed but active scheming of governments. There was an anxiety that no amount of exposure could "truly reveal the state's terrifying security capabilities."[33] Watergate proved that political leaders *were* conspiring to burgle opponents, eavesdrop illegally, and blackmail. As Richard Nixon famously admitted in his notorious interview with David Frost, "When the president does it, that means it is not illegal." Then, as if matters weren't absurd enough, the conspirators' funds were channeled through the Committee to Re-Elect the President — which has the acronym CREEP. That alone seems worthy more of Monty Python or Austin Powers than 1600 Pennsylvania Avenue.

The problem was that Western agencies were involved in activities that far exceeded those of Nixon's henchmen. Political assassinations and regime changes were on the Cold War agenda, and not just by the Reds.

- Iran: The CIA and British SIS colluded in 1953 to topple Prime Minister Mohammed Mossadegh after he threatened to nationalize the Anglo-Iranian Oil Company. The shah of Iran was subsequently able to rule with American support.

- Cuba: In the 1960s, there were numerous attempts to assassinate Fidel Castro in Operation Mongoose.

- Congo: The first democratically elected, postcolonial prime minister, Patrice Lumumba, was assassinated in 1961 in what is recognized as a joint Belgian, American, and probably British operation. President Mobutu's kleptocratic rule was subsequently buttressed by the United States for three decades.

- Chile: President Salvador Allende (elected in 1970) was overthrown in 1973 by a military coup led by General Augusto Pinochet. While there is no evidence that the CIA participated in the coup, it is clear that U.S. foreign policy makers supported it, not least because Richard Nixon stated in 1970 that Allende should not be allowed to take office.

- Nicaragua: Throughout the 1980s, the United States tried to do everything it could to overthrow the Sandinista government, including funding and training of the Contra rebels (as authorized by President Ronald Reagan).

The list could go on. Stronger nations have always interfered with the affairs of weaker nations. It is not exclusive to the West, nor did it cease with the end of the Cold War. But the resources and ambitions of the era's intelligence services *were* new.

This fact was not lost on President John F. Kennedy. He was fully aware of his deep unpopularity in the U.S. military establishment. Among his closest friends, he occasionally pondered the possibility of a military coup.[34] Was it so absurd to imagine rogue operatives doing on home soil what they engaged in abroad? After all, Kennedy had already vetoed Operation Northwoods, a plan suggested by the Joint Chiefs of Staff. The plan was to fabricate terrorist attacks "designed to simulate 'a Communist Cuban terror campaign in Miami' in order to provide grounds for the invasion of Cuba."[35] This was even after Kennedy had rejected a proposal to sabotage John Glenn's 1962 space flight in order to pin the disaster on Cuba. Historian Thurston Clarke writes, "If the chiefs were prepared to recommend deceptive, violent, and illegal actions on the U.S. mainland that risked harming civilians, it was not preposterous to imagine them cooking up a similar scheme to justify overthrowing a president whose policies they viewed as threatening national security."[36] That the president himself had these suspicions is, of course, grist for the mill to the conspiracy theorists who continue to comb through the details of November 1963.

But suspicion, and even paranoia, does not merely afflict the powerless. It also seems to be an inevitable side effect of high office. Former Soviet Union leader Joseph Stalin, the person with perhaps more responsibility than anyone for crafting the suspicion state, ended his days "as a lonely, deluded, and fearful old man" who acknowledged shortly before his death, "I don't even trust myself."[37] Former Chinese leader Mao Tse-tung saw enemies everywhere in his later years. When three of Beijing's leading physicians diagnosed his pneumonia, "he refused to believe them, suspecting a plot by [his chosen successor] Lin Biao."[38] Closer to home, Richard Nixon admitted long after his disgrace that he had been a "paranoiac, or almost a basket case, with regard to secrecy,"[39] and Harold Wilson, UK prime minister in the 1960s and 1970s, became convinced there were numerous MI5 plots against him.[40]

What happens if this paranoia seeps through an entire society?

The Corrosive Effect of Paranoia

It is hard to return to solid ground once on the path of paranoia. Suspicion generates an interminable peeling away of the onion layers; getting to the bottom of such fears is impossible. But paranoia is a prerequisite for survival in a dangerous and unpredictable world.

Government officials in Richard Nixon's time were advised after a spate of kidnappings to vary their routes to work in Washington because "we've got to think paranoid."[41] Corporate bosses are being told the same thing today.

Andrew Marantz recently described a newly recognized psychological affliction in *The New Yorker*: the "Truman Show" delusion. As he notes, technological developments have altered the types of delusions in America. In the 1940s, it was the Japanese controlling people through radio waves; then it was the Soviets via satellites; in the 1970s it was the CIA via implanted microchips.[42] Now, therapists are encountering a psychosis wherein patients believe they are constantly on camera and that "the films are being broadcast for the entertainment of others."[43] Those who know Peter Weir's film *The Truman Show* will recognize that the syndrome's name is apt. We might therefore say that the phenomenon of reality TV has spawned the fear of personal reality *as* TV.

If we find ourselves disorientated by the wilderness of mirrors without maps, guides, or a sense of direction, what hope is there? Could our disorientation explain the prevalence of conspiracy theories?

From Paranoia to Conspiracy

In John le Carré's *The Honourable Schoolboy*, George Smiley writes to his estranged and unfaithful wife Anne, "I have learned to interpret the whole of life in terms of conspiracy."[44] If Google is any indication (16,000,000 search results for "conspiracy theories"), millions share his outlook. This is yet another consequence of the culture of suspicion. Of course, one reason there are conspiracy theories is that people do conspire, as is abundantly clear. But to see *everything* through the lens of conspiracy is a matter of grave concern.

It sometimes proves catastrophic. A case in point is "The Protocols of the Elders of Zion," a document purported to be the minutes of a late-Victorian conclave of Jewish leaders. Their goal apparently was world domination through cultural subversion, cynical propaganda, and economic mastery. But the document is a forgery. Tsarist agents crafted it in Russia in around 1900, but that was no bar to thousands taking it very seriously.

It had a profound influence on the Nazis, and one historian, Norman Cohn, went so far as to describe it as a "warrant for genocide" in his 1966 book of the same name. Hitler and his acolytes were convinced that "an international Jewish conspiracy was manipulating world events."[45] The result was a conspiracy of their own. At Reinhold Heydrich's Wannsee Conference in January 1942, the "final solution" to the "Jewish problem" was devised. The resulting memorandum paved the way for the Holocaust.

Yet this horrendous outcome was not sufficient to consign the forged protocols to the rubbish heap. Various Islamists in the Middle East declare that it *still* represents the avowed intent of Israel. So Hannah Arendt was correct in arguing that the protocols' significance does not lie in their forgery; rather, "the chief political and historical fact of the matter is that the forgery is being believed."[46]

Conspiracy theories thus beget other conspiracy theories, and even more disturbingly, actual conspiracies. Don DeLillo declared in his 1978 novel *Running Dog*, "This is the age of conspiracy, the age of connections, secret links, secret relationships."[47] After Watergate, according to John le Carré, people learned "to translate almost all of political life in terms of conspiracy ... We as the public are absolutely right to remain suspicious and contemptuous, even, of the secrecy and the misinformation which is the digest of our news."[48]

So what are we to do? Not all politicians, journalists, priests, or executives are conspirators. How do we discern the false from the genuine conspiracy, treading the tightrope between absolute cynicism and naive credulity? Or are we doomed to grope impotently in the wilderness of mirrors?

Analyzing Conspiracy Theories

We will consider theological responses to the problem in the third part of the book. But for now, it will help to consider the nature of conspiracy theories themselves. Journalist David Aaronovitch offers an excellent starting point in his *Voodoo Histories*.

The Disingenuous Power of Questioning

Conspiracy theories can feel as elusive as quicksilver. This is because of one of the more threadbare weapons in the conspiracist's armory—the feigned innocence of "just" asking questions. After all, there is nothing to fear from questions, is there? Yet this enables the advocacy of what David Aaronovitch calls the " 'it's not a theory' theory" because "the theorist is just asking certain disturbing questions because of a desire to seek out truth."[49] We the audience are then left to make up our own minds. It is disingenuous. The questions are never neutral; the questioner is already convinced there *is* indeed a conspiracy.

The problem is that we can never categorically deny the possibility of a conspiracy taking place. We know enough of the abuses by the powerful to lack complete confidence in their probity, so a few pointed questions are sufficient. They create the smoke from which we extrapolate the existence of a fire.

Questions are not the same thing as evidence. Yet as former U.S. secretary of defense Donald Rumsfeld said in a press conference, "The absence of evidence is not evidence of absence."[50] Thus, the power of suggestion is enough to grant conspiracists authority. Nobody wants to be gullible. The opportunities for demagogues of all stripes are therefore many. One outspoken example from the deeper recesses of the Christian right is Texe Marrs, who seems to combine the passion of an end-times preacher with the ingrained skepticism of the professional conspiracy theorist. His targets include everything from Obamacare and the George W. Bush presidency to Zionist Israel, the Freemasons, and the Illuminati. He even appears to take "The Protocols of the Elders of Zion" with the utmost seriousness.[51] But woe to any who question his questioning. On one recording, he says, "Ladies and gentlemen, if you have a friend who says he does not believe in conspiracy, look him straight in the eye and tell them that they are ignorant. 'I love you brother, I love you sister, but you are stupid.'"[52]

This is nothing less than an unveiled power play to silence critics. Entering Marrs's world resembles (irony of ironies) an initiation into the Freemasonry that Marrs and others are so determined to expose. It offers a new lens by which to interpret the world, like Google Glass spectacles offering a view unavailable to the uninitiated.

The power of conspiracy theories to incite self-validating communities of fellow believers is another reason for their attractiveness. It is not only skeptics who are drawn in; life's casualties also often find a home there as well.

The Suffering Casualties of History

Conspiracy theories assume that power has been exploited for venal ends. Hidden from the gaze of the public square, faceless men and women plot and scheme. As they execute their schemes, people get hurt. The little people suffer; they are the distant dots that may or may not stop moving. The powerful tend not to care. Or that, at least, is how the standard conspiracy narrative runs.

So when people *do* suffer as a result of fortune's slings and arrows, they ferret around for culprits. Such scapegoats are invariably easy to identify. Big cultural or political shifts always result in losers as well as winners. Thus David Aaronovitch rightly notes, "There is a more than plausible argument to be made that, very often, conspiracy theories take root among the casualties of political, social, or economic change."[53]

This may be one reason that conspiracy theorists are as likely to be found among doves as hawks, the Christian right as Islamic jihadists, Marxist revolutionaries as small government libertarians. But often only when they have lost something. Plots are then unearthed, regardless of the ideological flavors of the accused. The farce is that some left- and right-wing groups find themselves fingering the same villains.[54]

Consider the cycle of United States presidential elections. Both political parties prime cohorts of lawyers to expose and exploit the slightest inkling of opponents' skulduggery. A campaign would seem incomplete without both candidates accused of scandal, deception, and character flaws. Then, once the result is declared, it is guaranteed that some from the losing side find justification, however weak, for the suggestion that the battle was lost unfairly. Media bias, campaign finance, hanging chads, voter fraud, and dirty tricks have all featured.[55] It is noticeable, though, how rarely the explanation is that the better or more popular candidate won! It is far easier to take solace from the honor of a victory being stolen.

When O. J. Simpson was on trial for the murder of his white wife, Nicole Brown Simpson, in 1994, opinion polls were telling. Three-quarters of African Americans considered him the innocent victim of police collusion, whereas comparable numbers of white Americans were convinced of his guilt.[56] When a sense of injustice is endemic, the rhetoric of conspiracy fits the available evidence with ease. This is certainly the case for writer Jawanza Kunjufu, who himself simply asks questions. Are these legitimate questions? Or aren't they?

> Can you explain how less than 10 percent of the world's population which is White own over 70 percent of the world's wealth?...
>
> Is it an accident that African American males comprise 6 percent of the U.S. population, but represent 35 percent of the special education children and 50 percent of the inmates?
>
> Could the above be happenstance, irony, luck, or a conspiracy?[57]

As wealth gaps widen and the sense of disenfranchisement grows, we should not be surprised by the accompanying power of conspiracy explanations.

The Implausibility of Conspiracy

The trouble is that conspiracy theorists fail to distinguish between fiction and reality. Too often, they attribute to human beings a greater power, consistency, and dominance than is justifiable. Leaders do, of course, become delusional about their own power (often a prelude to their downfall). So when the Polish Karol Wojtyła was elected the first ever Slavic pope in 1978, KGB chief Yuri Andropov slammed his Warsaw bureau chief for allowing a socialist to become pope. But "there was no good answer to this, for not even the K.G.B. controlled papal conclaves"![58]

Complexity makes the future impossible to predict, let alone plot. There are simply too many variables and divergent agendas. Peter Berger is surely right: "One of the elements that keeps history from being a complete bore is that it is full of 'surprises.'"[59] Too often history is characterized by "the unfolding of miscalculations," to appropriate Barbara Tuchman's compelling description.[60] The nature of reality is precisely what makes the future so unforeseeable. So how can complex conspiracy theories be even *vaguely* plausible?

The acceptance of conspiracy theories usually requires a degree of gullibility far greater than that needed to accept official statements or the possibility of incompetence. After all, consider the most notorious *proven* conspiracy of the 1970s, namely, Watergate. It was puny—a bungled burglary of political opponents covered up by senior politicians. They couldn't even keep it quiet, and it brought down an entire administration. Is it really credible that the silence of thousands required to fake moon landings could be preserved, for example, even now? For all its science-fiction allure, the effort required to place twelve men on the moon is much more plausible.

Conclusion

Actual conspiracies do, of course, exist. History is full of them. As we've seen, there is endless evidence for the abuse of power to exploit and oppress. It is only right for perpetrators to be exposed and brought to justice.

Yet resorting to a culture of conspiracy invariably undermines the legitimate cases against secret abuses that need to be made. There has to be a better way.

The contention of the rest of this book is that there *is* a better way, but it may come as a shock to many. I believe we can discover the framework, resources, and virtues to escape the wilderness of mirrors in one of the very narratives that the masters of suspicion presumed to understand well enough to deconstruct. In fact, this way may even prove to be the only way.

PART 3

REBUILDING TRUST:
HOPE FOR OUR AGE

PART 3

REBUILDING TRUST:

HOPE FOR OUR AGE

And what remains when disbelief is gone?
Philip Larkin, "Church Going"

A lie never lives to be old.
Sophocles (fifth century BC)

I believe in getting into hot water;
it keeps you clean.
G. K. Chesterton

INTRODUCTION

FLEEING OR YIELDING TO THE MATRIX

The most iconic and now most clichéd scene from *The Matrix* comes when Morpheus makes Neo the life-changing offer of the red pill or the blue pill. Take the blue pill, and Neo will be returned to his recognizable life. Take the red, and he will discover the truth he vaguely perceived in all its uncomfortable reality. He, of course, chooses the red. There is, however, a far more haunting scene.

Exhausted and disillusioned by the rigors of red pill life, one of Morpheus's crew, Cypher, decides to betray Morpheus to the sinister agent Mr. Smith in exchange for reintegration to the Matrix. His terms are revealing. He demands to be rich and important, which means he wants to be an actor! He barely cares that his reality will be entirely artificial. In fact, for him, the "real" is "just another four-letter word." He lives up to his name: a "cipher" can be a person of no importance or significance.

Many have similarly concluded that the very notions of reality and truth are suspect today, mere human constructs. If any reality is possible, none is more authoritative than another. There is something exciting, attractive even, in inventing reality. What is more, it seems to work. But only for a time. As theologian Alister McGrath put it, "Reality is what you are faced with when you are wrong."[1] Reality has a maddening habit of puncturing what we presumed were the hermetically sealed walls of our constructed realities.

The central reason the Christian worldview is coherent and sufficiently broad to encompass and respond to the culture of suspicion is its commitment to the principle of paradox. A paradox is not a contradiction. It is the juxtaposition of two palpably true statements that only appear to contradict one another because of our limited understanding. Quantum physicists know this well. Light is comprised of both waves and particles, despite the apparent impossibility of this. This principle, which physicists have embraced in the last hundred years, Christians have embraced for the last two thousand.

I do not claim to offer the sum of theology in the following chapters, or even the totality of what the New Testament calls "the gospel." Instead, I attempt only to draw together some elements that are most relevant to the contemporary crisis.

From the skeptic, I request a temporary suspension of disbelief. This should emphatically not be a suspending of critical faculties, but rather a willingness to try on unfamiliar glasses through which to view the world, in order to establish whether they do justice to the complexities of existence.

We come from the creator, each of us trailing wisps of glory.
Maya Angelou

The New Generation had matured to find all Gods dead, all wars fought, all faith in man shaken.
F. Scott Fitzgerald

In questions of power, let no more be heard of confidence in man, but bind him down from mischief by the chains of the Constitution.
Thomas Jefferson, third president of the United States

The trust of the innocent is the liar's most powerful tool.
Stephen King

CHAPTER 6

TRUST NO ONE?
An Ancient Hermeneutic of Suspicion

Three millennia ago, a Jewish monarch asked God a question that has haunted humanity ever since. Gazing into a cloudless, star-filled sky over Jerusalem, King David wondered aloud, "When I consider your heavens ... what is mankind that you are mindful of them, human beings that you care for them?" (Psalm 8:3–4). This can be taken in at least two ways. In the first place, what exactly *are* human beings? In the second, what, if anything, gives them significance in the universe? Why should the God of the cosmos, if he is there, bother with us at all? Despite secularism's apparent mastery in the West, these questions have refused to die.

Haunting the Twentieth Century: Why the Suspicion?

At the end of the nineteenth century, it was perfectly possible to remain optimistic about human nature. The heights of the supposedly "civilizing" mission of the "white man's burden" across Africa and elsewhere seemed to cement it (while concealing colonialism's darker face). While the United States had been devastated by civil war, Europe had enjoyed a century of peace. This would end, ninety-nine years after Napoleon's demise, with an assassin's bullet in Sarajevo.

How different twentieth-century Europe would be from nineteenth-century Europe. The decades after the First World War relentlessly undermined optimism. Europeans have been haunted by the question "Who or what are we?" Tragedy upon tragedy impelled responses leaning toward the negative and even nihilistic. Are humans merely sophisticated mammals who gained ascendancy by virtue of brain size and opposable thumbs (the "naked ape," coined by anthropologist Desmond Morris)? Are we a parasitical virus that consumes all in its path (as the machines in *The Matrix* claim)? Perhaps we really are the only animal that blushes, as in Mark Twain's famous aphorism, because we are the only one that "has occasion to."

We can well sympathize with the hapless Charlie Fortnum, protagonist of Graham Greene's *The Honorary Consul*, who describes why his marriage failed: "It didn't work out. She was an intellectual if you understand what I mean. She didn't understand human nature."[1]

Many of the twentieth century's greatest minds assumed they understood human nature. That is, until reality caught up with them and challenged their most cherished beliefs. Perhaps surprisingly, for many it was not the First but the Second World War that finally killed off those optimisms. Despite the smoldering ashes of "the war to end all wars," people still clung to utopian dreams. Historian and father of science fiction H. G. Wells could still write confidently in 1937 that "the little triumphs of [man's] present state ... form but the prelude to the things that man has yet to do."[2] Less than a decade later, he was in despair. "The cold-blooded massacres of the defenseless, the return of deliberate and organized torture, mental torment, and fear to a world from which such things had seemed well nigh banished—has come near to breaking my spirit altogether ... *Homo sapiens*, as he has been pleased to call himself, is played out."[3]

W. H. Auden trod a similar path. Much to the consternation of fellow humanists, however, Auden traveled far beyond nihilistic anguish. Only a matter of weeks after war broke out in 1939, Auden went to a cinema in a largely German-speaking area of New York. One of the films featured Nazi propaganda about the invasion of Poland. When Poles came onto the screen, fellow audience members started crying out, "Kill them! Kill them!" This appalling experience shook Auden's deepest liberal convictions that, in his words, had undermined "faith in the absolute."[4] He desperately needed philosophical grounds on which to invalidate a Nazi ideology that blithely dismissed his humanistic principles of equality, neighborly love, and forgiveness as "fit only for effeminate weaklings." In the face of totalitarianism, "it was impossible any longer to believe that the values of liberal humanism were self-evident."[5] So began his return to God, since only God could command people to "love your crooked neighbour with your crooked heart."[6]

Those who survived the Second World War, then, had few doubts about

the horrors of which mankind was capable. Oxford professor of English literature Lord David Cecil remarked that "the jargon of the philosophy of progress
taught us to think that the savage and primitive state of man is behind us ...
But barbarism is not behind us, it is [within] us."[7] Education, social cohesion,
and high culture could never again give legitimate grounds for hope. For Nazi
Germany was arguably one of the great paragons of all three. Nor could it any
longer be reasoned that enlightened emancipation from religion and superstition was a sure route to social freedom. Alister McGrath is withering: "The
greatest intolerance and violence of that century were practiced by those who
believed that religion caused intolerance and violence."[8]

Yet in our contemporary generation, there is confusion. If people are
essentially good, why is there so much evidence to support what is almost
a modern requirement to be suspicious? And if we are not essentially good,
what are we? Genetically predisposed to selfishness? Or could the concept of
sin have any resonance?

The popular philosophies that underpin our education systems and the
therapy culture of Oprah-endorsed pop psychology would vociferously repudi-
ate that. They are resolutely optimistic.[9] Is it a coincidence that many of these
arose out of the 1960s counterculture climate of California and Woodstock,
among the baby boomers who had not personally experienced world war?
The great man of letters Arthur M. Schlesinger Jr. noted how the influence
of theologian Reinhold Niebuhr changed over the years: "His emphasis on sin
startled my generation. We had been brought up to believe in human innocence and virtue. The perfectibility of man was less a liberal illusion than an
all-American conviction ... But nothing in our system prepared us for Hitler
and Stalin, for the death camps and the gulags." Then came the 1960s : "The
rebel young of those frenzied years, with their guileless confidence in the
unalloyed goodness of spontaneous impulses and in the instant solubility of
complex problems, had no feeling for Niebuhr."[10]

Reductionism is a constant hazard for Enlightenment-shaped mind-sets,
whether religious or secular. Views of human nature are too often reduced
either to a blind, naive optimism or to a bitter, desolate cynicism. The question that will occupy the rest of this chapter is whether or not there is a way
of holding positive and negative views of human nature in tension. Both poles
seem to have validity.

The biblical writers certainly assume that preserving this tension is both
possible and essential. From the earliest Jewish scriptures to the last New
Testament documents, they present a far more nuanced picture of human

nature than skeptics give them credit for. Perhaps this is sufficient warrant for revisiting them in the light of modern confusion. The chronological snobbery that dismisses ancient insights with a sly shrug will no longer do.

It is fascinating how the Bible never whitewashes its heroes of faith, and yet, for all their failings, even the slightest characters preserve a sense of dignified humanity. A case in point might again be the great King David. For all his greatness, he was not quite the paragon he has sometimes been made out to be.

When first introduced, David is an unprepossessing shepherd boy passed over by his father. The prophet Samuel is told by the Lord to anoint a more faithful alternative to Israel's first king, Saul. As Jesse parades all his sons before the prophet, he seems to have forgotten about David working in the fields (1 Samuel 16:10–12). It is a less than auspicious start—hardly the mythmaking so loved by propagandists ever since. But David is the one God chooses to anoint as king and thus declare as his *messiah* ("anointed one" or, in Greek, *christos*).

David does, of course, bear some hallmarks of the traditional hero. We next read of his famous encounter with the Philistine giant Goliath. Interestingly, the significance of this contest is not so much that it proves the boy David's great skills as his trust in the God who anointed him. Recalling hair-raising experiences while guarding his sheep, he knows who should get the credit: "The LORD who rescued me from the paw of the lion and the paw of the bear will rescue me from the hand of this Philistine" (1 Samuel 17:37). When David defeats Goliath without breaking a sweat, Saul's jealousy is naturally aroused—but then, God had placed David on a collision course the moment he was anointed king while Saul still held the throne.

Relations between the two "messiahs" rapidly deteriorate, with David forced to seek refuge in mountain caves (1 Samuel 22:1–2) and even feign insanity in foreign courts (21:12–15). One mark of David's integrity in the midst of his suffering is his refusal to kill his rival, despite at least two opportunities (chs. 24; 26). When Saul takes his own life, David unites the nation and consolidates its territory in ways unseen since the heady days of Joshua. He is a national hero, so the new capital, Jerusalem, is named the City of David (2 Samuel 5:7–12), much as the U.S. capital is named after the nation's first president, George Washington.

In subsequent chapters, the king's piety is clearly on display, even if it is occasionally presumptuous (such as his concern about building a permanent house for God—2 Samuel 7). Eventually, power goes to his head, as with monarchs and demagogues the world over. He begins to treat Israel as a personal fiefdom rather than a nation to serve. When he spies the stunning Bathsheba bathing, he simply assumes a *droit de seigneur* and takes her for himself, despite her marriage and his own large household (2 Samuel 11).

Bathsheba becomes pregnant; her husband Uriah takes his soldiering seriously and refuses to sleep with her; David has him killed. David has grossly abused his position *twice*. It takes a bold prophetic voice to confront him with his crime (2 Samuel 12). To give him his due, David responds with immediate contrition—but this is not enough to prevent extreme consequences. For immediately after this story, we read of the domino effects of his lust.

In 2 Samuel 13, we find David's children following in their father's footsteps. Amnon becomes obsessed with his half sister, Tamar. David committed adultery; one of his sons commits incestual rape (verse 14). When Tamar's full brother Absalom hears about this, he is naturally appalled and determined to avenge his sister. David murdered to conceal his crime; one of his sons commits fratricide (verses 28–29). A "private matter" spirals into full-blown civil war when Absalom revolts against his father, forcing the king to temporarily abandon his capital (2 Samuel 15). It is harrowing. Even though David eventually restores order, he never regains the stature of his early rule.

The complex depiction of David is not unique in the Bible. The same complexity is found in other great faith heroes: Noah, Abraham, Moses, Elijah, the apostles Peter and Paul, even Jesus' own family. The only exception is Jesus himself, a point explored in the next chapter. So what is it that gives the Bible's writers the confidence to tell the nation's story without hagiography? The answer surely lies in their nuanced view of human nature. They are never blind to, nor surprised by, both the greatest achievements and worst atrocities of which human beings are capable. Thus, suspicion *is* legitimate, but cynicism is not the last word. The possibility of redemption always remains.

The Ancient Paradox

C. S. Lewis captured with characteristic finesse in Narnia what Rowan Williams called "the dual sense of human dignity and human degradation that is central to the orthodox Christian tradition."[11] Here, Aslan addresses Prince Caspian's disappointment at not coming from "a more honourable lineage":

"You come of the Lord Adam and the Lady Eve," said Aslan. "And that is both honour enough to erect the head of the poorest beggar, and shame enough to bow the shoulders of the greatest emperor on earth. Be content."[12]

Despite the conspicuous appeal of pop psychological, "bring out the divine within you" viewpoints, today's greater challenge is to establish an apologetic for preserving any honor at all in the face of human shame. So it is with human dignity that we begin.

Divine Image Bearers

The enigma of human significance has become more perplexing since King David. The more we comprehend of the sheer scale of the universe, our biochemical makeup, and the contingencies of human history, the more elusive any sense of human dignity becomes.

As King David sang, "When I consider your heavens ... what is mankind that you are mindful of them?" (Psalm 8:3–4) — what, indeed? In the face of such enormity, clinging to human significance seems as futile as climbing a snowdrift in a blizzard.

No wonder, then, that Father Brown, G. K. Chesterton's ecclesiastical sleuth, once declared to a puzzled police inspector, "All men matter. You matter. I matter. It's the hardest thing in theology to believe." He then expands on this to the uncomprehending detective. "We matter to God — God only knows why. But that's the only possible justification for policemen ... If all men matter, all murders matter. That which he has so mysteriously created, we must not suffer to be so mysteriously destroyed."[13]

Father Brown is right. Purpose and meaning in this barren universe are only ultimately possible if our existence has been granted purpose and meaning by being created. This is precisely the point that captures David's imagination as he exuberantly answers his own rhetorical question in Psalm 8:

> You have made them a little lower than the angels
>   and crowned them with glory and honor.
> You made them rulers over the works of your hands;
>   you put everything under their feet.

PSALM 8:5–6

Like Father Brown, this royal poet does not explain God's reasons. It is enough simply to state that because God created us, we matter. Divine intention bestows human significance in ways that cosmic coincidence never could. But David goes further. He is convinced that not only are we created, but we also have dignity and honor because of our unique status within creation. Alluding to the created cosmic hierarchy, we are "a little lower than the angels"—whatever that might mean—and assigned the duty of responsible stewardship over the rest of creation.

Here, David clearly alludes to the creation narratives in Genesis. This is not the place to weigh all the scientific implications of the Bible. Suffice it to say there are several possible interpretations that do justice both to the findings of scientific inquiry and the contentions of this wonderfully literary text. We are free to argue about the mechanisms and timings until kingdom come (and no doubt we will). The one nonnegotiable, however, is its assertion of our shared createdness, as part of a cosmos designed with order, purpose, and beauty.

Within this order, then, human beings share many characteristics with their fellow creatures, whether physical, genetic, or social. It can be no surprise that we share features with chimpanzees (from DNA to group dynamics). It is rather more curious that human DNA is 50 percent identical to that of the banana, but then this is merely one mysterious quirk among countless others in the natural world. The issue at stake is whether or not there are any significant distinctions. The answer in Genesis is clear: "So God created mankind in his own image, in the image of God he created them; male and female he created them" (Genesis 1:27).

It is a uniquely high status to be made in God's image (what theologians call the *imago dei*). As Christopher Wright puts it, "Createdness is glory, not shame. Our shame lies elsewhere."[14] Whatever else it might mean—the Bible never actually defines God's image—it must at the very least mean human beings are to some extent like God in our very essence. This is how we *are*. For sure, there are differences; we are not created identical to God. Our resemblance, however, is intended to say as much about what God is like as about what we are like. It is then reflected in our social and relational capacities, our rationality and creativity, our individuality and moral consciousness. This is why, to paraphrase one of the thoughts (*pensées*) of Blaise Pascal, the infinite abyss of the human heart can only be satisfactorily filled with the infinite, namely, God himself. Or as the Old Testament teacher Qoheleth put it, God has "set eternity in the human heart" (Ecclesiastes 3:11). To be made in God's image means, therefore, to have a God-shaped hole.

Unsurprisingly, this brings both tremendous privileges and responsibilities. From the very origins of our species, we have the innate ability to relate to our creator and even to share some of the burdens of creation care. The instructions at the heart of this divine creation mandate are to "be fruitful and increase in number" (which is not, of course, unique to humans) and to "subdue" the earth (which is) (Genesis 1:28).

It is easy to see why, amid concerns of population explosions and rampant exploitation of limited resources, this verse is sometimes regarded with disdain and even indignation. It has certainly been used to justify all manner of environmental atrocity. It is clear from various biblical passages that this is not the original intention. Apart from anything else, the vocation to be gardeners implies patient care and responsibility for one purpose: so that the garden flourishes. All cultures that live off the land acknowledge this. It is only in our reductionist, post-Enlightenment era that the world has become *merely* a resource repository to be plundered.[15]

The most significant aspect of this responsibility is that it is *delegated*. This is the point made by both David and Genesis 1. God made us rulers under him; we are divine deputies, divine representatives. Just as a mirror reflects the one standing in front of it, so human beings are to reflect the one in whose image we are made. This demands acting in ways that reflect his character. It is inconceivable that this image-bearing stewardship should lead to wanton destruction and natural exploitation for self-aggrandizing affluence. Christopher Wright describes the duty as "servant-kingship," on the Old Testament model of kingship that was to be "exercised particularly on behalf of the weak and powerless."[16] Exploitation and abuse have no place.

The problem today is that positive authority seems inconceivable. This is partly because of our flawed understanding of freedom. If my freedom requires discarding all constraints, disciplines, or structures, then of course, another person's authority will impinge on me. But surely, some constraints exist for our good—a barrier on the edge of a skyscraper's roof, or even the divine command not to eat from Eden's "knowledge tree." But let's leave aside for a moment the place of authority in a broken and damaged world. Imagine a symphony orchestra assembled in Eden. Would there not still be a conductor? Even ensembles that do without a director still need *someone* to coordinate them. It is not just a matter of keeping starts and ends together, but also of balancing dynamics, drawing out the more reticent sounds, and enabling every individual to contribute to a sum greater than its parts. Such authority enables each artist to fulfill his or her potential. As Victor Lee Austin puts it, "It is not sin that makes authority necessary ... Rather, even if human beings were unencumbered by sin they would still need authority in order to flourish."[17]

Furthermore, there is something wonderfully empowering about this delegated authority right at the heart of the creation narrative. Just as an apprentice worker needs to be trusted with a task in order to develop (albeit under the boss's watchful eye), so God entrusts human beings with remarkable freedom to act and affect. This is symbolized by the almost comic biblical scene of Adam's naming of the animals, while he is simultaneously seeking a "suitable" partner (Genesis 2:18–20). It is clear that no one, or rather no thing, is suitable. So a woman is made from the same stuff as the man — fundamentally equal but distinctly different — and as is clear from Genesis 1:27, the creation mandate is addressed to both.

Wherever human beings flourish and enable others to flourish, the Judeo-Christian claim is that this derives from our creaturely *imago dei*. Whatever needs to be said about what is shameful in our nature, it is fundamental that human beings still bear God's image, albeit in a tarnished way.

This is why, even in the darkest periods of human history, there are glimmers of light, examples of astonishing courage or altruism: the kindness of strangers (like the return of an intact wallet or cell phone); a person's capacity to inspire or create beauty, whether aurally, visually, dramatically, verbally, or simply by relating to others; the public service of an individual genuinely unconcerned about popular recognition; the sleep-deprived, bedside vigil of a sick child's parent; an intense dedication to cracking a complex medical conundrum that plagues people half a world away; an acquaintance's sunny disposition that always lifts spirits or prompts a chuckle; a teacher who spots the potential in the child everyone else despairs of; an official with a sensitivity to bend the rules of excessive bureaucracy to help someone in trouble; an infectious love for living; the heroic, the sacrificial, the generous, or the gracious. The list could go on and on. Thank God.

These moments surprise us, but they never fail to enhance and enrich us. Without them, life would be bleak indeed. Aspects of human nature undeniably point to a deep-seated moral sense and altruism that defy rationalistic definitions. Such moments point to our createdness, for they are all pale reflections of the character of God himself. As such, they remind us that we share an original goodness, the vestiges of which clearly remain.

In her remarkable account of totalitarianism's European legacy, Marci Shore recalls a conversation with a Czech friend, Arnošt. Having survived Auschwitz, he immediately joined the Communist party because in the camps "the communists were the best people. They were absolutely beautiful, wonderful people." In other words, they were people who walked their talk, concerned for the most vulnerable. However, Arnošt could not leave it there. He added this biting coda: "Until they got into power. Then they were horrible."[18] Power changed them.

Of course, in the West, it is easy, but dangerous, to assume that the Far Left, or even the Far Right, are uniquely prone to this. We fall into the trap of this kind of thinking because liberal, democratic capitalism "won" the Cold War, as if what we represent is the ideal *via media* between extremes. Every regime, culture, or political system in history has been flawed, regardless of its glories. And after the twentieth century, few believe that those in power can be fully trusted with that power. Is this not why the heroes of today's blockbusting books and films tend to be embattled loners struggling to preserve their integrity in the fight against institutions or agencies? What these fictions rarely show us is how these heroes would manage if they wielded power themselves.

Even the most optimistic concede that something has gone wrong. It is interesting, therefore, that a New Testament text that engages with Psalm 8 offers this surprisingly understated observation.

But there is a place where someone has testified:

"What is mankind that you are mindful of them,
    a son of man that you care for him?
You made them a little lower than the angels;
    you crowned them with glory and honor
    and put everything under their feet."

In putting everything under them, God left nothing that is not subject to them. Yet at present *we do not see everything subject to them.*

HEBREWS 2:6–8, emphasis mine

Why is this? What has gone wrong? It is an issue that preoccupied Blaise Pascal. In his *Pensées*, he suggests, "The greatest baseness of man is the pursuit of glory. But it is also the greatest mark of his excellence."[19] Dick Keyes notes that because Pascal regarded this pursuit as essential to human nature itself, "people will pursue glory of one sort or another. The all-important question then becomes, *What glory will we pursue?*"[20] Or to put it another way, to what ends and to whose benefit will human beings use the freedom and power that flow from being in the *imago dei*? The key is to grasp the attraction of the original temptation. So to Genesis we must briefly return.

Deluded Glory Seekers

God's image bearers have remarkable dignity in the primordial garden. They have hard work to do, to be sure: the garden bursts with exuberant life and needs tending. But difficulty is itself a token of this dignity. The work is a joyful expression of their likeness to, and love for, the Creator. But it goes much deeper. In the garden, God shows himself to have a freedom-granting, generous-hearted, diversity-loving, gratuitously good character. This is illustrated by God's very carefully worded instruction in Genesis 2: "You are free to eat from any tree in the garden; but you must not eat from the tree of the knowledge of good and evil, for when you eat from it you will certainly die" (Genesis 2:16–17).

It is intriguing that most translations of these verses emphasize the notion of human beings as *free*.[21] Naturally, this is a multifaceted freedom. For a start, it is simple physical freedom. They are free to eat from any tree in the garden. Since the garden's dimensions are essentially inconceivable (in Genesis 2:10–14, it is said to be bordered by two known rivers, the Euphrates and the Tigris, and two unknown, the Pishon and the Gihon), the fact that there is only one single forbidden tree is tantamount to unrestricted roaming rights. After all, imagine having the warrant to harvest from all but a *single plant* in the Amazon delta or Yosemite or Germany's Black Forest. That is real freedom—to explore, to inhabit, to thrive on the grandest scale.

Yet the small, significant prohibition of that one tree points to another kind of freedom. This is the freedom to enjoy the relationship that the *imago dei* enables. Or not. Love ceases to be love precisely at the moment coercion begins. To be programmed to love (effectively what a world without any divine prohibitions becomes) is not to be human at all. It is to be an automaton, and therefore *nothing* like God. So the rejection of a relationship with God must always be possible. All it takes is eating from one forbidden tree.

In Genesis 3, the snake does all he can to make the temptation to reject God appealing. He starts with a subtle but slippery distortion of the tone and substance of God's instruction: "Did God really say, 'You must not eat from any tree in the garden'?" (Genesis 3:1).

Note the artful omission of the crucial word *free*, as well as the deliberate twisting of God's prohibition to make it sound decidedly miserly. It demands a refutation, and to give Eve her due, she tries: "We may eat fruit from the trees in the garden, but God did say, 'You must not eat from the tree that is in the middle of the garden, and you must not touch it, or you will die'" (Genesis 3:2–3).

The problem is that she does not fully restate the generosity of God's provision, leaving the negative insinuations about God's prohibition unchecked. This is clear from her bizarre insertion of "you must not touch it." This is pure fabrication—as if the snake's approach has disoriented, as well as challenged, its human prey. Of course, if eating this fruit is so dangerous, there is no conceivable reason for wanting to touch it. Avoiding physical contact is a matter of wisdom. Nevertheless, Eve's response is, strictly speaking, incorrect. Touching the fruit is *not* fatal. Her refutation is only half right.

The ground is thus laid for the snake's trap to be sprung: "'You will not certainly die,' the serpent said to the woman. 'For God knows that when you eat from it your eyes will be opened, and you will be like God, knowing good and evil'" (Genesis 3:4–5).

A direct contradiction and a seductive proposition. What Old Testament scholar Dale Ralph Davis sometimes calls "serpent theology" has its global launch here. Yet because it is based on distortion and spin-doctoring, it perhaps needs a more Orwellian-sounding brand. So I think *SnakeThink* is even better. Not only does the snake set himself up as an alternative guide to reality; he dangles the ultimate carrot in front of his preys' faces (yes, Adam is silently, and thus culpably, present). Eating from this tree will make them "like God."

The irony is cruel. They do not need to eat anything to be like God; they were *created* like God. *SnakeThink* is cunning, though. It suggests that somehow they are missing out. Human beings do not yet know good and evil, whatever that might mean. In *SnakeThink* this is apparently worth having. It has all the appeal of the conspiracy theorist exposing a despot's dastardly stratagems to keep secrets concealed. After all, God would *never* want any human being to be like him, would he?

What is so attractive about this forbidden knowledge (apart from the obvious appeal of its being forbidden)? Much ink has been spilled over this conundrum. Is it because God fears the ghastliness of human sexual congress (as if the knowledge in question is the proverbial biblical sense of "knowing")? This view prevailed for some time, especially among those shaped by the ancient Greek views of gender that regarded women as inherently inferior to men. Yet this is palpably absurd within the context of the narrative that explicitly highlights the need to "multiply" (Genesis 1:28) within the goodness of the divine creation. It must be something else.

Perhaps it is merely a matter of factual knowledge, of knowing that good and evil exist. Yet one could argue that Adam and Eve already did know.

Within a biblical framework, doing what God forbids is by definition evil and is already a matter of public reality. Perhaps it is the knowledge of firsthand experience? Yet it is hard to see what is so alluring about the opportunity to experience evil. Much more plausible than either of these theories is the suggestion that the knowledge on offer is about determining one's own reality rather than accepting the givenness of reality. It is a matter of *deciding* what is good and evil rather than conceding to it. As such, eating of this tree is a bid for autonomy. It is a power grab, a wresting of ultimate authority from its rightful owner.

This, then, is the nature of sin. As far as the biblical writers are concerned, this changed everything. And it explains everything. However, Francis Spufford is surely to be commended for seeking a new vocabulary for this phenomenon in his quirky but sparkling *Unapologetic*. *Sin* is a hopelessly outdated term, even if the concept it signifies clearly is not; it is so overburdened by cultural baggage as to be virtually unusable. Spufford's controversial if memorable solution is to summarize it as the "human propensity to f*** things up" or "*HPtFtU*"![22] He is certainly onto something. However, it doesn't quite do justice to the (anti)relational element of the problem. So here is another suggestion: "living in God's world as if (it was) mine" or, for symmetry's sake, "*LiGWaiM*."

Power is not by itself negative. As we've noted, its potential to engender the flourishing of others is tremendous. Within the creation narratives, great power and responsibility had already been delegated to human beings. The problem occurs when it is wielded autonomously, without accountability to, and intimate relationship with, the creator of reality. When the man and the woman (together) eat the fruit, they are not crossing some impersonal boundary marker. Their act signifies both a rejection of a personal relationship with God and a unilateral declaration of independence. They are claiming God's world as their own, and thus an entitlement to rewrite the rules. This is sheer folly. In fact, these are the kinds of people the Bible calls "fools." As Dick Keyes notes, "The overarching attribute of the fool is not low intelligence or lack of education but a lack of humility before God and other people."[23]

So the cruel irony is that the first creatures made in God's image are coaxed into becoming somehow "like God," only to find they lose the very thing they sought: their original perfection and divine likeness. It has made them somehow *less* human, not more. Of course, the divine image is not altogether lost, but it is marred, twisted, and ruined—much as a great Old

Master painting would be after being slashed by a vandal's blade. It is still possible to make out the picture's grandeur and beauty; however, the scars and drooping folds of canvas are impossible to ignore. The undeniability of both aspects of human nature is what led Pascal to declare, "The greatness and the wretchedness of man are so evident that the true religion must necessarily teach us both that there is in man some great source of greatness, and a great source of wretchedness."[24]

Genesis takes a grim, downward turn in the following chapters, as if things are spiraling out of control. In the story, death comes into the world, but not through natural causes. Cain kills his brother. The fallout from LiGWaiM then takes its accumulative toll, both on individuals and in society. One bad decision (to tell a lie, say) inexorably leads to others, propelling the perpetrator into such a complex web of sin that they feel unable to extricate themselves without deep shame and humiliation.

Contemporary Resonance

Two of the most captivating TV shows ever made have surely been Breaking Bad (2008–2013) and Mad Men (2007–2014). As well as being brilliantly scripted, acted, and crafted, their huge narrative arcs have depicted precisely this phenomenon. Neither show shies away from it. In contrast to so much screen mediocrity, with its cheap and facile resolutions, Walter White's and Don Draper's transgressions are always detrimental.

So the story of Genesis might be ancient, but it remains hauntingly contemporary. The traditional Judeo-Christian contention is that this paradoxical amalgam of human greatness (as divine image bearers), and human wretchedness (because we claim autonomy from God) has great plausibility. So does it measure up to the glories and horrors of human behavior from, say, the last century better than its reductionist alternatives?

The Plausible Paradox

When James Angleton had to face the scale of Kim Philby's betrayal after the latter's defection, his sanity was irreparably damaged. When I was able to ask John le Carré how his fictional mole hunter George Smiley avoided this fate, his response was fascinating: "He starts with a deep human pessimism. He can't go much lower in his expectations or disappointment at other people's betrayals."[25] In other words, nothing surprises him. This is crucial to his genius, since, like G. K. Chesterton's Father Brown, it enables him to inhabit the worlds of all those he is pitted against. In the labyrinthine complexities of his duel with Karla, he can plan multiple moves ahead.

Yet Smiley is honorable, despite his complexity and even ruthlessness. As such, he reflects le Carré's conviction that it takes the actions of a few individuals to thwart collective, corporate, or institutional agendas.

But if that deep pessimism is both realistic and expedient, is this integrity plausible? Furthermore, can it only be found in individuals, and not institutions? History seems to indicate this. Le Carré describes the most exciting encounter of his life as meeting the remarkable Soviet dissident Andrei Sakharov. He had been "king of a closed society (he was their nuclear weapons supremo), but he realized that what he was doing was wrong and so spoke up, showing true heroism and integrity, at great personal cost."[26] Le Carré, in fact, alluded to the problem by suggesting that Smiley, "like Scott Fitzgerald, was able to hold two contradictory things as simultaneously true."

So human beings do have potential for great glory and great shame, especially when we wield power over others. This, it seems, is the human condition. Indeed, this is precisely what we should expect if the Judeo-Christian claim is correct, unpopular though this seems. Blaise Pascal was well aware of the controversy involved in articulating the problem of human sin: "Certainly nothing offends us more rudely than this doctrine, and yet, without this mystery, the most incomprehensible of all, we are incomprehensible to ourselves."[27] G. K. Chesterton wrote that original sin is "the only part of Christian theology which can really be proved,"[28] because of what John Bennett termed "the stubbornness of evil in society," which no philosophy can overcome and no political regime can legislate away.[29] Remarkably, that enlightened archskeptic, Voltaire, rejected all of Christian doctrine as superstition, except the notion of original sin, to which he returned in his later years.[30]

Graham Greene found himself having "to find a religion to measure my evil against."[31] He said, "The basic element I admire in Christianity is its sense of moral failure. That is its very foundation. For once you're conscious of personal failure, then perhaps in future you become a little less fallible."[32]

To paraphrase Andy Crouch, this is the paradox that makes it possible to expect, and to find, a Dietrich Bonhoeffer or Oskar Schindler amid the rise of Nazism; an Aleksandr Solzhenitsyn in Stalin's gulag; a Nelson Mandela or Desmond Tutu despite apartheid; a Rosa Parks or Martin Luther King Jr. when surrounded by the horrors of Jim Crow.[33]

The Moderns, Exposed

Reinhold Niebuhr insisted that the doctrine of original sin stands in judgment over *every* political system.[34] Yet for some, it still comes as a shock to find that this framework is necessary for accurately diagnosing the Enlightenment mind-set. The West's dominant narrative for the last two and a half centuries has been the struggle (with regional variations) for liberation, especially from material want and political oppression. This is undeniably a noble struggle aided by rapid developments in science and technology.

As modern revolutionaries swept away all perceived impediments to liberation, such as monarchies and aristocracies, the church, and other vested interests, a grim irony emerged. Old authorities were simply displaced by new ones. These were arguably much worse, enslaving as many as or more than they liberated. Instead of divine diktat channeled *through* earthly agents (as had once been claimed), divine authority was simply replaced *by* human beings.

The human displacement of the divine has continued apace. If the premodern European believed in a being with the divine attributes of omniscience, omnipotence, and providence (who was thus worthy of adoration), the modern Westerner sees each appropriated by human ingenuity. Of course, if God is dead, as many claim, this is inevitable. But what happens when *we* become the arbiters of good and evil?

Human Omniscience: The Panopticon

Twentieth-century leaders had at their disposal power that was previously undreamed of. Long before the surveillance potency of PRISM (the National Security Agency's program in collaboration with Government Communications Headquarters, its British counterpart), many governments on both sides of the Iron Curtain went to astonishing lengths to unearth people's secrets, all in the name of national security. The urge is as old as the hills, with some past regimes peculiarly adept at these dark arts. The tempestuous reign of England's Elizabeth I (1558–1603) would undoubtedly have collapsed had it not been buttressed by the intelligence networks of Lord Burghley and his canny spymaster Sir Francis Walsingham.

Today, espionage has advanced far beyond intercepting letters. It is now possible to eavesdrop on muffled conversations far out of earshot, film assignations, and track movements from the other side of the planet. If knowledge is power, then the ultimate knowledge (seeking effectively to abolish the notion of secrecy) is the ultimate power. Of course, the more data is collected, the harder it is to sort the important from the flotsam—but this merely spurs programmers to devise ever more complex algorithmic filters. The goal is to have access to the kind of knowledge once possessed by the gods alone. As a character in one of David Sipress's *New Yorker* cartoons demanded, "Get me everything on everybody."[35] For the first time in history, this is not as ridiculous as it sounds, and in fact, it sounds alarmingly similar to the goal of Keith Alexander, former director of the NSA. As a result of the documents released by Edward Snowden in 2013, it seems the NSA and the GCHQ have a "collect it all" strategy.[36]

French philosopher Michel Foucault identified the perfect emblem of this: Jeremy Bentham's "Panopticon." Bentham devised this circular prison in the 1780s, with all the rows of cells arranged around an open space occupied by a central security tower (equipped with louvered shutters). Each cell had solid walls on three sides, but the fourth, inward-facing wall was replaced by bars. As a result, a minimal number of security staff could control the maximum number of inmates. It created what Bentham called "the sentiment of an invisible omniscience."[37] Hence the name Panopticon, which is coined from Greek words meaning "all-seeing." The mere possibility of observation was a sufficient incentive for good behavior. The same psychological cunning is at work in the prevalence of CCTV cameras. As David Lyon points out, "For Foucault, the disciplinary gaze of the Panopticon is the archetypical power of modernity."[38] Power has been depersonalized in the hands of anonymous people. Where God had once been uniquely all-seeing, now unseen humans usurp the privilege. This is perhaps the most powerful form of social control.

Human Omnipotence: The Atomic Bomb

After the first atomic bomb tests, one of the key scientists behind its development, J. Robert Oppenheimer, reflected on the myth of Prometheus, and on "that deep sense of guilt in man's new powers, that reflects his recognition of evil, and his long knowledge of it. We knew that it was a new world, but even more we knew that novelty itself was a very old thing in human life."[39] Shortly after seeing the fireball glowing at the test site, Oppenheimer is said to have had a passage from the Hindu scriptures, the Bhagavad Gita, flash into his mind: "If the radiance of a thousand suns were to burst at once into the sky, that would be like the splendor of the Mighty One." And he was also reminded of another line from the Hindu scripture: "I am become Death, the shatterer of worlds."[40] Never before had mankind possessed such "divine" destructive power.

With every scientific advance, there have been ethical dilemmas and more sinister applications. As a symbol of human ingenuity to exploit power in order to control others, nuclear arms are hard to beat. Zeus's thunderbolt has been displaced by Oppenheimer's mushroom cloud. No wonder historian Norman Stone described atomic devastation in apocalyptic terms: "A biblical fate awaited Japan, once the Americans could establish a proper base for the delivery of fire and brimstone."[41]

Human Providence: The Inevitability of Progress

In the premodern world, the belief in a divine creator entailed a divine purpose behind reality. In more theologically sophisticated schemes, this would be captured by the notion of divine providence—God implementing a benign purpose that could be trusted even in the face of trauma and tragedy. In other words, history was going somewhere. Despite dispensing with God, modernist thinkers were reluctant to lose the optimism of providence. It was simply rebranded as "progress."

There is no doubt that when it comes to medicine or technology, the evidence for progress is overwhelming. As satirist P. J. O'Rourke brilliantly quipped, "If you think that, in the past, there was some golden age of pleasure and plenty to which you would, if you were able, transport yourself, let me say one single word: 'dentistry.'"[42] Countless examples of human innovation have irrevocably improved our lives.

But would such progress be found in the political and social realms as well? It was axiomatic for Karl Marx that it would be. For him, full Communism was the final outworking of human social development. It was a matter of scientific inevitability once human beings cast off their chains. We can, should, and will make this happen.

We may naturally dismiss this as the absurd bravado of a fundamentally discredited ideology. Yet the fact remains that confidence in progress stubbornly persists. Some historians have identified progress as the "dominant motif in Western society" and "the working faith of our civilization."[43] It manifests itself in so many ways. If there is optimism about a plotted revolution or euphoria at an election victory, isn't this because people think progress is possible? We must simply apply ourselves, collaborate widely, spend wisely, work efficiently—in other words, do whatever it takes—and *nothing* is beyond our grasp. We don't need God; we can improve our world ourselves! The present must inevitably be better than the past. Any social development or liberalization will be an improvement, because, it is said, "we have history on our side." This spurs us to further change and improvements, ad infinitum. It is not just a matter of "things can only get better," but also "things *will* only get better."

Human Adoration: The Logic of Worship

Megalomaniacal leaders have demanded exclusive allegiance from their subjects since time immemorial. The Roman emperors demanded their subjects' worship in temples scattered across their territories. In the Bible, the prophet Daniel spoke of a king who would "exalt and magnify himself above every god" (Daniel 11:36). Anthropologists have proven that all cultures have displayed a compulsion to worship. The extraordinary fact is that this persisted even after God's death was announced. The veneration demanded by both Joseph Stalin and Adolf Hitler constitutes worship in all but name. And it continues today as well.

Until his death in 2006, President Saparmurat Niyazov ruled Turkmenistan with an iron grip and the most arbitrary of diktats. Among his prohibitions were beards, singers lip-syncing at concerts, and TV news anchors wearing makeup. Yet, the most brazen of his impositions was the notorious 246-foot-high golden statue of himself, which gently rotated to enable his face to catch the sun.[44] Further east, North Korea's Kim Jong-un has extended his father's and grandfather's personality cults, despite the hope that his years in Europe might have rubbed off a little. These national patriarchs have displaced divinities.

Westerners are probably too cynical and empowered to be sucked into such overt farcical behavior by political leaders. Yet fanatical nationalism is not so far removed from the cult of personality stoked by dictators. This is especially true when the world is perceived in the absolutist "you're for us or against us" terms of "us" and "them." Is blind allegiance to one's country not just as dangerous as blind adherence to an ideology or a single leader? It is of tremendous significance that in the British Parliament, the leader of the second-largest political party is automatically granted an official title (as well as official car and salary). He or she is "the Leader of Her Majesty's Most Loyal Opposition." The assumption is that one can be both a loyal patriot *and* opposed to government policy. It would be an impossible job if patriotism brooked no dissent.

Contemporary Suspicions ...

In the decades following the Second World War, dissenters against modernity started to dominate public discourse in the West. As the bitter realities of Joseph Stalin's regime came to light, many Western Marxists began to reject the very basis of their own ideology. They were not sudden converts to capitalism, however. Instead, they rejected ideologies altogether. Armed with the hermeneutic of suspicion, they now regarded all ultimate meanings as "deodorants to cover the smell of our own self-interest," to adopt Dick Keyes's pungent analogy.[45]

In a way, this follows a trajectory similar to that of airport security. Because just one terrorist attempted to conceal explosives in drinks and toiletries, millions face airport delays at security the world over. Because power has been abused so appallingly, we must now be suspicious of *any* who wield it. Nothing can ever be taken at face value. However, this analogy needs extending.

It is indeed true that our suspicions should be alerted because of the actions of a few. However, within the biblical framework founded on Genesis, the "few" were, in fact, the original man and woman in the garden. The Bible has a hermeneutic of suspicion all its own — one that predates all human philosophers, French, post-Marxist, or otherwise. It is called sin. While it can never be divorced from an appreciation of human image bearing, it can never be ignored. The self-interest that lies at the heart of all individuals is the self-interest of *LiGWaiM*. So we can and must agree that people do "construct meanings for themselves — philosophies, religions, ideologies, and rationalizations — all in a vain attempt to evade the truth of God."[46] They always have.

... Because of a Personal Preference

SnakeThink makes eating forbidden fruit both attractive and wise. It is immaterial that it is delusional. The right to call the shots is simply too alluring. Then, because there is safety in numbers, it helps to have this preference buttressed by like-minded companions. In fact, the psalmist put this in strikingly contemporary terms:

> Why do the nations conspire
>   and the peoples plot in vain?
> The kings of the earth rise up
>   and the rulers band together

against the LORD and against his anointed one, saying,
"Let us break their chains
and throw off their shackles."

PSALM 2:1–3

That this is a manifestation of *SnakeThink* is clear in their battle cry. Divine authority is an oppressive straitjacket.

It takes courage to admit this, which is why novelist Aldous Huxley's confession in his 1937 book *Ends and Means* is so startling. He freely concedes his "motives for not wanting the world to have meaning; and consequently assumed that it had none ... [thus he] is concerned to prove that there is no valid reason why he personally should not do as he wants to do, or why his friends should not seize political power and govern in the way that they find most advantageous to themselves."[47] Huxley is simply admitting to using a philosophical deodorant.

This raises something of a conundrum. It means that theological and metaphysical questions can never be exclusively intellectual. The nature of *LiGWaiM* is such that we *always* have an incentive for *SnakeThink* to be true. Just as we can never be impartial observers of our environment because we are participants in our environment, so no one can be neutral here. We all have a vested interest in there *not* being a divine authority.

This can never be a justification for ignoring our doubts, objections, or dilemmas: they must be faced. But the detached neutrality someone might bring to a pure mathematical problem is simply impossible when it comes to God. The Bible's ancient hermeneutic of suspicion will never allow for that. As Jeremiah pronounced long ago, "The heart is hopelessly dark and deceitful, a puzzle that no one can figure out" (Jeremiah 17:9 MSG).

SnakeThink is so insidious that it can even motivate believers with perfectly sound theology to act without integrity. Theologians can use their learning to find valid reasons for justifying *any* course of action, concealing private agendas behind appeals to a revelation of divine authority. Personal preference trumps divine authority. This was one of the greatest flaws in the project known as Christendom, whereby the church wielded political and military power to achieve its own ends. In some ways, this is even worse than the brazen, anti-theistic conspiracy spoken of by the psalmist in Psalm 2.

... *Because of Failed Promise*

Even if *SnakeThink* does have explanatory power, because it is based on a delusion it still must fail.

When Timothy Garton Ash met Major Risse, one of the Stasi agents assigned to Garton Ash's surveillance, their conversation was striking. Despite being drawn to Communism by its aspirations for creating a better world, Major Risse is forced to reflect on what went wrong. His diagnosis is bald: human nature. He told Garton Ash that Communism failed to allow for what he called "the inner *Schweinehund*" and that the system could only have worked if people had been angels.[48]

When an ideology promises liberation, the result is often the exact opposite. For all its promises of community and comradeship, emancipation and exhilaration, disappointment is inevitable. For, as Harry Emerson Fosdick famously wrote, "At the very best, a person completely wrapped up in himself makes a small package."[49]

... *Because of Human Limitations*

It is a fact of existence that we are limited in every conceivable way: physical proportions, life span, stamina, speed, intelligence, capacity for love—the list goes on and on. One of the few guaranteed lessons from history is that it bears out our finitude. A person's perspectives are always partial and provisional to some extent. However good our intentions or motivations, however extensive our preparation and research, we can never fully master a situation.

This fact alone should keep us honest about human beings, however gifted or remarkable. It is in itself the basis for a degree of skepticism about hyperbolic claims to supremacy or superiority. But the greater tragedy is that our limitations extend even to our propensity to LiGWaiM. Hence, this sharp witticism from nineteenth-century writer Elbert Hubbard: "Die, v.: To stop sinning suddenly."[50] Before that point, we simply cannot help ourselves. LiGWaiM is what we all want.

Our Schizophrenic Nature

It should be clear why facile reductionism in describing human nature is entirely out of place. We are too complex.[51] We can see this in three ways.

Utopias/Dystopias

We have the propensity to dream of something better. The brightest and noblest minds might apply themselves to create utopias; the bravest and most courageous might act to inaugurate them. But revolutions tend to eat their children. As psychoanalysts are quick to tell us, what we strive for tends to have a parallel shadow side. Utopian dreams all too quickly become dystopian; hopes for heaven on earth rapidly lead to its opposite. Christendom paved the way for crusades, pogroms, and the Inquisition. The French Revolution paved the way for Robespierre's Terror and Napoleon. The Russian Revolution paved the way for Stalin's purges and the Gulag.

It matters little what cause is defended or dream implemented; *LiGWaiM* always rears its head. You may cast off the chains of the aristocrats, the bourgeois, the workers, the wealthy, anti-Semites, the educated, the racists, the male chauvinists, the homophobes, the whites; but have no illusions that their replacements will be much better. Gene Veith is surely right: "If Eurocentrism is a fault, one would think Afro-centrism would be similarly narrowminded. If patriarchy is wrong, why would matriarchy be any better?"[52]

This leads to the second complexity.

Perpetrators/Victims

The problem is that each of us indulges in *LiGWaiM*. Conflict is inevitable. And because we are all interconnected, people get hurt. We are, in fact, *all* victims of others' *LiGWaiM*. Furthermore, we are all victims of our forebears' *LiGWaiM*. The transatlantic slave trade is a case in point, resulting in victims at all manner of social, structural, and international levels.

Victimhood is a tragedy. It leaves scars and open wounds, which are sometimes lifelong. One Auschwitz survivor wrote that it left him "held captive there as a life prisoner, bound and fettered with chains that cannot be undone."[53] Victimhood always entails loss, as Andy Crouch observes: "Innocence cannot be replaced, and innocence is always lost, along with many other infinitely precious things."[54] Victimhood is a desperate reality of this flawed and complicated world, and it rightly spurs people to work on behalf of the voiceless and the powerless, the victims of others' grand utopias.

Victimhood is particularly heinous because it is often perpetrated by the very people with the power to bring about the flourishing of others. Andy Crouch writes, "When we think about distorted and damaging power ... what comes to mind ... is the strong imposing their will upon the weak, resorting deliberately or casually to acts of violence and exploitation. This, we have every reason to think, is power at its worst."[55] One exile from Vladimir Putin's Russia described how the president used every tool at his disposal to maintain his own power rather than to help the vulnerable: "For less sophisticated people, he relies on brainwashing ... For more sophisticated but less honest people, he needs to bribe them. For honest, sophisticated people, he uses repression."[56] In a very different context, Joyce Rebeta-Burditt describes the impact of others' addictions, pains, and choices in these striking terms: "Alcoholism isn't a spectator sport. Eventually the whole family gets to play."[57]

Yet the inescapable truth is that victims are *always* perpetrators of *LiGWaiM* as well. This is not to suggest for a moment that a victim of injustice must also be a perpetrator of *that* particular injustice (as if "they had it coming to them"). Rather, being a victim in one sphere never precludes being a perpetrator in another. Does this not explain the perpetual problem of one generation's victims becoming the next generation's oppressors?

Matters become considerably more complex, however, when an entire system is constructed on injustice. The acknowledgment of this fact is one of the most remarkable aspects of Václav Havel's thought. He insisted that Czechoslovak Communism in the 1970s was "post-totalitarian," because the whole population had become complicit in propping up the regime. So "in the post-totalitarian system ... everyone in his or her own ways is both a victim and a supporter of the system."[58] Thus Marci Shore writes, "What I learned from Havel about the moral ambiguity of being both a victim and an oppressor was my entryway into postcommunist Europe ... It was the beginning of my fascination with those historical moments in which there are no innocent choices."[59]

Is this not true of *all* contemporary life? We do not live under totalitarianism, but are we not constantly faced with less than innocent choices? In a world of more than seven billion individuals, *LiGWaiM* is so devilishly complex, its tentacles so widespread, that trying to frustrate it is beyond the wit of any of us. There have been inspiring attempts, such as South Africa's Truth and Reconciliation Commission, but even its greatest champions will admit its shortcomings. It is absolutely right that every individual should work to mitigate the effects of their own *LiGWaiM*; we should all seek to make intentional, ethical choices. Yet we know that even trying to do the right thing can have unintended negative consequences and may even make things worse, despite our best intentions.

In *The Gulag Archipelago*, Aleksandr Solzhenitsyn describes witnessing the vicious abuse of fellow prisoners, only to realize he could easily have acted similarly in the same circumstances. The Siberian camps didn't merely teach him about the depths of human evil and sin; they taught him about his own: "Gradually it was disclosed to me that the line separating good and evil passes not through states, nor between classes, nor between political orders either—but right through every human heart—through all human hearts ... even in the best of all hearts, there remains ... an uprooted small corner of evil.[60]

Justice Pursuers/Fugitives

Confronting the reality of the world entails, at the very least, the recognition of others' victimhood. It means listening to the voiceless, powerless, and defenseless, which will naturally lead to the pursuit of justice. For without the pursuit of justice, there can never be the proper recognition of crimes perpetrated or appropriate punishment or compensation for victims. No wonder some spend a lifetime pursuing it. If we cannot understand that, it may well be because we have not suffered enough.

Integral to this pursuit is the need for truth. Only then can consequences be determined. This is why postapartheid South Africa invested so much in its pioneering Truth and Reconciliation Commission. For all its flaws, it was an impressive and desperately needed attempt to expose the atrocities and failings of the old regime. To be indifferent is to betray a lack of solidarity with our common humanity and to ignore the inevitability of our own victimhood. German Lutheran pastor Martin Niemöller famously said of the Nazi regime:

> First they came for the Communists, and I did not speak out—
> because I was not a Communist;
> Then they came for the Socialists, and I did not speak out—
> because I was not a Socialist;
> Then they came for the trade unionists, and I did not speak out—
> because I was not a trade unionist;
> Then they came for the Jews, and I did not speak out—
> because I was not a Jew.
> Then they came for me—
> and there was no one left to speak out for me.[61]

He knew this firsthand. He suffered for seven years in a concentration camp. But what happens when there is no one left to "speak for me"? What happens when the hope of justice in the world is a forlorn one? As former United Nations secretary-general Kofi Annan wrote, "The slowness of international justice can be a problem when the pace of politics is intense."[62] A posthumous recognition (or even pardon) of a victim of injustice may help relatives and friends, but is little compensation for the victim. Then, what is far worse is that many who perpetrated the twentieth century's most terrible atrocities never faced justice. After all, Joseph Stalin died in his bed (albeit as a paranoid and irrational wreck). This was no consolation to his victims, either contemporary or subsequent, which brings us to the knotty problem of God and justice.

Is God indifferent? The answer for many is that, despite the persuasive power of Western liberalism (which finds the notion of divine justice abhorrent), we *need* him not to be. Otherwise, this is indeed a cold and terrifying universe. Inhabiting a universe in which God is indifferent to sin is no different from a universe that is godless. In fact, it is probably worse. Film director Stanley Kubrick once said, "The most terrifying fact about the universe is not that it's hostile but that it is indifferent ... However vast the darkness, we must supply our own light."[63] But hasn't history proved again and again that our own light has been woefully insufficient and ineffective? And if God *does* exist but does *not* act against atrocity and sin, what would that reveal about his character and nature?

Croatian theology professor Miroslav Volf witnessed firsthand the brutal breakup of Yugoslavia in the 1990s. He is resolute in his conviction of the necessity of divine justice. In fact, he goes so far as to suggest that the path of genuine nonviolence is only possible after injustice where divine justice is unimpeachable:

> In a world of violence [one could argue that] it would not be worthy of God not to wield the sword; if God were not angry at injustice and deception and did not make the final end to violence God would not be worthy of our worship ...
>
> My thesis that the practice of nonviolence requires a belief in divine vengeance will be unpopular with many Christians, especially theologians in the West. To the person inclined to dismiss it, I suggest imagining that you are delivering a lecture in a war zone ... Among your listeners are people whose cities and villages have been first plundered, then burned and leveled to the ground, whose daughters and sisters have been raped, whose fathers and brothers have had their throats slit. The topic of the lecture: a Christian attitude toward violence. The thesis:

we should not retaliate since God is perfect noncoercive love. Soon you would discover that it takes the quiet of a suburban home for the birth of the thesis that human nonviolence corresponds to God's refusal to judge. In a scorched land, soaked in the blood of the innocent, it will invariably die. And as one watches it die, one will do well to reflect about many other pleasant captivities of the liberal mind.[64]

In fact, as cultural critic Mary Eberstadt has convincingly argued, it was precisely the fact that Adolf Hitler, Joseph Stalin, Mao Tse-tung, and their toadies did not believe that a god was going to hold them to account that gave them the confidence to commit their atrocities with such abandon.[65]

Conclusion

The problem should now be obvious. What about ourselves? If Václav Havel is right that in the extremes of totalitarianism no action is entirely innocent, then in the face of divine justice, where do we now stand? We are created in the *imago dei*, but we are equally perpetrators of *LiGWaiM*. This paradox is the only plausible explanation for the realities of the last century in particular. So what now?

The answers to this question are as surprising as they are revolutionary.

125 Rebuilding Trust: Hope for Our Age

> Nearly all men can stand adversity, but if you
> want to test a man's character, give him power.
>
> *Abraham Lincoln*

The great question which, in all ages, has disturbed mankind
and brought on them the greatest part of those mischiefs
which have ruined cities, depopulated countries, and
disordered the peace of the world, has been, not whether
there be power in the world ... but who should have it.

> *John Locke*

> Power belongs to you, God, and
> with you, Lord, is unfailing love.
>
> *Psalm 62:11 – 12*

CHAPTER 7

TRUST THIS ONE!
Dominion in Safe Hands

The prophet Daniel had few illusions about power, as we have seen. He foresaw a time when kings would exalt themselves as gods. It is no surprise that his preoccupations invaded his dreams. One in particular woke him up in a cold sweat — a dream full of fantastical beasts and terrifying monsters worthy of the darkest Tolkien nightmare. However, these monsters weren't Daniel's greatest anxiety.

> In my vision at night I looked, and there before me was one like a son
> of man, coming with the clouds of heaven. He approached the Ancient
> of Days and was led into his presence. He was given authority, glory and
> sovereign power; all nations and peoples of every language worshiped
> him. His dominion is an everlasting kingdom that will not pass away, and
> his kingdom is one that will never be destroyed.
>
> DANIEL 7:13 – 14

Two Hebrew idioms require brief explanation: "son of man" simply means "human being," while "the Ancient of Days" is a title for Yahweh, Israel's God. Daniel thus eavesdrops on an astounding celestial event: God grants *all* power and authority over human affairs to a single human being. Moreover, this is no temporary role; it is an eternal mandate. One could be forgiven for imagining that such supremacy should be restricted only to God. But inexplicably, it is placed in the hands of a finite human being, who is to be worshiped by the whole of humanity. Worst of all, this is God's initiative.

Is it any surprise Daniel flinched? His reaction seems almost understated:

"I, Daniel, was troubled in spirit, and the visions that passed through my mind disturbed me" (Daniel 7:15).

Why on earth was God granting a human being divine supremacy? Is this not the dream of megalomaniacs whose ambitions become the stuff of nightmares? As one Romanian novelist, Alexandru Ivasiuc, said of the brutal years of Communist rule under dictator Nicolae Ceaușescu, "We are 22 million people living in the imagination of a madman."[1] Other twentieth-century dictators differed in scale rather than ambition, and with the benefits of weapons and surveillance technologies, their grip on power seemed unassailable. It is salutary to remember that despotic regimes always fall eventually, so aspirations to thousand-year reichs are risible. However, this is scant consolation for those writhing beneath their iron fists. So the vision of a human being with eternal divine power is the greatest nightmare conceivable. After all, the maturity of a political constitution is indicated by such things as open elections, the separation of powers, the limitation of political mandates, and fixed elected terms. The introduction of checks and balances was central to the genius of America's founding fathers. Thus, many would wholeheartedly endorse these five accountability questions for the powerful, first articulated by the British political firebrand Tony Benn.

1. What power have you got?
2. Where did you get it from?
3. In whose interests do you exercise it?
4. To whom are you accountable?
5. And how can we get rid of you?[2]

These questions always irritate those in power, even if they once gained it in an insurgency campaign against incumbents. Yet Daniel's vision seems to fly in the face of every political theorist ever known. This man will have absolute power, granted to him by God, accountable to no one apart from God. And there is no way to get rid of him.

Daniel's qualms were undoubtedly informed by his knowledge of the old covenant, Israel's constitutional foundation given by God through Moses. Even though monarchy was to have an integral place within the nation's history, there is an ambivalence about it. At one stage, Moses warns the Israelites against desiring kings in order to be like the surrounding nations. Kings like that will surely accumulate countless horses, wives, and wealth at the people's expense (Deuteronomy 17:14–17). The prophet Samuel extends the warning. Kings send the nation's sons to war and turn her daughters into "perfumers and cooks and bakers" (1 Samuel 8:13). The day will come, said Samuel, when "you will cry out for relief from the king you have chosen, but the LORD will not answer you in that day" (8:18). It seems that Moses and Samuel understood the human heart sufficiently well to be budding conspiracy theorists themselves.

Of course, the goal was for Israel's kings not to be like other nations' monarchs. Moses insisted they devote themselves to God and his covenant, symbolized by one of the newly crowned king's first duties: to write out the law in his own hand (Deuteronomy 17:18). Few of David's descendants seem to have been especially influenced by the practice.

Jesus of Nazareth had similar concerns about the powerful, whether fellow Jews or Gentiles such as Judea's Roman occupiers. He berated the former for their religious hypocrisy (Matthew 6; 23); the latter had a reputation for "lording it over" people as if their only significance was to do their masters' bidding (Mark 10:42).

Jesus insisted on a radically alternative model. His own.

The conundrum is that he based it on Daniel's nightmarish vision of absolute power. His favorite title was "Son of Man," with its claims to authority that deliberately echo Daniel 7. There can be little doubt the title was used to claim authority and allegiance.

The Jesus Conspiracies

Before we can consider why Jesus might have used this title, there is a perplexing obstruction that, if left unresolved, would render all further discussion fruitless. This is the complex tangle of claims insisting that the historical figure of Jesus of Nazareth (the man who actually lived) must be distinguished from the so-called Christ of faith (the figure Christians worship as divine). The problem is that many increasingly regard this Christ of faith as a fiction, originally created to bolster the power and prestige of an imperial dictator. In other words, he is camouflage for a conspiracy.

In one of the earliest New Testament documents (written perhaps within twenty years of the crucifixion), the apostle Paul describes Jesus in astonishing terms. As a young adult, Paul's zeal for the Judaism of his upbringing was beyond question. From his earliest moments, he would have faithfully and regularly intoned the *Shema* (Hebrew for "hear"): "Hear, O Israel: The LORD our God, the LORD is one" (Deuteronomy 6:4). This ancient creedal statement lay right at the center of Judaism's greatest distinction: monotheism. Look at what Paul does with it:

> Even if there are so-called gods, whether in heaven or on earth (as indeed there are many "gods" and many "lords"), yet for us there is but one God, the Father, from whom all things came and for whom we live; and there is but one Lord, Jesus Christ, through whom all things came and through whom we live.
>
> 1 CORINTHIANS 8:5–6

Far from denying Jewish monotheism, Paul insists that Jesus' divinity is entirely consistent with it. He offers no explanation for how — yet to his mind, it is the only plausible conclusion to draw from the testimony of Jesus' life and ministry. N. T. Wright describes this as "possibly the single most revolutionary christological formulation in the whole of early Christianity, staking out a high christology [the doctrine of Jesus' identity] founded within the very citadel of Jewish monotheism."[3] It is staggering.

Within the next ten years or so, Paul then wrote to believers in Philippi from prison (Philippians 1:7). This letter was therefore written before at least three of the gospels and certainly within living memory of Jesus' life. One of its most famous passages is the early Christian hymn found in Philippians 2. Since it is integrated so perfectly into the letter's themes, it could well have been written by Paul himself. However, some scholars argue that another person composed it, in which case it is even older than the letter. Either way, the hymn concludes with an astonishing climax:

> Therefore God exalted [Christ Jesus] to the highest place
>   and gave him the name that is above every name,
> that at the name of Jesus every knee should bow,
>   in heaven and on earth and under the earth,
> and every tongue acknowledge that Jesus Christ is Lord,
>   to the glory of God the Father.
>
> PHILIPPIANS 2:9–11

The resonances with Daniel's dream are obvious, but there is an even more breathtaking Old Testament allusion from an even more ancient prophet:

> Turn to me and be saved,
>   all you ends of the earth;
>   for I am God, and there is no other . . .

> Before me every knee will bow;
> by me every tongue will swear.
>
> ISAIAH 45:22–23

New Testament scholar David B. Capes observes that the phrases "every knee will bow" and "every tongue will confess" (alluding to Isaiah 45:23) "belong to one of the most important monotheistic passages of the Old Testament and refer originally to the worship of Yahweh."[4] The divine name, Yahweh, that was revealed to Moses was considered so holy by the pious that it should not even be uttered, hence its euphemistic substitution with LORD (*Adonai* in Hebrew). However, Paul is brazen. The man Jesus of Nazareth is identified *as* Yahweh, the Almighty God of Israel and the cosmos. The world will one day "acknowledge that Jesus Christ is Lord"—in other words, that Christ is Yahweh! Within thirty years of his death, Jesus of Nazareth was clearly worshiped as God.

Some will merely retort that Paul was responsible for deifying Jesus and thus creating what became Christianity. So it is striking that Mark (who worked alongside the apostle Peter), John, and Matthew all echo the same beliefs, though in terms that are complementary with rather than identical to Paul's.

Take this conversation between Jesus and his opponents recorded in John's gospel. It must surely qualify as one of the Bible's strangest. Jesus has again been accused of being in league with the devil, but after denying it, Jesus complicates matters considerably by claiming superiority to Abraham, the revered father of Israel: "Your father Abraham rejoiced at the thought of seeing my day; he saw it and was glad." To which his hearers responded, "You are not yet fifty years old ... and you have seen Abraham!" Jesus had the last word: "Before Abraham was born, I am!" (John 8:56–58).

It was a serious enough matter to claim such antiquity, despite clearly being in his early thirties. But Jesus was suggesting something even more incendiary. The grammatical incongruity of saying "I am" about an ancient historical moment points to his shocking theological claim. For "Yahweh" is shorthand for the fuller revelation of God's name, meaning, "I AM WHO I AM" (Exodus 3:14). This points to Jesus' uncreated, eternal nature. John clearly has Jesus claiming identity with God the Father. This explains the reaction of Jesus' audience. If he was merely claiming to be ancient, they would have dismissed him as deranged. But it was precisely because he claimed divinity that "they picked up stones to stone him" (John 8:59). Stoning was the pious response to blasphemy.

In summary, then, it can easily be proved that "the New Testament bears credible and early witness to the unified doctrinal core, in particular with regard to Christology, centered on Jesus and his apostles, a core that is, in turn, grounded in Old Testament messianic prophecy."[5]

Of course, for the early church, the problems were only just beginning. These beliefs placed them on a collision course with imperial Rome, quite apart from the many intellectual challenges they were presented with. It would take decades, even centuries, of serious engagement to find theological formulae that did justice to the New Testament's nuances. For example, how is it possible to retain the resolute monotheism of Judaism with the newfound belief in Jesus' divinity, without resorting to tritheism (the belief in three different gods)? And then, what is the relationship between Jesus' divine nature and his human nature?

These were the questions that preoccupied the church's first leaders and thinkers and that the emperor Constantine was so desperate eventually to settle in the fourth century. It certainly wasn't his intention to impose an alien notion of Jesus' divinity on the church. In fact, it is arguable that he was exploiting the political benefits from adopting Christianity precisely because of its central belief in Christ's divinity.

It is interesting, therefore, to note that theological aberrations have historically tended to arise from the obliteration of paradox in order to preach something simpler and theoretically more plausible. One can learn a great deal about a culture from the aspects of Christology that are emphasized, and perhaps even more from those that are ignored. As Robin Griffith-Jones rightly suggests, "Every generation has depicted the Jesus which that generation needed: the Emperor, the liege-lord, the philosopher, the political radical, or the gentle Jesus, meek and mild."[6] The challenge has *always* been to present the totality of the Jesus of the New Testament.

This is why the ones who suffered for their faith in the church's first centuries were the believers in the paradoxes of the God-man. Their convictions about Jesus as Lord meant they could never accept Caesar as Lord. Gnostics, on the other hand, were no threat to the status quo, since their beliefs were "spiritual" and otherworldly. The grubby realms of imperial politics were an irrelevance to their piety. N. T. Wright summarizes the point perfectly:

> One of the best answers to the new "myth of Christian origins" is the fact that, in the second and third centuries, it was the orthodox, not the Gnostics, who were being thrown to the lions and burnt at the stake.

This is a point that needs to be rubbed in whenever anyone says, as they frequently do, that the canonical gospels, and the portrait of Jesus they enshrine, were designed to gain power and prestige, and ultimately, social and political favoritism.[7]

The Personification of Truthful Power

The twentieth century witnessed countless individuals willing to sacrifice their lives for their nations, their heroes, or their beliefs. These convictions ranged widely from the political and revolutionary to the religious or deeply personal, and, of course, a person's readiness to die proves neither the validity nor the coherence of the motivating belief. Yet the motivations are always intriguing and challenging. Why do it? Why pay the ultimate price?

For the early Christians, and indeed for the majority of Christian martyrs ever since, the reason is simple: Jesus himself. But what is it about him that prompts such allegiance? He never commanded armies or roused rabbles into revolt. In fact, he denounced such tactics. He never wrote books or espoused a new philosophy. He never established a political power base or lobbied for office. There has quite simply never been a leader like him. In fact, I want to suggest that one of the many characteristics that drew people to him is precisely the way he subverted human power. Despite laying claim to be Daniel's cosmic Son of Man, his was authority with a difference.

That did not mean he was reticent about it. He never seized power. His authority was merely a given. In fact, the sheer regularity with which he spoke about himself in exalted terms suggests that the common reduction of him as a great moral teacher must be dispelled. A morally upright teacher, for example, would never say things like this: "I am the way and the truth and the life. No one comes to the Father except through me. If you really know me, you will know my Father as well. From now on, you do know him and have seen him" (John 14:6–7).

This is even more daring than his blasphemous declaration in John 8. Not only is he claiming to be the unique door to knowing God; he makes one of the New Testament's most profound statements about his identity and indeed about cosmic reality. If correct, his statement means ultimate truth and reality are not actually to be found in ideas or systems of human thought. Truth (with a capital "T") is not essentially philosophical; it is personal. H. Richard Niebuhr thus described Jesus as the "Rosetta stone of faith," the one through whom all things can and should be interpreted, and this metaphor powerfully expresses something of what Jesus is saying.[8] He is the path to reality, the personification of reality, the one who truly lives in reality and who sustains those seeking to live in reality.

This is crucial. Václav Havel diagnosed the subtle horrors of life under Communism. One of its hardest aspects was the way in which authority became anonymous. Despite the socialist dream of universal equality, pyramids of power persisted. Those at the top were as inaccessible to the ordinary worker as medieval monarchs had been. What made totalitarianism worse, though, was the impossibility of ever knowing who had authority over what in the Kafkaesque labyrinth of state bureaucracy. Power is depersonalized so that it makes little difference who holds the reins, just like in Jeremy Bentham's Panopticon prison. The system continues regardless of the identity of its "faceless people, puppets, those uniformed flunkies," with everyone blindly following what Havel described as the rituals of power. When power is anonymous, "individuals are almost dissolved in the ritual."[9]

This is an extreme example, but do not elements of this problem exist today? Consider democratic political systems. In an effort to prevent the concentration of power, constitutions are drawn up to preserve the status of an office rather than its occupants. The United States has, at the time of writing, its forty-fourth president, and the United Kingdom has its fifty-third prime minister. While incumbents can have a considerable impact, the office will outlast them all. In a world that is suspicious of those who hold these offices, there seems to be no realistic alternative.

This is fundamentally different from the way Jesus reveals ultimate reality. Because he *is* the truth and the life, the cosmos has a personal intelligence at its core. By proclaiming this, Jesus makes this authority approachable. Furthermore, truth is simply *who he is*. Authority is simply *what he has*. This inevitably gets worked out in his ministry, as shown in Matthew's gospel:

- After the Sermon on the Mount: "When Jesus had finished saying these things, *the crowds were amazed at his teaching,* because he taught as *one who had authority,* and not as their teachers of the law" (Matthew 7:28–29, emphasis mine).

- During a storm on the lake: "Then he got up and rebuked the winds and the waves, and it was completely calm. The men were amazed and asked, 'What kind of man is this? Even *the winds and the waves obey him!*'" (Matthew 8:26–27, emphasis mine).

- When presented with a paralyzed man: "'I want you to know that *the Son of Man has authority on earth to forgive sins.*' So he said to the paralyzed man, 'Get up, take your mat and go home.' Then the man got up and went home. When the crowd saw this, they were filled with awe; and they praised God, *who had given such authority to man*" (Matthew 9:6–8, emphasis mine).

- Training his disciples: "Jesus called his twelve disciples to him and *gave them authority* to drive out impure spirits and to heal every disease and sickness" (Matthew 10:1, emphasis mine).

There is little in the Gospels to dispel the reason that Daniel's vision was so nightmarish. Both confirm the Bible's contention that divine power is vested in one individual. Indeed, one of the other features of totalitarian Czechoslovakia that so concerned Václav Havel was that "the centre of power is identical with the centre of truth."[10] Surely, this is precisely the problem with Jesus. Or is he different from megalomaniacal dictators?

The Power of the Powerless

A thought experiment is perhaps necessary here. Suppose for a moment that handing absolute power to one individual might not be so nightmarish after all. What virtues in that individual might make it positive?

At the very least, we would hope for a sense of responsibility to harness and guide that power. This would ideally entail a deep commitment to justice, especially for the most vulnerable. At the same time, could there not be extenuating circumstances that warrant a degree of mercy? It would be important for this superpower to be approachable—for anyone and everyone. Otherwise, justice and mercy would be available only to those with access. This individual would ideally be consistent, impartial, and trustworthy.

Yet if there was one characteristic to crown all the others in this fantasy virtue list, it would surely be altruism—a profound commitment to the flourishing of others. This is what characterizes authority at its best.

It would be hard to deny that such a person has the right to govern. This is why the character of political candidates is deemed almost as important as their policies and also why the nineteenth-century statesman George Canning declared he must travel a road "through character to power; I will try no other course; and I am sanguine enough to believe that this course, though not perhaps the quickest, is the surest."[11]

When leaders exhibit these virtues, even if imperfectly or partially, others are always inspired to follow. The challenge in contemporary culture is their rarity or, more accurately, our presumption of their rarity. That explains our reluctance to trust; it also explains the clamor for checks and balances, public inquiries, and regulatory bodies.

Jesus never ran for office. He merely proclaimed his authority as the Son of Man revealed—and there is a take-it-or-leave-it quality to this proclamation. Yet it is fascinating how many of the characteristics from our virtues wish list are essential to his nature. Of course, it might be argued that the list was framed precisely to make Jesus the perfect fit. However, it is a testimony to his influence that these characteristics are valued in leaders today at all, because they certainly would not have featured on the ancient world's wish list. Jesus was a subversive radical from the start. He transformed our hopes and expectations of what leadership should be about. As C. S. Lewis articulated brilliantly in his Chronicles of Narnia series, Aslan, the analogue to Jesus, first appears "as a rebel against the established order."[12] And his subversive work continues. Three ways in particular stand out: status, weakness, and defeat.

Subverting Status Anxiety

Power conveys status, so the greater the power, the greater the status—and the greater the anxiety about gaining that status. Jeff Connaughton, who is profiled in George Packer's The Unwinding, is a long-term operator in Democratic Party politics. Having started out as a starry-eyed idealist, he soon became jaundiced. He discerned two kinds of people in Washington, DC: "those who crossed the room at a party to greet someone they knew, and those who waited for the other person to cross the room."[13]

This obsession with status means that the constant preoccupation is to calculate relative rankings on pecking orders. Philosopher Alain de Botton defines status anxiety as "a worry ... that we are in danger of failing to conform to the ideals of success laid down by our society and that we may as a result be stripped of dignity and respect; a worry that we are currently occupying too modest a rung or are about to fall to a lower one."[14] There is nothing especially modern about this. But Jesus refused to follow its rules. The Son of Man never made anyone cross a room to get to him.

He never stood on ceremony, being quite happy to be interrupted by and occupied with the problems of the lowest of the low. His followers were slow to grasp this. On one occasion, people brought their children to him, perhaps for a blessing. The disciples took it upon themselves to act as their boss's gatekeepers and began rebuking the parents. Jesus used the moment to explain something vital about the status anxiety–free society he was inaugurating: "Let the little children come to me, and do not hinder them, for the kingdom of heaven belongs to such as these," he said (Matthew 19:14). If even the lowest on the status ladder have a valued place in the kingdom, does the ladder not then cease to have significance?

The subversive quality of Jesus' act pales in comparison with perhaps the most unsettling act of his ministry on the night before he was arrested. Stripping to his underwear and wrapping a towel around his waist, he fell to his knees to wash his friends' feet. In Jewish culture, only the most menial of servants might be expected to do this. For some, only Gentile servants or others who could be demeaned (like women or students) would do it. Peers would only do it on very rare occasions as a mark of affection, but seniors would certainly never do it for their inferiors. The duties associated with status operated in one direction only: upward. What Jesus did as he washed and dried his disciples' feet (John 13:4–5) was an "act of humility ... as unnecessary as it is stunning."[15]

Peter, for one, could not handle this breach of cultural norms. Yet John's narrative offers a stunning repudiation of the rights we naturally associate with status: "Jesus knew that the Father had put all things under his power, and that he had come from God and was returning to God" (John 13:3). It is one of the most startling, apparent non sequiturs in history: he has divine power; therefore he must wash feet! Yet Jesus knows exactly what he is doing by stooping so low. He was once again exposing the futility of status anxiety. He simply did not care about earthly status.

Nor should his followers. For the Son of Man wields his awesome power unlike *anyone* else, before or since:

> Jesus called them together and said, "You know that those who are regarded as rulers of the Gentiles lord it over them, and their high officials exercise authority over them. Not so with you ... For even the Son of Man did not come to be served, but to serve, and to give his life as a ransom for many."
>
> MARK 10:42–45

It is inconceivable that a Roman emperor, British monarch, or even a democratically elected politician would volunteer to wash the feet of his contemporaries, let alone seek to introduce such a profoundly countercultural model of leadership.

Redeeming Human Weakness

Karl Marx believed that change comes from the strength of the powerless, not from the weakness of the powerful.[16] His confidence for the inevitable revolution derived from the knowledge that once the world's workers had united, they would easily overwhelm the small ruling elites. They might have been powerless for generations, but their strength came from their numbers.

It took Václav Havel's genius to turn the phrase against Marx and his disciples in *The Power of the Powerless*. He realized that regimes would totter if everyone simply started living within the truth (as he put it) instead of tacitly accepting lies. Whole countries pretended not to notice their emperor's distinct lack of clothing. Of course, this was because they were terrified— totalitarianism had discovered how to dominate people from within. But this psychological oppression could be overcome if individuals overcame fear and lived within the truth.[17] In many ways, this is what happened in 1989 when the Berlin Wall fell. The crowds in East Berlin simply overwhelmed the hapless guards. The combination of numbers and truth was too great to be denied.

But here is the shock: In both cases, revolution came about when those who were previously weak joined forces and thus became strong. The Son of Man's revolution was achieved by doing precisely the opposite. This is how Paul's Christ hymn begins:

> [Jesus], being in very nature God,
> > did not consider equality with God something to be used to his
> > > own advantage;
> rather, he made himself nothing
> > by taking the very nature of a servant,
> > being made in human likeness.

PHILIPPIANS 2:6–7

No one expected *that* from God's Son of Man. Pomp and circumstance would be more fitting, surely? The trappings and status of authority, the unrestrained adoration of crowds, the creative power to conjure up a palace and pleasure gardens at the click of a finger—these are what we might expect from the one Daniel dreamed about. However, this reveals more about our own dreams and aspirations than God's.

There is a subtlety in Paul's words here that is often overlooked. A viable fleshing out of the first line could read, "Who, *because* he was in very nature God, did not consider equality with God something to be used to his own advantage." In other words, it was in God's character to be profoundly altruistic. He would never exploit his powers. He would do whatever was necessary in order to love—even if it meant making himself "nothing," someone whose presence does not register or seem to matter, like a menial servant, a homeless veteran, or a statistic on lists of genocide victims. This is the strong becoming weak—*because* he is God.

It was humiliating enough for the Creator to become a creature. To conceive of what that was like is impossible. But consider the incongruities of Jesus' inauspicious start. His paternity was suspect. His parents clearly weren't married when he was conceived. He was born in a borrowed accommodation where the only place to put him was a farmyard food trough. Within days, his family became refugees from a king's lethal paranoia. When they could eventually return home, they lived in a northern area of the country disdained by Jerusalem's religious elite. It is highly likely that Jesus then had to shoulder family responsibilities as the main breadwinner through carpentry—the fact that Joseph is never mentioned after Luke 2:39 (while Mary and Jesus' siblings are) suggests he died when Jesus was young. None of this was an ideal start for an aspiring religious leader, let alone God's means to change the world. He had very little going for him.

But it was at Jesus' crucifixion that his deliberate weakness and vulnerability were most grimly on display. Jesus was defeated, executed on an instrument of torture regarded by the Romans as so atrocious it was used only for non-Roman criminals. This is worse than frailty; it is abject failure.

Yet here is the strangest thing: it was the whole point. As one of G. K. Chesterton's characters brilliantly put it, "The cross cannot be defeated ... for it is Defeat."[18]

Defeating Defeat through Defeat

If defeating defeat through defeat sounds absurd, then Paul's challenge when preaching "Christ and him crucified" is beginning to register. But Paul isn't fazed; in fact, he maintains that Jesus' death was God's deliberate purpose:

> Since in the wisdom of God the world through its wisdom did not know him, God was pleased through the foolishness of what was preached to save those who believe. Jews demand signs and Greeks look for wisdom, but we preach Christ crucified: a stumbling block to Jews and foolishness to Gentiles, but to those whom God has called, both Jews and Greeks, Christ the power of God and the wisdom of God.

1 CORINTHIANS 1:21–24

A crucified messiah or king has always been utterly implausible. This is because a cross is emphatically the last place anyone would expect cosmic authority to show, let alone assert, itself. In fact, the very concept of Christ crucified is a contradiction in terms. Who ever heard of a king on a cross? Kings reign in palaces; they do not die on death row. If they do, it suggests their overthrow in a coup d'état. It suggests failure.

Of course, different cultures take issue with different aspects of Paul's message. In the first century, the Jews searched for celestial signs to corroborate the claims of David's long-sought successor, and so they would have at least expected a few military skirmishes and the odd victory thrown in. To put it bluntly, they wanted a David-like hero to slay their Roman Goliath; they could never accept one slain by the Romans.

On the other hand, the Greeks found it impossible to respect a god willing to get his feet muddy on earth. For people profoundly shaped by the unique heritage of their philosophers (literally "lovers of wisdom"), the game was already lost at the incarnation, when God took on human flesh. The crucifixion hardly mattered—it merely made Paul's message more preposterous. Wisdom seems absent.

Today it seems unscientific to believe in God becoming human; it is alien to a secular mind-set. Furthermore, is it not incongruous with the way power "works"? As Tim Keller put it, "This is unnatural biologically—who ever heard of the survival of the weakest?"[19] This cannot be Daniel's Son of Man, surely? D. A. Carson notes of the passion narrative in Matthew's gospel, "It is difficult to imagine a portrait more calculated to depict Jesus' utter powerlessness."[20] The irony of course, as Andy Crouch points out, is that "there is no point in this story where Jesus gives up power" because nothing happens outside his purposes.[21] But he does relinquish the status, privileges, and, above all, immunity that were his birthright.

Nevertheless, Paul was convinced that Jesus was exactly who he said he was, and that God was indeed at work through him. It looked pathetic and absurd, but why should that matter? Why should God act according to human conventions or expectations? Why should God squeeze into boxes limited by human imagination? In fact, God's defiance of the world's expectations ought to be central to Christianity's appeal.

Yet here is the paradox: The cross has become both Christianity's symbol and creed. This is because even though it was a defeat, it was not an end. Despite appearances, the cross was Jesus' greatest victory. This does not fit with the prevalent pick-and-mix approach to Jesus, what Henry Maier called "an easier, faster, no-fuss, microwavable God."[22] The cross will always be a stumbling block until one can accept that there was a need for the rescue of humanity.

This is why Jesus' famous last utterance was not "I'm finished," but "It is finished" (John 19:30). In other words, his work was done. And it was achieved through the subversion, and even rejection, of worldly patterns of wielding power. Graham Tomlin wrote, "God still works in and through what is to conventional human understanding, weak, powerless and apparently irrational rather than through what is strong, powerful and reasonable. In the light of the cross, human power counts for nothing before God."[23]

This explains why a power-seeking culture has no place among the followers of the crucified Messiah. It also explains how Paul can subvert the imagery of a Roman victory march through the city streets, an honor granted to generals after spectacular conquests. The technical term for this procession was a "triumph"; it was a tangible symbol of imperial power. How ironic to describe the cross as such: "Having disarmed the powers and authorities, he made a public spectacle of them, triumphing over them by the cross" (Colossians 2:15).

This, then, is how God in Christ fulfills Daniel's vision of the all-powerful man. The cross shows how God wields power. It was precisely because he was God that Jesus did not seek to exploit the privileges of heaven, but made himself a nobody—and then died in the lowest of ways. The Son of Man became a slave to give his life as a ransom for many. The contrast with how human beings handle power couldn't be greater.

Most of us would likely say that some things are worth suffering for, and many today certainly suffer for their beliefs. But what on earth could be worth the suffering of God's Son of Man? The New Testament consistently proclaims it was nothing less than the restoration and rescue of a humanity that has been "living in God's world as if (it was) mine" (LiGWaiM). And God's shocking, scandalous means of bringing this about was nothing less than the Son of Man suffering the consequences of humanity's sin.[24]

Paul writes, "God made him who had no sin to be sin for us, so that in him we might become the righteousness of God" (2 Corinthians 5:21). Jesus willingly took on himself what we deserved so we could be granted what we did not deserve—his righteousness and a perfect, unimpeded relationship with the Creator from whom we had alienated ourselves.

This is why the renowned Victorian preacher Octavius Winslow summarized the events of Jesus' final hours by asking who delivered Jesus to die:

"Not Judas, for money; not Pilate, for fear; not the chief priests, for envy; but the Father, for love."[25] Before the cross, the ground is level and all are equal—equally created in God's image, equally LiGWaiM, and equally loved. All can find genuine forgiveness and restoration here. This is the case, regardless of any and every distinction or division that human society erects. Every culture's pecking orders, career paths, and social ladders are laid flat and rendered pointless before the cross.

Of course, Good Friday by itself would have seen Christ's work completed, but not publicly vindicated and paraded. This is why Easter Sunday shows the great victory, because in the apostle Peter's words, "it was impossible for death to keep its hold on him" (Acts 2:24). The resurrection happened and changed everything.[26] And if God has vindicated the crucified criminal, then, as Philip Kern asks, "what of the values that condemned him?"[27] Worldly power, lording it over others, ruthless ambition that vaunts self over others—all of this is rendered null and void. This is the great victory of Christ's cross and resurrection. Such is the unprecedented and startling power and wisdom of God at work.

It is all a matter of how those final hours on the cross are interpreted. A ghastly failure? That will always be the reading of the person trying to squeeze God into the box of human expectations. A triumph? Only if we accept that God defies our expectations. It is a question of being willing to accept that God can subvert power patterns if he wishes.

This is why the words of the weather-beaten military officer who witnessed Jesus breathe his last are so remarkable. Here was a Gentile who had undoubtedly spent his professional life seeing people die across the Roman empire, probably often at his own hands. "When the centurion, who stood there in front of Jesus, saw how he died, he said, 'Surely this man was the Son of God!'"(Mark 15:39). He is not, in fact, making a statement about Jesus' divinity, since the biblical phrase "Son of God" does not mean what theologians later meant by "God the Son" (the second person of the Trinity). God's firstborn son in the Old Testament initially referred to the nation of Israel (see Exodus 4:22). Then, after the monarchy had been established and the king became a representative for God's people, he became the son of God. This is why Psalm 2 (with its proclamation in verses 6–7 about God's new king becoming his son) was used at Jerusalem coronations.

So "Son of God" was a royal title. It is no less remarkable for that, however. What it means is that the centurion somehow saw through the trappings of worldly power to the way God does power. God's king dies on a cross.

Power for the Powerless

It makes little difference which gospel account we turn to; they all offer a consistent impression of Jesus, the servant of the powerless. In the aristocratic culture of Rome and the hierarchical world of first-century Judaism, the powerless were most of the citizens. Luke's gospel is traditionally regarded as the one that is most concerned for the social outsiders who were drawn into Jesus' orbit. Paul described him as "our dear friend Luke, the doctor" (Colossians 4:14), which suggests the gospel writer had himself been a slave (the majority of doctors at that time were). Luke therefore would have had a deeply personal interest in the matter. It is breathtaking when we consider how countercultural Jesus was—and still is.

- Jesus was conspicuously countercultural in honoring women. Luke emphasizes the importance of women in the stories of his birth and childhood (his mother Mary, obviously, but also Elizabeth and Anna in Luke 1–2). Then there are the integral followers like Martha and Mary (Luke 10:38–42), Mary Magdalene, Joanna, and Susanna (Luke 8:2–3). Individual women are commended for their faith as role models, and they are central figures in some of Jesus' parables (Luke 15:8–10; 18:1–8). His is not the behavior of an aspiring megalomaniac.

- A central theme in Old Testament ethics is care for society's most vulnerable, which in ancient Israel meant foreigners, widows, and orphans (Deuteronomy 10:18; 24:17–22; 27:19). It isn't surprising, then, that we see Jesus doing this (Luke 7:1–10; 13:10–13; 21:1–4). Luke also takes special notice of the times when Jesus cares for vulnerable families, at risk perhaps because a widow is left with only one child (Luke 7:12–15). We've also noted Jesus' willingness to welcome children, and the fact that adults have much to learn from them (Luke 18:16). His is not the behavior of an aspiring megalomaniac.

In Jesus' day, it was commonly assumed that wealth was a sign of divine approval. People drew the obvious conclusions about the poor. Yet Jesus took special interest in the poor (Luke 4:18; 6:30; 14:11–13, 21) and didn't hesitate to warn the wealthy about the false confidence that results from riches (12:16–21; 16:19–31; 18:18–27). Because wealth inevitably brings power, currying favor with the wealthy is a tried and tested policy of the ambitious. But Jesus refused to do it. This is not to accuse Jesus of an inverted snobbery. He was perfectly at ease in the company of the powerful and was always responsive to genuine approaches. His is not the behavior of an aspiring megalomaniac.

- In first-century Judea, people were ostracized for many reasons. A disease like leprosy was one. Collaborating with the Roman occupiers was another. Those who lived and worked on the wrong side of the tracks, the sinners and tax collectors, were particularly reviled by the religious establishment. But Jesus went out of his way to heal the diseased (Luke 6:18; 7:21), to hang out with sinners (Luke 15:1–2), and to associate with collaborators (Luke 19:1–10). Even worse, some of his parables were simply inflammatory. In more than one, religious types are the hypocrites, whereas the marginalized are models of faith (Matthew 21:28–32; 22:1–14; Luke 18:9–14).

    Supreme in this litany of power subversion is the cross itself. Conventional kings expect their subjects to die for their crown and country. But Jesus was the only king who died so his subjects could live. In the apostle Paul's words, "God demonstrates his own love for us in this: While we were still sinners, Christ died for us" (Romans 5:8). Nobody in another religious system, philosophy, or ideology has offered anything quite like it. His is emphatically not the behavior of an aspiring megalomaniac.

As a young believer, Ian Morgan Cron struggled to grasp something of this extraordinary grace-filled God. It eventually fell to an elderly African-American woman to help him, offering him a phrase that is as poignant as it is profound: "Miss Annie ambled the five or six feet that separated us and took my hand. 'Son,' she said, rubbing my knuckles with her thumb, 'love always stoops.'"[28]

Such is the essence of Jesus' love. He is never coercive, never proud, never in pursuit of hidden agendas. His authority works as it was always meant to work—creatively finding ways to help others flourish, even at enormous personal cost. Andy Crouch writes, "None of [Jesus'] power is reserved for carefully guarding privilege or meticulously accounting for status; every bit of it is poured into this one end [of restoring power to its original purpose]."[29]

Is it any wonder that people were attracted to him in droves, despite their confusion and misunderstandings, despite their cultural stumbling blocks and biases, despite their sins and failures? It is salutary to be reminded of this fact, because many people today assume Jesus is only interested in religious and 'holy' people. The blame must lie squarely at the feet of Jesus' imperfect followers, for we have evidently failed to live like our servant king.

His is truly transformative power. It revolutionizes those swept up in its path, and, above all, it confronts contemporary cynicism about what power can be.

Why Nietzsche Does Not Have to Be Right ...

Friedrich Nietzsche longed for a culture that saw strength and courage as the supreme virtues.[30] His famous expression, "the will to power," is much misunderstood. It does not mean a will to have power so much as having the power to exercise one's will.

It's easy to see why the Christianity of Nietzsche's upbringing was anathema to the philosopher, and why those who appropriated his ideas for their own political ends were equally contemptuous of it. The cross appalled him. As Graham Tomlin suggests, it wasn't the apparent irrationality of Christianity that Nietzsche despised, but the depravity of its myth of the "crucified God," a narrative he regarded as "seductive, intoxicating, anaesthetizing, and corrupting." In it, Nietzsche can see "only passivity and negativity" rather than the strength and courage he longed for.[31]

The operative word in Tomlin's analysis is "only." It exposes the perennial problem of reductionism. Even a casual reading of the gospel accounts shows that Jesus never lived absentmindedly; he was deliberate about everything, even silently refusing to defend himself during his kangaroo trial (Matthew 27:11–14). He was passive during the trial, not because of coercion but self-control, not out of passive aggression but dynamic, vital, self-sacrificial love.

This is the crucial point. The hermeneutic of suspicion has reduced *all* human interactions to power plays, a kind of social survival of the assertive. It sees no possibility of an alternative, which means there can be no grounds for optimism whatsoever. It makes cynicism both inevitable and prudent. Yet this reductionism flattens the possibility of authority ever being wielded for the flourishing of others and ignores the genuine human capacity for love that is derived from being created in the *imago dei*.

Conclusion

The greatest problem with this reductionism is that it completely fails to account for the Son of Man himself. He shows it is possible to wield power the way God does—to show a kind of power that emerges from a position of powerlessness, yet serves and loves and sacrifices.

The Christian contention is that Jesus is the *only* person in history ever able to do this without sin, without even the slightest hint of self-service. He is the *only* bulwark against the ultimate decline into a culture of suspicion, alienation, and paranoia. He has always been relevant. But I cannot help sensing that his gospel has never felt more like *good* news than it does now. Without him, we would surely be doomed to succumb to the same irresistible cynicism about power that Friedrich Nietzsche and Michel Foucault showed.

Andy Crouch sums it up well, nicely adapting Lord Acton's famous aphorism: "Love transfigures power. Absolute love transfigures absolute power. And power transfigured by love is the power that made and saves the world."[32]

> It is the duty of every man to promote the happiness
> of his fellow creatures to the utmost of his power.
> *William Wilberforce*

> Church should be everyone arriving with one piece of the jigsaw.
> *Milton Jones, comedian*

> The church should be the safest place on earth.
> *Larry Crabb*

CHAPTER 8

THE SAFEST PLACE ON EARTH?
A Community with Integrity

London's Royal Academy of Arts presented a fascinating exhibition in 2013. Simply titled *Australia*, it assembled an unprecedented collection of artwork dating from the colony's earliest days to the present. One image in particular haunted me — *The Expulsion*, a 1955 print by Margaret Preston. An Aboriginal couple faces us in the foreground, the man clearly distraught as he appeals to heaven with one arm raised high, while the woman seems more focused on the infant nursing at her breast. Behind them is a padlocked gate, and beyond the gate, we can glimpse a beautiful garden. But the print's most chilling element is the garden's guardian: a resplendent, sword-wielding, and golden-winged angel. He is the focal point, not the young family. And it is clear: the angel looks European.

In a brutal revision of Genesis, Preston depicts the theft of an Australian Eden. Like humanity's divine expulsion from paradise, Aboriginals were expelled by imperialists with the gall to claim a divine mandate for their civilizing mission. For when Western imperialism brought "enlightened" Western culture to Africa, Australasia, and the Americas, it also brought the church. Preston's image thus chimes with a story that former South African archbishop Desmond Tutu has often enjoyed telling: "When the missionaries first came to Africa, they had the Bible and we had the land. They said, 'Let us pray,' so we closed our eyes. When we opened them, we had the Bible and they had the land."[1]

It was, of course, more complex than this. More often than not, missionaries actually collided, rather than colluded, with their colonial masters. They championed the welfare of indigenous people above the profit margins of investors and were inadvertent defenders of vulnerable languages by codifying

157

them as part of the Bible translation process.[2] Yet their work, and indeed their presence, could never be entirely disentangled from imperialism, bringing about a tension that Nelson Mandela, for one, recognized. Describing South African missionary colleges (often established by flouting government indifference or opposition), he says that although "they were often colonialist in their attitudes and practices," he felt their "benefits outweighed their disadvantages."[3]

The impression many have today of churches and of organized religion generally is far less nuanced. People are grimly mindful of the church's history as yet another agent of oppression, and thus are scared off. Ross Douthat, himself a Roman Catholic, acerbically described the sex abuse scandal horrors in the Roman Catholic archdiocese of Boston as a story "perfectly calculated to discredit the message of the Gospel ... No external enemy of the faith, no Attila or Barbarossa or Hitler, could have sown so much confusion and dismay among the faithful as Catholicism's own bishops managed to do."[4]

It is a simple but tragic fact: churches of all hues and persuasions have been complicit in injustice. Far from being the refuge of the downtrodden, wounded, and lost, they have easily become havens for the judgmental, controlling, and dangerous. No wonder people find it hard to trust the church.

It was never meant to be like this. And thankfully, it doesn't have to be.

The God with a Plan up His Sleeve

Jean Vanier, who founded the first L'Arche community in France in the 1960s (a thriving Christian refuge for those with disabilities and their caregivers), is quoted as saying, "People are longing to rediscover true community. We have had enough of loneliness, independence, and competition."[5] Take note: he was not thinking of the physically or mentally disadvantaged; he meant the whole of Western culture.

In our pursuit of consumer convenience, we have sought to obliterate dependence on others, as if this is a bad thing. To be sure, many have found themselves driven to this mind-set by bad experiences, but not all have. It is as if we have decided not to trust because we want everything, from my café lattes to my lifestyle, "my way." Does this not explain, in part, why the baby boomer generation struggles with the indignities of old age? All the way up to and beyond retirement, they have prized independence too highly. This is tragic, for as business philosophers Fernando Flores and Robert Solomon suggest, "A person incapable of trust is a person who is something less than fully human, less than fully socialized, less than fully a member of society."[6] We are *meant* to be dependent on one another; it is how we are wired.[7]

Perhaps it should not be as surprising as it is to find the controversial and radical Slovenian philosopher Slavoj Žižek advocating a community along the lines of the original Christian "community of outcasts." "This is why I and many other leftist philosophers ... are so interested in rereading, rehabilitating, and reappropriating the legacy of Paul," he said.[8] It is therefore worth returning to Paul, not to reappropriate so much as to reread, and if necessary, rehabilitate.

What was so special about Paul's vision for the Christian community? His regular term for church (*ekklesia*—essentially "a gathering") was the same one used in the Septuagint (the Greek translation of the Old Testament) for the assembly of Israelites (see Deuteronomy 9:10, for example). But it is the location that is most surprising, even for modern Christians. Paul does not describe denominations as churches (they didn't exist yet), nor does he describe all the various groups of believers who might live in the same city as "the church."[9] And he would never dream of calling a building a church.

Instead, the church is primarily the gathering of all believers *in heaven, now*! He speaks of the church as a permanent celestial assembly gathered in the presence of God in fulfillment of God's eternal purpose.[10] In his letter to the believers in Ephesus, Paul writes, "God raised us up with Christ, and seated us with him in the heavenly realms in Christ Jesus" (Ephesians 2:6). This is what might be termed the "cosmic" or "invisible" church—and it refers to all believers who have ever lived, including those still alive.

At the same time, "church" also describes local, visible expressions or outposts of the cosmic church. So Paul can write to the church in the Greek city of Corinth. If there were several congregations in a city, they were each churches—Paul never grouped them together as "the church." Christian thought on the church (the doctrine of ecclesiology) has developed considerably since Paul, but we can never depart from his foundation. If someone has taken up Christ's call to follow him, they are incorporated into this cosmic body and have an onus to be part of the local outpost. This is where Paul's next surprise lies.

God has a secret weapon up his sleeve. He had apparently mandated Paul to spread the news of Christ's boundless riches to Gentiles across the Roman world and to make known what God had kept under wraps for centuries. So what was this great secret? "His intent was that now, *through the church*, the manifold wisdom of God should be made known to the rulers and authorities in the heavenly realms" (Ephesians 3:10, emphasis mine).

This may seems quite obscure on first reading, especially if one is unfamiliar with Paul's language. In essence, he explains that God is battling evil forces ("the rulers and authorities in the heavenly realms") in a war Jesus has already won. But where is the evidence of that victory? What is God's secret weapon to let the world know it has happened? It is the church, no less! If that seems quite the miscalculation today (in light of its reputation), we easily forget how utterly ridiculous it would have sounded in Paul's day.

Rodney Stark, an eminent sociologist of religion, has devoted considerable efforts to estimating the numerical growth of the early church. His first assumption is that believers must at some point have accounted for more than half of the Roman Empire. How else could one explain the political expediency of Constantine changing the official religion? This means there must have been nearly thirty-four million believers by around AD 350. Comparing different demographic models projecting back to the first century, the results are startling. Stark calculated there would have been no more than eight thousand Christian believers in the whole of the Roman Empire in AD 100.[11] When Ephesians was first read, the figure would have been even smaller. This puny band of believers was God's secret weapon to change the world?

Leaving aside the quantity of the converts, consider their quality. The first disciples were not the most impressive bunch: fishermen and tradesmen, joined by at least one collaborating tax collector, all following a hillbilly carpenter who ended up on death row. Commissioning this lot hardly looked like a world-changing strategy. In fact, the general status and reputation of Christian believers in subsequent centuries improved little. The church's message and community life appealed primarily to society's outsiders and the downtrodden, especially in the empire's great urban centers. That explains why Paul could say of the first Corinthian believers, "Not many of you were wise by human standards; not many were influential; not many were of noble birth" (1 Corinthians 1:26; note he doesn't say "not *any* of you" were wise, influential, or noble!).

Yet, as the most visible manifestation of the Son of Man's lordship, this *was* God's strategy. As far as Paul is concerned, what matters is not what these converts have been or done. Of far greater significance is what happens when they are gathered together by the shared experience of God in Christ. No one here is enslaved to his or her history (however reprehensible) or present circumstances. This is why Christianity will never initially appeal to those who take pride in their achievements or status. But it has been a timeless factor in the attractiveness of the Christian community for the broken, the hurting, the guilty, and the downtrodden. In short, the church is a community of grace — people drawn together by God's bewildering kindness to live in a community characterized by unconditional kindness. This is nothing less than what is expected from those who have accepted the authority of the crucified Lord.

On the surface, it all seems rather inconsequential. Yet Paul insists that encountering a counter-community like this will bear witness to God's divine purpose, even today. Our contemporary urbanized and technological world is by default a graceless and suspicious world. A society that insists on giving everyone their just deserts ends up becoming a fragmented society indeed, one in which survival depends on constant vigilance against predators and competitors. In such a dismal environment, a genuine Christian community will blaze with solar intensity, simultaneously exposing the shortcomings of the surrounding culture and attracting those desperate for something better. This is why Francis Schaeffer wrote that a community of Christians is "the final apologetic."[12] Lesslie Newbigin similarly suggested that "the only answer, the only hermeneutic of the gospel, is a congregation of men and women who believe it and live it,"[13] because a church's dynamic of grace is a visual aid for interpreting the message of God's love for the world.

How tragic, then — how reprehensible — for the church merely to ape the gracelessness of the environment around. In what Larry Crabb calls "unspiritual community," people inevitably make every effort to ensure they are "safe *from* people and never enjoy safety *with* people."[14] No wonder we often find ourselves attempting to draw a missional veil between Christ (who is innately attractive) and Christians (who are not). Of course, we should beware of antireligious propaganda that exploits high-profile failures in order to tar all Christians with the same brush. Still, many individuals' experience of local church life fails to come close to its high calling. What then? The challenge is immense, and it always has been. Our cultural wallpaper may have changed, but human nature has not.

The key has always been to allow "Christ crucified" to shape community life. The particular challenge today is to grapple with the relationship between being a grace-filled community and the wielding of community power. How do we do this? Through a self-sacrificing, unconditional love (*agapē*, in the Greek) best seen in Jesus, who came to serve and not be served. In his gospel, Mark applies this self-sacrificing love to Jesus' followers: "Whoever wants to become great among you must be your servant, and whoever wants to be first must be slave of all" (Mark 10:43–44).

The Revolution of a Cross-Shaped Church

When considering the great Christ hymn of Philippians in the previous chapter, I deliberately omitted the most important verse. Despite the song being a remarkably early christological statement, Paul's purpose in including the song was not primarily doctrinal but rather ethical. He introduces it with the highly charged words, "In your relationships with one another, have the same mindset as Christ Jesus: Who, being in very nature God ..." (Philippians 2:5–6). This means Christians, out of love, must be willing to serve and even make the ultimate sacrifice for the beloved. As Jesus himself said, if the *Son of Man* came to serve, how much more should his followers be willing to serve? This is what theologians since the great Reformer Martin Luther have called *theologia crucis*, a theology of the cross. This is not simply a question of leadership; it is a matter of imitating Jesus in our life together.

The Inevitability of Brokenness

N. T. Wright is correct when he writes, "*Agapē* sets the bar as high as it can go. The first thing to do before we can discuss it is to acknowledge that we have all failed quite drastically to clear that height."[15] Herein lies the paradox: A community of grace is one that will welcome all comers—it is truly inclusive. This means its membership can *never* be everything it should be. So perhaps we should not be surprised to find that Christian communities are not all they might be cracked up to be. A church cannot means-test applicants; it cannot devise morality filters or peccadillo detectors. Instead it must welcome whoever crosses the threshold and face the consequences. It is not really fair to ask, "Is this the best they can come up with?"

This is what makes Christian community a challenge for all concerned. We accept others not because of *their* righteousness but because of *Christ's*. As Dietrich Bonhoeffer put it, "Our community with one another consists solely in what Christ has done to both of us."[16] If it did not, there would always be some who can't make the grade. This is a huge relief to those who are all too aware of their brokenness and their bent toward "living in God's world as if (it was) mine" (LiGWaiM). But there's a catch. The thing that makes joining the community so attractive (and indeed possible) is the very thing that demands so much of its members. Because each is accepted by divine *agapē* through

Christ's self-sacrifice at the cross, none should fail to offer the same *agapē* to others. Being inclusive is never enough by itself. It must be accompanied by a culture of confession and forgiveness. Those unwilling to be part of this cannot ultimately remain included.

Having explained in Ephesians 3 God's purpose in letting the church loose on the world, Paul urges believers to live it out. The local church must reflect the character of the cosmic church. "I urge you to live a life worthy of the calling you have received," Paul writes (Ephesians 4:1). Paul had no illusions about what this would require: "Be completely humble and gentle; be patient, bearing with one another in love. Make every effort to keep the unity of the Spirit through the bond of peace" (Ephesians 4:2–3).

It is why, in our failings, we have no alternative but to return again and again to the one place where we start over: the God of the cross. As Larry Crabb puts it, the cross reminds us that "we are not our problems. We are not our wounds. We are not our sins. We are persons of radical worth and unrevealed beauty."[17] Why else would Christ have died for us? So Paul crescendos to his clinching summary: "Follow God's example, therefore, as dearly loved children and walk in the way of love, just as Christ loved us and gave himself up for us as a fragrant offering and sacrifice to God" (Ephesians 5:1–2).

We imitate God by walking in the way of love (*agapē*) because we are dearly loved (*agapētos*) children. He loved us *first*. Any confidence of cross-won forgiveness is thus never a justification for failure to forgive others; instead, it is the supreme motivation for love. C. S. Lewis was right: "To be a Christian means to forgive the inexcusable, because God has forgiven the inexcusable in you."[18]

This is what lies behind David Smith's excellent insight that, for Paul, "the greatest threat to the believing community was not located in differences of opinion concerning theology, but rather in the loss of contact with the God of kindness and mercy, a loss which would lead inexorably to the return of the human pride and arrogance which the revelation of God in the gospel had destroyed."[19] The willingness to maintain this contact is the only thing that can sustain the church's work in progress, for a work in progress it must always be.

So there is no room for rose-colored glasses, as anyone who has worked in Christian ministry for even five minutes knows all too well. People always bring their baggage with them. Without honesty about human nature, pretense and hypocrisy are inevitable. But without a sense of common affliction, how can it ever be safe to admit one's flaws? Is this not the secret of organizations like Alcoholics Anonymous—admitting to a problem in public is only possible when there is confidence in numbers? C. S. Lewis put it beautifully: "Friendship ... is born at that moment when one man says to another: 'What! You too? I thought that no one but myself ...'"[20] Only then can we love those who are truthful about themselves and be truthful to those who love us. Otherwise, as Dietrich Bonhoeffer wrote, "We dare not be sinners. Many Christians are unthinkably horrified when a real sinner is suddenly discovered among the righteous. So we remain alone with our sin, living in lies and hypocrisy."[21] Or to put it in more contemporary terms, as Larry Crabb wrote, "We all play it safe because none of us feel safe in the group—not really."[22]

However, this is the wonder of a grace-centered community. In contrast to the legalists (who impose tough and often arbitrary criteria for membership) and the licentious (who regard private lifestyles as irrelevant for those who are forgiven anyway), a grace-filled people will always be seeking to grow in Christlikeness. He is now Lord. Without that, the grace we claim to share can only ever be what Bonhoeffer called "cheap grace":

> Cheap grace is the grace we bestow on ourselves. Cheap grace is the preaching of forgiveness without requiring repentance, baptism without church discipline, Communion without confession ... Cheap grace is grace without discipleship, grace without the cross, grace without Jesus Christ, living and incarnate.[23]

For Bonhoeffer, and indeed for Paul, grace is costly because it cost Christ the cross. What Bonhoeffer calls repentance is simply jargon for turning my back on a *LiGWaiM* lifestyle and accepting Christ's lordship. This is the revolution brought about by the cross. A theology of the cross is thus not a proposition to which we merely give intellectual assent or the benchmark for testing another's theological reliability. It must be lived out—just as Paul told the Philippians. Our mind-set is to be *the same* as Christ's because he is the Lord. Otherwise, it makes a mockery of the claims on our lips.

If accepting that the lordship of Christ seems a fearful thing, then we must simply rehearse the wonders of the previous chapter. The Son of Man never lords it over us—he stoops to wash our feet and stretches his arms on a cross to die for us. His commitment to us is beyond dispute. His call to us is nothing less than a call to embrace a cosmic reality and become more, not less, than the people we were created to be.

Me-ism or We-ism?

Jean Vanier wrote that "community ... is a place of pain, of the death of ego."[24] No wonder it is hard. No wonder people love the idea of it, but keep the real thing at arm's length and subject to their own terms. Even tougher is the fact that growing in Christlikeness is always a painful and possibly protracted process. Impatience with others' failings and personal blind spots are other causes of people leaving in disgust and disillusionment. They forget that a Christian community is by definition full of broken people who are all works in progress.

Furthermore, community must be lived out corporately because it can *only* be lived out corporately. Forgiving love in seclusion is a contradiction in terms. If I never interact with others, I never have others to forgive. Nor, for that matter, do I have anyone to forgive me. But for the proud, the cultural alienation we experience in a suspicious world can almost seem preferable to the exposure within a mutually trusting community.

Eugene Peterson is surely right in his criticism of much of contemporary church life: "What is being sold, on inspection, doesn't turn out to be community at all. Americans are good at forming clubs and gathering crowds. But clubs and crowds, even when—especially when—they are religious clubs and crowds, are not communities."[25]

True Christian community is not a gathering of like-minded individuals who share enough in common to make gatherings effortless and enjoyable. It is emphatically not like a Meetup-enabled gathering of Tolkien-obsessed stamp collectors in rural Kansas or Elvis-impersonating software developers in downtown Leipzig. The whole point of a community born at the foot of the cross is that it is made up of *differences*. The church ought to defy all sociological theories. In fact, I heard someone once describe church as "a collection of the very last people you would ever want to go on a vacation with." This runs completely counter to the nature of all other social gatherings.

Far too often, churches are culturally uniform because they (unwittingly perhaps) exclude those who do not socially conform. C. S. Lewis once warned a group of Cambridge graduates that they would face no greater temptation than the urge to create an inner ring of community that was special because it excluded others.[26] This is not always the case—it has been a privilege and joy for me to have worked at All Souls, Langham Place since 2005, a church made up of people from more than sixty-five nationalities with all kinds of different social groupings represented (in part a reflection of the vast diversity of central London). However, we still suffer from our fair share of blind spots; people always drift toward those most like themselves. We are, and always will be, a work in progress. It is inevitable.

This is why divine grace is fundamental to a church community's existence, growth, and survival. It is the only way we will be able to shift from a 'me-ist' mind-set (constituting community around those most similar to me) to a "we-ist" mind-set (that is prepared to allow those unlike me to be included in the "we"). This is essential and urgent for a despairing, cynical, and suspicious world. If the church is indeed to be God's final apologetic, it must receive our fullest attention. This means facing up to the relationship between the church and power. Can we embrace what it means to be a community of outcasts?

An Eye for "the Other"

The greatest social division in the old Jewish mind-set was the canyon between Jew and Gentile. It was not the only one, however. The ancient Jewish cycle of prayer began with the three benedictions, in which a devout man would pray, "Blessed be [God] that He did not make me a Gentile; blessed be He that He did not make me a boor [i.e., an ignorant peasant or a slave]; blessed be He that He did not make me a woman."[27] Race, social status, and gender—do they not lie at the heart of humanity's most intractable and durable divisions? There are plenty of others, of course, but few are as universal.

The tragedy of gender-induced vulnerability continues. In 2007, World Vision included this statement in a report to the United Nations Commission on the Status of Women: "The majority of the world's women and girls will experience violence; whether it's physical, psychological, or sexual violence, it plagues every community and many homes."[28]

Discrimination because of skin color or ethnicity is rife, often fomented in the fires of extreme nationalism, which is patriotism's dark side. The last century of European history has witnessed the worst of this, of course, but it is by no means unique. There is something irrational about nationalism because it extends to its logical extreme George Bernard Shaw's quip that patriotism is the conviction that "your country is superior to all other countries because you were born in it."

Human beings have a grim track record when it comes to the treatment of "the other" and the powerless. So it is astonishing to find that, nearly two thousand years ago, Paul wrote these words to the Galatian Christians:

In Christ Jesus you are all children of God through faith, for all of you who were baptized into Christ have clothed yourselves with Christ. There is neither Jew nor Gentile, neither slave nor free, nor is there male and female, for you are all one in Christ Jesus.

GALATIANS 3:26–28

Paul was ahead of the game. This is nothing short of a social revolution. There was literally no one else writing this kind of thing in the ancient world. When the Galatians put their trust in Christ (going public by being baptized), they were adopted into the divine family. Paul's metaphor of being clothed with Christ is a bit like the old discipline of school uniforms. Their advantage is that they provide a sense of cohesion and corporate identity. They also provide a respite (however temporary) from the peer pressure of wearing the right brands. Similarly, being clothed with Christ provides the deepest possible cohesion and identity, individual as well as corporate, theoretically removing all pressure to compete. If the analogy breaks down slightly (as all analogies do), it is from the paradox that Christlikeness never flattens or crushes individuality (unlike uniforms). Quite the reverse — it honors and glories in our diversity. As the saying goes, when human beings freeze water, we make ice cubes; when God freezes water, he makes snowflakes.

Being clothed with Christ cannot and must not leave us unchanged, however. It transforms ambitions and working practices, spending and giving habits, socializing and neighborliness, family life and sex life, political and ethical concerns, intellectual, physical, and spiritual activity. The list is endless, because the lordship of Christ is endless. At the very least, it must transform how we treat one another. Christ loves us all equally, and therefore we love all equally. There can be no status distinction for the Christian. Is it any wonder that Jerusalem's and Rome's most marginalized flocked to Christ from the start?

This does not make everyone identical, of course. I did not stop (how could I?) being English, privately educated, or male when I came to Christ at age eighteen. Nor are some of the distinctions between people necessarily negative. What did have to stop, however, was any sense of superiority or inferiority that these might have given me. There is no social ladder in God's family; as previous generations would remind us, the ground before the cross is flat.

This is the genius of the church. Because Christ forgives our *LiGWaiM* at the cross by reconciling us to God the Father, we are reconciled to others who *LiGWaiM*, even though they are radically different from us. Because we share both in bearing God's image and in enjoying Christ's rescue, the value of even the most vulnerable, broken, and despised is absolute. The church should be the safest place in the world. Because we all sin, we should have nothing to hide; but because Jesus died, we should have nothing to prove.

As Alan Jacobs quirkily put it, "The grace of God gives hope to the waverer, the backslider, the slacker, the putz, the schlemiel."[29] All have a place. All can have hope. The question is, do they? This is what motivated Christian social activism from the start, whether the recipients of care were Christian or not. It ensured that others took notice of the heart of the believers, despite the weirdness of their beliefs and their non-Roman origins. By the fourth century, the emperor Julian was so frustrated by the Christians' impact that he launched a campaign to start pagan charities. In AD 362, he urged a pagan high priest in Galatia to up his game because Christianity was growing as a result of believers' "moral character, even if pretended."[30]

Yet, despite inevitably mixed motives for it, philanthropy is always spurred on by the model of Christ himself. He poured out *agapē* to the vulnerable, the weak, the forgotten. Therefore, so do his people. This is power and authority exploited for the genuine flourishing of others, however "other" they might be. This is Philippians 2 love. This is certainly not suggesting that Christians have been the only philanthropists. For example, much Enlightenment thinking simply decoupled the *agapē* ethic from its theological moorings. What is indisputable is the uniqueness of Christ's original example of *agapē*. No other king, no other lord, has loved like that. No other ruler has loved and sought to forgive his enemies. The bar truly is set as high as it can go. Despite the church's frequent failures, this still makes a difference.

In the horrific aftermath of Hurricane Katrina, senior politician and atheist Roy Hattersley wrote a surprising column in which he acknowledged that primarily Christian organizations stepped in to provide disaster relief. "Notable by their absence," wrote Hattersley, "are teams from rationalist societies, free thinkers' clubs and atheists' associations — the sort of people who not only scoff at religion's intellectual absurdity but also regard it as a positive force for evil." While he may have overstated his case a bit, he concluded with an extraordinary admission:

> It ought to be possible to live a Christian life without being a Christian or, better still, to take Christianity à la carte ... Yet men and women who, like me, cannot accept the mysteries and the miracles do not go out with the Salvation Army at night.

The only possible conclusion is that faith comes with a packet of moral imperatives that, while they do not condition the attitude of all believers, influence enough of them to make them morally superior to atheists like me. The truth may make us free. But it has not made us as admirable as the average captain in the Salvation Army.[31]

If this kind of indiscriminate but transformative love is a feature of relationships with those beyond church walls, how much more should it lie at the church's heart? As Dick Keyes rightly notes, "The ethics of the New Testament tolerate too much ambiguity to affirm a sense of tribal identity," however that tribal identity is formed.[32] This is why Keyes goes on to identify several essential features of genuine Christian community.[33] It all begins with grace, of course. What else could hold diverse but equally broken and flawed people together? Otherwise, we will only love others when they are lovable. Grace loves even when they are not.

But of the other characteristics Keyes articulates, these two are the most telling.

- Crossed boundaries: Christ crossed the ultimate boundary to love us (descending from heaven to the lowest of the low at the cross); we must be prepared to do the same in our churches. Do our Christian communities reflect the diversity of the communities in which we live? Or are they more segregated?

- Reconciliation: Because of our flaws and because we tend to cling to our prejudices long after our inclusion into the community, there will be many we haven't treated as those who are clothed with Christ. Fundamental is a shared spirit of truth and forgiveness, especially when an imbalance of power has meant some have clearly come off worse. The vertical reconciliation brought about by Christ is inseparable from the horizontal reconciliation among his people (e.g., 2 Corinthians 5:18–20; Ephesians 2:14–18).[34]

I have taught in the former Yugoslavia on many occasions, and there is much about this beautiful but traumatized region that is utterly beguiling. One moment in particular stands out, however. Our small event had drawn a few people from Serbia, Croatia, and Bosnia—all of them had been affected by the Balkan crisis of the 1990s. It just so happened that our event coincided with the seventeenth anniversary of the 1991 Vukovar massacre. More than 250 people were killed in what was later officially recognized as a war crime. Two delegates at our event had been at Vukovar—a Bosnian forced to fight for Serbia, and one Croatian from the town. The former had been under orders to fire into the town. The latter's mother was shot and wounded. But here they were in the same room learning, praying, and praising God together—much had happened in both men's lives since. Furthermore, on the event's last night, representatives from Bosnia, Serbia, and Croatia stood up and prayed publically for one of the other countries. I didn't understand a word they were saying, but it was one of the most unforgettable experiences of my life. Such is the reconciling power of grace.

Never imagine reconciliation is easy. There is no magic wand to wave after betrayal. The healing process takes immense courage and patience. It may take years. The business of reconciliation requires small steps. Like a pilgrimage, the long journey to establish trust begins with just a few steps. Perpetrators must be willing to acknowledge their wrong and seek forgiveness. Victims must also show a readiness to forgive. Each must first be willing to trust and to be trusted. Then, as Onora O'Neill rightly states, "Trust often invites reciprocal trust: and when it does, we have virtuous spirals."[35]

Perhaps this seems utterly naive and fanciful. Can this really be possible in the church, an institution so tarred by a centuries-old reputation for negativity and even oppression? Furthermore, it is all very well to wax lyrical about events from two thousand years ago, but is this sort of community even possible in our justifiably suspicious and cynical age? It is countercultural at so many levels. In fact, in a secularized or postmodern society, to become part of a church is now an act of significant social deviance, just as it was in the apostles' day. The only way such a group can survive is if it is, as Peter Berger writes, a "countercommunity of considerable strength," with mutual dependence and trusting love of such quality that it can withstand any external incomprehension or opposition.[36]

The key to it, ironically, lies in grasping the true nature of leadership. For it is only when leadership is characterized by serving in love rather than exercising controlling power that the church can be the paradigm-shifting community it was always meant to be. Love is the only viable alternative to power games.

Success or Service? Cross-Shaped Servants of the Cross-Shaped Community

The New Testament letters were written to churches and individuals in response to specific problems or questions. The root issue behind many of them was leadership. Who should hold it, what is it for, how should it be exercised? It is sometimes said that in a democracy, we get the leaders we deserve. While that may not necessarily be the case in the church, it is certainly true that churches will invariably reflect the people who lead them, and leaders will reflect the leadership models that most influence them. So the questions are crucial. What constitutes success in Christian leadership?

For too long now, power has felt like a threat—especially church power. People are fearful of losing their identities, their personalities, and their freedom if they join up. This does, of course, happen in religious groups, including churches. It can happen through controlling leaders or intransigent institutions. Indeed, one explanation for the massive shift in Latin America from Catholicism to Pentecostalism has been that the latter is primarily a bottom-up, grassroots movement in contrast to the common perception of global Catholicism.[37] It is a generalization, of course, but there is a cruel irony to the prevalence of controlling leadership in some Pentecostal circles.

This should not and must not happen in a church led by people following in Christ's footsteps. As Andy Crouch observes, "Unchecked power, driven by self-interest, scarcity, grandiosity, and aggression, is deadly to God's original fruitful purposes."[38] Victor Lee Austin writes that authority done right fosters "a rich texture in society, not a flattening of initiative and purpose."[39] This is leadership that inspires the flourishing of the other rather than the aggrandizement of the self. This is service that washes another's filthy feet. This, then, is *successful* ministry—although the adjective is not one the New Testament especially values. Faithfulness is of infinitely greater concern than success. This is why Paul, for one, seems unconcerned about conversion statistics, attractive church programs, public relations plans, or therapy skills. Of course, these may all have their place in contemporary ministry—but if they ever supersede taking up a cross to serve like Christ, then all is lost.

Every job description includes certain expectations of applicants. Church leadership is no exception. When Paul establishes criteria for choosing elders (local congregational leaders), he includes marital faithfulness, self-control over tempers and alcohol, financial honesty, hospitality, and holiness (Titus 1:6–8). Elsewhere, he adds gentleness and the respect of outsiders (1 Timothy 3:1–7). The interesting thing is that these characteristics are all marks of the Christian life. This does not suggest that everyone is suited for leadership, of course, but it is a reminder of the essence of Christian leadership: all are to share Christ's mind-set (Philippians 2:5).

There are naturally responsibilities and demands specific to leadership. Paul tells Timothy that elders should not be recent converts—too much responsibility too early might make them conceited (1 Timothy 3:6). They should also be able to teach well (1 Timothy 3:2; Titus 1:9). But above all, nothing may detract from Christ's model of servant leadership. As Jesus said, "Whoever wants to become great among you must be your servant, and whoever wants to be first must be slave of all" (Mark 10:43–44). The importance of this in a cynical generation cannot be overstated. Dietrich Bonhoeffer was prophetic, writing in 1939 from his underground seminary:

> The question of trust, which is so closely related to that of authority, is determined by the faithfulness with which a man serves Jesus Christ, never by the extraordinary talents which he possesses. Pastoral authority can be attained only by the servant of Jesus who seeks no power of his own, who himself is a brother among brothers submitted to the authority of the Word.[40]

So if trust in church leaders and by extension in the church is dependent on this, how might power and authority be wielded differently now? The answer is not contemporary at all, of course. But therein lies the tragedy and shame. If only the church had been more determined to live and serve like its Lord.

Authority That Limps

Just as the ethical expectations for leaders are no different than the expectations for believers in general, so is the assumption that leaders are LiGWaiM perpetrators like everyone else. This is why the power balances intrinsic to pastoral ministry (considered in chapter 3) are always a risk. In Bonhoeffer's terms, leaders are therefore always brothers among brothers and sisters among sisters. All alike require grace.

Jesus' apostles had to learn this the hard way. They constantly got things wrong. Peter had to be rebuked on several occasions: once by Jesus for (temporarily) being a satanic spokesman (Mark 8:33); then by Paul for actions that were inconsistent with his gospel message (Galatians 2:14–16). In fact, Jesus' words about servant leadership were prompted by James and John sidling up to him to reserve the best seats on heaven's high table. "Let one of us sit at your right and the other at your left in your glory" (Mark 10:37). Jesus' response is chilling. "You do not know what you are asking," he says. They do not yet understand that for Jesus, the *only* way to glory is through suffering and death. Not only that, it is the only way to lead.

The yearning for the glory fast track is perennial. It is just one of many ways in which all-too-human flaws can undermine the Christlikeness of a minister. Humanity is diverse in both its glory and its shame. What is undeniable is that anyone in Christian leadership will battle with *something*.

Paul, however, did not consider church leadership a lost cause. He did not give up, because God is at work, and he could testify to an extraordinary reality in his own life. Despite acknowledging he was the chief of sinners (he had been a tenacious and brutal hunter of Christians before his conversion), he noticed that when he was at his weakest (through failing health, disasters, persecution, or his own failings—or all of the above), extraordinary things still happened. When he pleaded for his afflictions to be taken away, he sensed God saying no. Paul wrote, "[The Lord] said to me, 'My grace is sufficient for you, for my power is made perfect in weakness'" (2 Corinthians 12:9). It was as if Paul's afflictions enabled his ego to get out of the way so God could roll up his sleeves and really get down to work.

This is what prompted Paul's enigmatic declaration that "when I am weak, then I am strong" (2 Corinthians 12:10). Graham Tomlin put it like this: "True power begins with a realisation of one's powerlessness before God, when the point is reached where a person grasps the ineffectiveness of their own power, whether rational, moral or social, before God."[41]

Taking a cue from that peculiar tale of Jacob's divine wrestling match (Genesis 32:22 – 32), wise believers know we should never trust a leader without a limp. In other words, leaders who never acknowledge frailties or, even worse, faults and temptations, are unlikely to have the humility required for God to work through them.

Power and Plurality

It is interesting how often the New Testament assumes that church leadership is plural. Decision making is a corporate business, even if specific responsibilities are divided up. For example, the decision to send Paul and Barnabas from Antioch on their preaching journey took place when the church elders were meeting together in prayer and worship (Acts 13:1 – 3). Their practice was then to appoint groups of elders in each of the churches they planted (Acts 14:23). The idea that any church would be led by one individual in splendid isolation seems entirely alien to the early church (even if there were strong and dominant characters like Paul around). Since then, many different governance practices have developed within different theological traditions. Each has its own good qualities and its pitfalls. The point here is that for trust to grow, there must be active accountability. What is needed, therefore, is a deep recognition of how power operates in institutions. In particular, leaders need to be doubly aware who is likely to be most vulnerable in their communities.

It is instructive to see how the Jerusalem church dealt with this in the first weeks of its existence. One of the most impressive features of the first Christians was their spontaneous willingness to share assets, so that "there were no needy persons among them" (Acts 4:34). They were victims of their own speedy success, however. Within a short time, they were operating food runs for considerable numbers of widows. Then an old bias reared its ugly head. "The Hellenistic Jews among them complained against the Hebraic Jews because their widows were being overlooked in the daily distribution of food" (Acts 6:1). This was not actually a division between Jews and Gentiles, nor even between Jews and Christians. The division was more subtle. These widows were all Jewish converts to Christianity. It is just that some were from Jerusalem and Judea, while others were Hellenized—culturally more Greek, therefore. But Peter and the other leaders took this very seriously and put processes in place to prevent this perceived discrimination from recurring.

Because those who lead are often drawn from those who have cultural power outside the church, it is hard for them to see such discrimination. All the more reason, therefore, to aim for a plural and diverse leadership.

Power and Privilege

Respect for those in positions of authority is not wrong or even necessarily harmful. Furthermore, it is recommended by the New Testament. Peter tells his readers to "show proper respect to everyone, love the family of believers, fear God, honor the emperor" (1 Peter 2:17). Remember that this honor was owed even to an unelected, hostile, foreign, imperialistic, and brutal monarch, with whom early believers probably disagreed about nearly everything. Then the writer to the Hebrews has sound, even wry, advice for those within the church. "Have confidence in your leaders and submit to their authority, because they keep watch over you as those who must give an account. Do this so that their work will be a joy, not a burden, for that would be of no benefit to you" (Hebrews 13:17).

Of course, we see a word like *submit*, and we run for the hills. Yet the key factor is whether or not a leader is worthy of respect and trust. Furthermore, all leaders have "to give an account," for they are accountable to Christ. Peter describes the role of a leader as being that of a shepherd of God's flock, "not pursuing dishonest gain, but eager to serve; not lording it over those entrusted to you, but being examples to the flock" (1 Peter 5:2–3).

This must mean leaders should never insist on respect and honor, but should earn them. In my experience, many are motivated to do precisely that—to begin with, at least. The problem comes as they become overly comfortable with the respect they have earned, enjoying the privileges it generates within the community.

Jesus was particularly troubled about the religious authorities of his day: "Everything they do is done for people to see … They love the place of honor at banquets and the most important seats in the synagogues; they love to be greeted with respect in the marketplaces and to be called 'Rabbi' by others" (Matthew 23:5–7).

As I've already mentioned, every congregation's temptation is to place their pastor on a pedestal, and every pastor's temptation is to want to be there. Power is alluring, especially for those who have grown accustomed to wielding it for a long time.

Power and the Vision

Divine authority easily gets displaced by human authority. It happens in churches unwittingly. A leader's "God-given vision" (which may or may not be in line with a Christlike model for the church) becomes all-encompassing. Thus, to disagree with or even reject that vision becomes more grave than a challenge to the leader; it becomes a challenge to God.

There are vital questions to ask: Is the vision that is purported to be God's means for maturing this local church merely a means for exercising power over people? Is it erecting an artificially narrow boundary for the congregation by which to manipulate those within it and to expel those who do not conform? Of course, there is no such thing as a boundary-less community, and local churches can never cater to everyone's particular needs—which may be why God raises up a diversity of local churches within a city, as well as a diversity of membership for each one. These questions should prompt leaders to regular, honest self-examination.

Those who fall into the trap of usurping God's authority are often the ones who brook no dissent or even thoughtful inquiry. They might repeat a simplistic mantra that everyone needs to rally behind. Or they might resort to that other proven tactic, namely, pejorative labeling. As we saw in chapter 3, adjectives mutate into nouns. A term that legitimately *describes* someone's action or view can then become an identity by which to *encapsulate* and thus reject the person. Thus, a liberal or conservative perspective turns the person into "a liberal" or "a conservative." A disloyal statement means someone is "a traitor"; a sexist remark makes someone "a sexist." Ironically, this is a matter of the powerful exploiting the hermeneutic of suspicion in order to control the weak. Such is human ingenuity that the same tools for exposing abuse of power can be twisted to reinforce the abuse. In the end, as Stephen Arterburn and Jack Felton write, "Labeling attempts to dehumanize critics so that dismissing them or their opinions becomes much easier."[42] C. P. Snow rightly reflected, "When you think of the long and gloomy history of man, you will find far more hideous crimes have been committed in the name of obedience than have been committed in the name of rebellion."[43] The church is no exception. Sometimes a little rebellion may be just what was necessary to protect the common good, especially when leaders are so wrapped up in their own visions that they lead people away from Christ rather than toward him.

Followers on The Way — but is it *Via Dolorosa* or Wall Street?

Like any new movement, religious or otherwise, the first Christians devised a name for their new beliefs. It was simply known as "the Way," a common word that could equally mean "path" or "street" (Acts 9:2; 19:23; 24:14). It was an ingenious choice. Whenever they made appeals for people to trust in Jesus, all they were doing was inviting people to join them on the same road they were walking. There was certainly no superiority or condescension, making it clear that just as life is a journey, so is the experience of trusting Christ. No one on the Way could claim to have made it or be the finished article. Thus, it had a drawing power best summed up in the adage that defined evangelism as "simply one beggar showing another beggar where to find bread."

To see how the institutional church's relationship to public power changed from the earliest decades of the Way, we need to return to the fourth-century Roman emperor considered in chapter 7.

Constantine emerged victorious from an imperial power struggle. He shrewdly calculated that Christianity suited his political needs admirably as the empire's official religion. Likewise, Christians recognized the benefits of supporting him against his rivals, who had no love for the Way.[44] Since then, as Graham Tomlin notes, "Christianity in the Western world has tried to influence society from a position of authority."[45] This was the birth of what became known as Christendom. It evolved over a long period, of course, but Constantine's edict had momentous consequences.

The emperor was impatient for a final decision to be made about Christology, not necessarily because he had strong views either way, but because the confusion played havoc with his political agenda. In fact, he rebuked *both* men at the center of the debate (Arius and Bishop Alexander of Alexandria) for causing so much trouble. So in AD 325, he called some eighteen hundred bishops from around the world to Nicea for the first great church council, although only perhaps three hundred made it. The council's subsequent statement (known as the Nicene Creed) resoundingly declared the combined humanity and divinity of Christ. Far from being an imposition of imperial power, this was an example of Christians getting their house in order on a very important issue.

The real problems actually came afterward. It was one thing to rule out the views of Arius (Jesus was only human, not divine) as incompatible with Christianity—there *was* a basic contradiction there. But then Constantine exiled the two Arian bishops who had voted against recognizing Jesus' divinity. The relationship between church and state was thus forever muddied.

It has been a two-way street ever since. The church discovered that easy access to the corridors of state power offered a shortcut to achieving its goals. It suited Constantine too: the church helpfully asserted that divine providence must have brought about his victory. This is not to deny that divine providence must have brought it about (that is a corollary of believing in a sovereign God). But it is a different matter altogether to suggest that divine providence legitimizes a ruler's every enterprise, any more than voting for a candidate endorses everything the candidate does while in power.

Paul, for one, carefully subverts this notion. He controversially asserts that worldly authorities are established in power by God and therefore the law should be obeyed (Romans 13:1–7). But does this mean he approved of everything Rome did or stood for? Of course not! Furthermore, what could be more politically subversive than asserting that Jesus is Lord (1 Corinthians 12:3)? From the start, therefore, Paul asserts there are clear limits to civil obedience. If the state ever seeks to trump the supremacy of Christ, disobedience is not merely advisable but imperative.

At issue is never whether Jesus is on the side of a candidate, a cause, or a creed. Of far greater significance is whether or not they are on *his*. This is why it is always alarming for a corporation, a state, or even, dare I say it, a church denomination to claim to have an exclusive mandate from heaven. Jesus could never be a Communist, a capitalist, a conservative, a liberal, a modernist or postmodernist, a feminist, a relativist, an individualist, a Democrat or an imperialist, a monarchist or Republican. Choose your cause; Jesus is not a member. However, this is not to say that there are no aspects of any, or even all, of these views that conform in some way to a Christ-centered worldview (and through the centuries, Christians have been numbered among advocates of all of these).

Ever since, under many different cultural guises, the church has walked a dangerous political path. The closer Christian leaders have been to the establishment, the less prophetic their ministry has become. For it is not as if the lordship of Christ has no bearing on the political realm. If Jesus truly is the King of kings (e.g., 1 Timothy 6:15; Revelation 19:16), any other authority is unavoidably relegated and relativized. No wonder megalomaniacs have hated Christ.

Wariness about imperial power is no justification for Christian silos, however. Quite the reverse. Christ's lordship should inspire and profoundly affect activity in all spheres of life. Martin Luther explicitly applied the Philippian Christ hymn to how German rulers should govern: "Let the prince then empty himself of his power and supremacy in his heart and concern himself with the needs of his subjects as though they were his own needs. For this is what Christ has done for us, and this is a genuine work of Christian love."[46] Yet not even Luther managed to tread this difficult path consistently. Too often, the church has allowed its mission to be indistinguishable from that of the state, instead of speaking truth to power even when doing so might threaten its privileges. This, after all, is what Jesus did when interrogated by Pilate.

Could this not be the reason the church is today tarred with the same cynical brush as all other human institutions? People are understandably suspicious that it has acted just like every other institution. Having enjoyed centuries of privileged status in the West, where it has often dominated and occasionally subdued others, it is surely paramount, as Graham Tomlin suggests, that the church rethinks "its notion of power and how it operates, if it is to play a significant part in this post-authoritarian world."[47]

This appeal is not motivated by a cynical pragmatism; it is driven by a yearning to retrieve the ancient, authentically Christian model for power, in an effort both to be faithful to Christ and to offer an alienated and suspicious world a genuine alternative to the wilderness of mirrors. It is an appeal for believers to walk the Way and to call others to join in doing the same. This walk is not the route to power and success, but the dangerous path of sacrifice and love. When Jesus called people to follow him by taking up a cross (Mark 8:34), he did not mean his disciples were to die for sin; he simply anticipated that followers would join him in experiencing the world's incomprehension and scorn.

In Jerusalem, there is still a street named Via Dolorosa (Way of Sorrows) because it is reputedly the road down which Jesus stumbled toward crucifixion. This is the street down which the church must walk. Yet we are so attracted by other streets for our models of power. Under the British Empire, the church often looked to the twin London authorities of Whitehall (the heart of government) and the ironically biblical-sounding road, Threadneedle Street (the Bank of England).

Today's influences are more likely to come from Pennsylvania Avenue, Hollywood Boulevard, Wall Street, and Madison Avenue. The latest fads in politics, entertainment, business and management, or marketing and communications are as likely to inform how the church operates today as British imperial paternalism and prejudices did a century or so ago.

I do not mean to ignore the many fine exceptions to this trend or to imply that the church has nothing to learn from these "streets." It is simply a matter of where the church's agenda, methodology, and character are derived from. In the end, all of these streets travel in the opposite direction of the Via Dolorosa. Church history indicates that whenever the church has forgotten this, the message of a foot-washing, crucified King is subtly but inexorably marginalized.

On the Road Together:
Toward a Community Hermeneutic

Living in community (which is simply another way to speak of sharing one's life) is a courageous activity. Because of LiGWaiM, grace is the only thing that can make it possible. Andy Crouch wrote, "No one gets out of any serious experiment in human community—church, marriage, family, or otherwise—without discovering, and becoming, an enemy."[48] The only hope is to walk the Via Dolorosa, having the same mind-set as Christ and therefore being willing to love others unconditionally.

Agapē is demanding. Sometimes it is difficult to know which is harder: a willingness to forgive or to be forgiven. Both require humility. *Agapē* also demands a determination to live with openness and integrity. It means a constant acceptance of our lack of completeness, but a joy in our progress. In other words, it is like any long journey on any road. John Stott was right when he wrote many years before he died, "Life is a pilgrimage of learning, a voyage of discovery, in which our mistaken views are corrected, our distorted notions adjusted, our shallow opinions deepened and some of our vast ignorances diminished."[49]

If everyone within the community of believers has this mind-set, then there is hope that, unlike any other community, the church really will be the safest place on earth. It won't be perfection, but it will be walking the road that leads to perfection.

> In the movies, it's always wrapped up in the end.
> *New York fire chief after 9/11*

Here is the world. Beautiful and terrible
things will happen. Do not be afraid.
Frederick Buechner

> How long will it take?... Not long, because "no lie can live
> forever." How long? Not long, because "you shall reap
> what you sow" ... How long? Not long, because the arc of
> the moral universe is long but it bends toward justice.
> *Martin Luther King Jr.*

CHAPTER 9

EVERYTHING *IS* CONNECTED!
Relishing the True Story

Each year, the Jewish family gathers around the table. The plan is to enjoy not only great food but also a great story. It is an increasingly countercultural act. But the digital age has not (yet) managed to eclipse this millennia-old tradition.

The youngest child asks an ancient question: "Why is this night different from all the others?" The annual *Seder* (Passover) gathering of ritual and story, family and food, can now begin. The evening sustains Jewish identity and corporate memory by harking back to Israel's inauguration at Mount Sinai (Exodus 12–20). Nothing that follows that event in the Old Testament can be understood outside its light.

> In the future, when your son asks you, "What is the meaning of the stipulations, decrees and laws the LORD our God has commanded you?" tell him: "We were slaves of Pharaoh in Egypt, but the LORD brought us out of Egypt with a mighty hand. Before our eyes the LORD sent signs and wonders—great and terrible—on Egypt and Pharaoh and his whole household. But he brought us out from there to bring us in and give us the land he promised on oath to our ancestors. The LORD commanded us to obey all these decrees and to fear the LORD our God.
>
> DEUTERONOMY 6:20–24

This story is not isolated but rests within another, grander story. For the Old Testament does not start with the people of Israel, but with the cosmos. So like all great stories, it has a beginning, a middle, and an end and confronts us with a "relentlessly narratival" view of the world.[1] The claim, then, is that every cosmic event has a place within this narrative, however implausible that initially appears. Stories are as essential to mental health as oxygen is to physical health. They help us make sense of the perplexing world we thought we understood and offer us a trajectory, charts by which to navigate life's currents. It is mere conceit that presumes these waters are entirely uncharted.

Stories are thus crucial for creating or intensifying a sense of identity or purpose amongst fellow travelers. Take the account of Rosa Parks's simple courage in that Alabama bus, or of the defense of the Alamo, or of the epic 1940 conflict in England's skies between the Luftwaffe and the RAF. Many such events would remain obscure had great storytellers not immortalized them. So while Rosa Parks was not the first to defy the Jim Crow bus laws, she was the first one civil rights lawyers believed could withstand the ensuing legal battles.

The best stories paradoxically confront our fantasies, rubbing our noses in the awkwardness of reality. As the English philosopher Roger Scruton rightly observes, "Fantasy replaces the real, resistant, objective world with a pliant surrogate. And it is important to see why this matters. Life in the actual world is difficult and embarrassing."[2] Good stories force us to reappraise the world we thought we knew, drawing back the curtains on unimagined vistas, exposing the paucity and egocentrism of our perspectives. In contrast, private fantasy offers no surprises or disturbances. Marilyn Chandler McEntyre puts it wonderfully: "A story is an invitation, and a challenge, and a choice."[3] The "relentlessly narratival" Bible is all of these things—and much more besides.

The Stories with Heroes Just Like Us

The heroes of ancient Indian or Greek myth were invariably *not* like us. We could learn from them, certainly. We might sympathize with them, take pity on them, or be outraged at them—but we could never presume to identify with them. Greek culture, for instance, was aristocratic, a culture that mythologized princes and demigods who "mere mortals" could only gaze up at in wonderment. So the highest form of dramatic art, according to the great philosopher Aristotle, was *tragedy*, in part because it always concerned true heroes. They will always display some flaw despite their aristocratic grandeur, and this will always bring them down. As we observe their inevitable demise, we experience a beneficial, almost religious feeling of purification—what

Aristotle called *catharsis*. We can thus return to our ordinary, humdrum lives subtly improved.

Taking its cue from its Jewish inheritance, Christianity changed everything. According to the French philosopher Luc Ferry, it introduced "the notion that humanity was fundamentally identical, that men were equal in dignity—an unprecedented idea at the time, and one to which our world owes its entire democratic inheritance."[4]

We might never have entirely identified with petulant Achilles or haughty Oedipus, but we certainly could with Abraham's faintheartedness or Simon Peter's impetuosity. As social reformer Vishal Mangawaldi notes, "If extraordinary things can happen to simple people … then all of us can be heroes."[5]

The Bible is unique in ancient literature. It insists that the whole of life is not merely *informed* by the story it tells but is *part* of the story it tells. This implies that life—our lives, everybody's lives—is a story with an Author.

But we recoil from this thought. We perceive a threat to our freedom and individuality—even though the Bible's narrative never once suggests either. As will have become clear, this is because we have had too many negative experiences of people claiming "author's rights" over us. We no longer trust *anyone* who claims such authority. This is because of a succession of stories we've been told and believed in.

What follows is a very crude précis of a millennium of Western thinking that will enable us both to trace how the overarching story of our culture has shifted and to draw together all the threads from this book. Regard each bullet point as the exposed tips of an archipelago of icebergs, each representing a wealth of submerged thought and experience.

The Stories We've Grown Out Of

While great storytellers might order these differently in terms of relative importance, a story will invariably contain five elements, which can then be applied to the elements of a person's worldview:

1. *Origins:* The narrative's background and introducing the characters.
2. *Problem:* The challenge or the antagonist(s) that conflicts with the protagonist(s).
3. *Solution:* The conflict escalates as the protagonist applies the solution.
4. *Goal:* The conflict ends in a victory.
5. *Outcome:* The consequences of the vision.

Premodernity

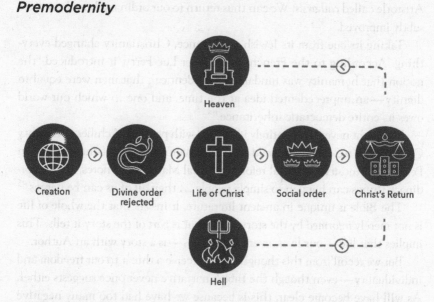

The geography of medieval stories was almost as important as their trajectory. The premodern person lived in a three-tier universe: God in heaven above, the Devil in hell below, and our world in between. God's final judgment at Christ's return determined where individuals would end up, on the basis of a life lived between these two cosmic realities.

Human existence is bookended by divine creation and divine judgment—time is linear; everything has a purpose; human life has significance. This biblical (by and large) narrative was preserved and disseminated in a largely illiterate age through the means of stained-glass windows, rituals and sacraments, traveling poets, and the great medieval tradition of mystery plays.

However, there were significant flaws with it (even for the contemporary Christian mind), not least in the matters discussed in the previous chapter. For if God holds authority over the world and if human systems are providentially established, then it is easy to appeal to divine mandate to preserve the political status quo. In fact, if sin (in a crude form of *LiGWaiM*) is simply a matter of rejecting divine providence, the church can easily degenerate into a convenient tool for preserving an aristocratic social order. Rebelling against that order is tantamount to rebelling against the divine order, which is punishable at the final reckoning. A peasants' revolt could then be construed as tantamount to Adam and Eve's original fall.

This preserving of the status quo is one of many chains that the newly enlightened sought to cast off. An easy appeal to Old Testament prophets would have been enough to expose the *LiGWaiM* of the powerful, but thinkers and revolutionaries had grander schemes. They did not simply seek to raid the palaces and usurp the thrones; they sought to plunder heaven too.

Modernity

Evolution   Chains of Oppression   Revolution   Utopia   Death

History is rarely neat, but even good historians find a satisfying set of dates hard to resist. So modernity sometimes gets dated from 1789 to 1989, the period when Western Enlightenment apparently gained the political power to implement its aspirations, from the French Revolution to the collapse of the Berlin Wall and Communism.

In essence, modernity luxuriates in the noonday light that obliterated the gloom of superstition and myth. Scientific, empirical observation and the fearless pursuit of reason trumped everything else. Religion in all its forms withered under its glare, as did the apparent absurdities of monarchy and aristocracy.

Of course, enlightened thinking was neither static nor monolithic; it evolved through the genius of many contributors and adversaries. But as suggested in chapter 4, the supreme legacy of Charles Darwin, Karl Marx, and Sigmund Freud (among others) was the intellectual justification for discarding God. We patently did *not* live in a three-tier cosmos, but in a "closed" universe. There was no need for the hypothesis or assistance of God. This is the world John Lennon appealed for us to "Imagine"—and for moderns "it's [really] easy if you try." After all, when you go "up," there is no heaven above (as Yuri Gagarin gleefully informed us on his return from the first human orbit of the earth). If there is mystery in the cosmos, it is only a matter of time before it is demystified by the accumulated wisdom of science.

Modernity spins a compelling story, of course. That much is obvious from the way it has managed to inspire optimism and even self-sacrifice in its believers. The flaw was that it insisted on holding on to the trappings and structure of premodernity's story while dismissing the other two tiers of reality.

1. *Origins*: The cosmos is not created but the result of random forces. Humanity is simply the present stage of an inexorable evolutionary process.

2. *Problem*: Humanity is in chains (because of superstition, religion, the powerful).

3. *Solution*: Enlightenment and revolution (forcibly overthrowing old orders) are the keys.

4. *Goal*: Utopia will result, the perfect new society populated by autonomous citizens living in glorious equality and liberty.

5. *Outcome*: But then what …? Aspirations for life after death are dismissed as pipe dreams. As Bertrand Russell famously said, "When I die, I rot" (although as some flippantly point out, he was wrong; he was cremated). We are left to make the best of our human lot.

In the meantime, modernity's utopian vision of what theologian Peter Leithart dubs "the modern trinity of control, progress, and freedom"[6] propels it forward, the ends by which all means are justified. As the English political philosopher John Gray writes, "Any society that systematically uses science and technology to achieve its goals is modern. Death camps are as modern as laser surgery."[7] In September 1959, Soviet premier Nikita Khrushchev addressed a jubilant Moscow crowd: "The dreams mankind cherished for ages, dreams expressed in fairytales which seemed sheer fantasy, are being translated into reality by man's own hands."[8] It was exhilarating, all-embracing, infectiously optimistic—and deeply flawed, as many realized even then. This is one of many Communist jokes from the era:

> What's the difference between a Soviet fairy tale and a Western fairy tale?
>
> A Western fairy tale begins: "Once upon a time there was …"; a Soviet fairy tale begins: "Once upon a time there will be …"[9]

This fairy-tale optimism is hardly confined to the East. We in the West still cling to the myth of progress. We know the future is as uncontrollable as it is unforeseeable—but we moderns still believe that things will only get better. Quite how that improvement is defined, however, is a very different, and sometimes fatal, matter.

Postmodernity

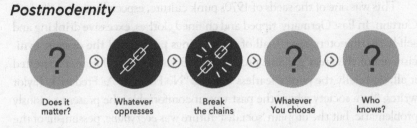

| Does it matter? | Whatever oppresses | Break the chains | Whatever You choose | Who knows? |

Reactions to the modern story have been many and varied. But sadly, as Roger Scruton has been at pains to articulate, their roots do not lie in irrepressible hope, but inconsolable grief. Modernity's flaws might be palpable, but the alternatives are not very palatable. So, for example, Scruton points to the German composer Richard Wagner as one of the great artists to prepare the way for modernism: "Acutely conscious of the death of God, Wagner proposed man as his own redeemer and art as the transfiguring rite of passage to a higher world."[10] John Lennon echoed this, but with angry resignation in his 1970 song titled "God." After the litany of all that he no longer believed in (including Jesus, Kennedy and — shock, horror! — the Beatles), the only thing left was ... himself.

Yet the self is not enough. Human beings can never be enough. How can we, finite and flawed beings that we are, ever fill the God-shaped hole? And so what Scruton calls high culture "hurts because it is bereft."[11] "It is," he goes on to write, "as though the high culture of our society, having ceased to be a meditation on the common religion, has become instead a meditation on the lack of it."[12]

Few contemporary writers have done this as honestly as Julian Barnes. The opening lines of his brilliant meditation on mortality, meaning, and religion, *Nothing to be Frightened Of*, are startling: "I don't believe in God, but I miss Him." His philosopher brother's response is blunt: "Soppy!" he scoffs.[13] Barnes finds little to convince him that God exists, and he is clear that the God he misses is the "New Testament one" of "Western Europe and nonfundamentalist America," rather than Buddha or Allah.[14] But his brother's scorn cannot deter his grief.

The consequences of this divine disappearance are devastating. For no God means no Author; and no Author means no Story. Just a myriad of exiles, each unavoidably bewitched by their own private, disconnected stories. We are dislocated and adrift in a pitilessly indifferent universe. It was no longer possible to claim the modernist dream of progress, purpose, or meaning. In fact, it is no longer possible to claim much at all for "true" reality.

This was one of the seeds of 1970s punk culture, especially east of the Iron Curtain. In East Germany, ripped and chained clothes, excessive drinking and self-harm, impotent rage—all of these things proclaimed the deepest cynicism about the great socialist project. East Berlin's political masters detested it all, especially the punks' fearless mantra: "No Future!" As Frederick Taylor writes, "In a society where the past was uncomfortable, the present seriously problematic, but the utopian 'socialist' future was *everything*, pessimism of the kind that punks luxuriated in was considered deeply anti-social."[15] Yet who could blame them in an age that had lost its stories?

1. *Origins*: Who knows? It's hard to know whom to believe, so simply choose the most amenable origins myth.

2. *Problem*: We are in chains to whatever curbs our right to be who we should be (often it is the very utopian vision proclaimed by modernists as offering hope).

3. *Solution*: Cast off those chains by whatever appropriate means (e.g., through engaging in identity politics, undergoing counseling, consulting a personal shopper, exploring a new spirituality, etc.).

4. *Goal*: We can be what we want until we prefer something else; above all, we should never allow anyone else's utopian vision to oppress us.

5. *Outcome*: Who knows? We don't really know where we've come from or where we're going—so settle for living in the present.

This lostness explains why Julian Barnes suggests that "when we killed—or exiled—God, we also killed ourselves."[16] Reflecting on the first human beings to fly—French balloonists like the pioneering photographer Nadar—Barnes knew that science had filled us with wonder, with never-before-seen views: "We have lost God's height, and gained Nadar's; but we have also lost depth."[17] The loss of God has led to fragmentation and the loss of identity. Václav Havel wrote, "It's as if we're playing for a number of different teams at once, each with different uniforms, and as though ... we didn't know which one we ultimately belonged to, which of those teams was really ours."[18] This is a unique agony. In one address at the Library of Congress in Washington, DC, Havel explained that when we lose God in the modern world, we lose four key things: meaning, purpose, responsibility, and accountability.[19] He seemed to imply that the dismissal of the divine has consequences far too catastrophic and too costly to be done flippantly.

George Orwell anticipated this pain in 1940, vividly suggesting that for two centuries, the West had been sawing away at the branch on which we had perched. When the inevitable collapse came, we were dumbfounded by that "little mistake." For we then discovered that "the thing at the bottom was not a bed of roses after all, it was a cesspool full of barbed wire ... It appears that amputation of the soul *isn't* just a simple surgical job, like having your appendix out. The wound has a tendency to go septic."[20] More than half a bloody century later, who could disagree?

G. K. Chesterton is reported to have said that that when people stop believing in God, they don't then believe in nothing; they believe in anything. Similarly a denarrated culture does not stop telling stories altogether; instead, it clings to *any* stories. And so we return to the lair of the conspiracist.

Conspiracy

When Malaysian Airlines flight MH370 mysteriously vanished in March 2014, 239 people lost their lives. We may never know what really happened, but the uncertainty offers scope for inexhaustible creativity. Almost immediately, sinister explanations started springing up across the Internet. After all, in our surveillance-drenched world in which the NSA can trace my every text or tweet, the notion that a huge jet aircraft could somehow just fall off the radar seems unthinkable. So it stands to reason that darker forces must be at work. Well, perhaps there were. But in a denarrated world, conspiracy theories are the most satisfying stories. That is why they mushroom when tragedy strikes.

Talk of satisfaction may seem incongruous, since conspiracy theories thrive on the negativity of fear and paranoia. However, they have a subtle appeal. In a chaotic, unpredictable, and irrational world, these theories claim to discern order. As the great playwright David Mamet says, "It is in our nature to dramatize."[21] He does not refer to being melodramatic but rather to the fact that we yearn for narrative significance in the events of our lives, however mundane they might be. We long to play a heroic, if small, part in something bigger than us.

Related to this, is the sense of being under observation. It grants a kind of validation, a significance in a meaningless world. The essayist Susan Sontag was on to something when she said, "I envy paranoids; they actually think people are paying attention to them."[22] For the conspiracist, the coincidental or accidental also gains significance within a wider narrative. Otherwise, life's experiences are, in novelist Douglas Coupland's words, "just a string of events entered into a daybook" rather than a coherent narrative, which gives a "false linearity imposed on chaos as we humans try to make sense of our iffy situation here on earth."[23]

It is here that the narratives of history and fiction converge. So accustomed are we to the vocabulary and craft of fiction (whether written or cinematic) that we forget its artificiality. Good editing ensures that every detail has a purpose. Whether in the terse prose of an Ernest Hemingway or the obsessive scene setting of a Marcel Proust, a sensitive reader knows nothing is accidental. The merest description provides narrative weight.

Conversely, real life is full of the mundane, inconsequential and coincidental. It is also full of the tragic, the unjust, and the desperately sad. Yet as historian Richard Hofstadter recognized, the paranoid mentality insists on "leaving nothing unexplained and comprehending all of reality in one overarching, consistent theory."[24] Everything *has* to be connected.

It is not just a matter of granting significance to the insignificant, however. Conspiracists do not merely want to connect all the dots; they want the line to end satisfactorily. Because life doesn't do that, conspiracy theories attempt to improve on meaningless and unrelated events by offering closure to tragedy. William Manchester, author of the classic elegy *Death of a President*, made precisely this point on the thirtieth anniversary of John F. Kennedy's assassination:

> If you put the murdered President of the United States on one side of a scale and that wretched waif [Lee Harvey] Oswald on the other, it doesn't balance. You want to add something weightier to Oswald. It would invest the President's death with meaning, endowing him with martyrdom. He would have died for something. A conspiracy would, of course, do the job nicely. Unfortunately, there is no evidence whatever that there was one.[25]

So here is the real irony: conspiracy theories represent not a connection with reality but a flight from it. They yearn for a narrative order that only the transcendent or divine can offer. After debunking the modernist's confidence in historical progress, the postmodernist must offer only silence. An event can only have the significance we choose to grant it. But as Graham Greene said of writing convincing fiction, "Only God and the author are omniscient, not the one who says 'I.'"[26] But if there is no God, there is no Author. We are alone together, a horde of individual "I's," each bound by our subjectivity to opinion and conjecture. And when these "I's" get together, events tend to go awry.

The rise of the conspiracy theory mind-set was bound to happen in a denarrated culture. Celebrated novelist Donna Tartt is absolutely right when she writes that a good novel "enables non-believers to participate in a world-view that religious people take for granted: life as a vast polyphonous web of interconnections, predestined meetings, fortuitous chances and accidents, all governed by a unifying if unforeseen plan."[27]

But what if there was more to the religious worldview than meets the eye? What if this actually offers an escape route from a lost, denarrated, and fearful wilderness of mirrors because it is uniquely robust enough to withstand it? In other words, what if it is actually—dare I say it—*true*?

The Story So Good—Because It's True

Could it not be that the reason all human cultures have worshiped is that it is then that we are at our healthiest? This would certainly fit with the notion of being in the *imago dei*, created with eternity in our hearts. Psychologist Dan Allender suggests this means that "eternity pulses through my blood, and its course will never allow me fully to forget that I will one day stand face to face with a holy, just, and righteous God."[28]

We can suppress this, of course; we can try to reason our way out of it. But the quirks and wonders of life have an uncanny habit of wrong-footing us. The Hungarian composer György Kurtág makes a remarkable confession:

> Consciously, I am certainly an atheist, but I do not say it out loud, because if I look at Bach, I cannot be an atheist. Then I have to accept the way he believed. His music never stops praying. And how can I get closer if I look at him from the outside? I do not believe in the Gospels in a literal fashion, but a Bach fugue has the Crucifixion in it—as the nails are being driven in. In music, I am always looking for the hammering of the nails ... That is a dual vision. My brain rejects it all. But my brain isn't worth much.[29]

C. S. Lewis expressed the point perfectly:

> The Christian says, "Creatures are not born with desires unless satisfaction for those desires exists. A baby feels hunger: well, there is such a thing as food. A duckling wants to swim: well, there is such a thing as water. Men feel sexual desire: well, there is such a thing as sex. If I find in myself a desire which no experience in this world can satisfy, the most probable explanation is that I was made for another world."[30]

Could it be, then, that my longing for an Author, which no human author can ever adequately satisfy, indicates the reality that there is an Author "out there"?

Eternity

On the assumption that the claims by and about Jesus of Nazareth are valid, we have seen that the God he reveals is an Author with a difference: he rules over his creation not with force (despite his unlimited power) but with love. He subordinates his power to his love. So just as a writer's books inevitably reflect her passions and character, so it is with the divine Author. He is writing the grandest story of them all, one that embraces the entire cosmos and yet that includes a place for the lowliest of creatures. It is not a totalizing story but a grace-soaked story. It offers forgiveness and hope to all, despite ourselves. In complete contrast to the postmodern mirage of liberty being achieved by casting off all authority, true freedom is only discovered through finding our place *within* the Author's story.

This is as all-embracing and life-affirming as it is possible to be — light-years from the caricature of Christianity "as a pale, wan, disembodied spirituality that seeks to repress desire so that we may pursue the colorless path of religious duty."[31] That is certainly what it has become at times, and the church, perhaps in part because of its pursuit of power and public influence, has appeared only to offer this. But it is not what the foot-washing Son of Man offered.

So while the premoderns had a worldview largely shaped along biblical lines, it is arguable that medieval Christian leaders' participation, and even collusion, with worldly power introduced fatal flaws. So let us return to the story outline for one last time to see how it might be adjusted. For a start, there is no need to adhere to a simplistic geographical account of three tiers. This is not to deny the realities of heaven or hell; it is merely to avoid any unnecessary distraction for overliteralism. This is, of course, as crude a generalization as all the other story outlines we have considered.

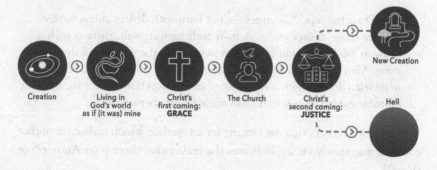

Creation — Living in God's world as if (it was) mine — Christ's first coming: **GRACE** — The Church — Christ's second coming: **JUSTICE** — New Creation — Hell

1. *Origins:* The cosmos exists because of divine initiative. Christians might disagree about the mechanics of how God did this, but the fact of it cannot be denied or marginalized. Without creation, the divine story is meaningless and groundless:

> You are worthy, our Lord and God,
>> to receive glory and honor and power,
> for you created all things,
>> and by your will they were created
>> and have their being.
>>> REVELATION 4:11

2. *Problem:* Humanity has sought to wrest the initiative for living from God—this is *LiGWaiM*. This places conflict, and even conspiracy, at the very heart of the universe, as already seen in Psalm 2:

> Why do the nations conspire
>> and the peoples plot in vain?
> The kings of the earth rise up
>> and the rulers band together
>> against the LORD and against his anointed, saying,
> "Let us break their chains
>> and throw off their shackles."
>>> PSALM 2:1–3

3. *Solution:* The conflict between Creator and creatures is, of course, complex, but the greatest surprise comes with another divine initiative. The crucifixion and resurrection of the foot-washing Son of Man inaugurates a new kingdom and redemption of those who are *LiGWaiM*. Jesus' first coming heralds the start of the era of the church, God's new society, which is as simultaneously glorious and flawed as its members:

> When you were dead in your sins ... God made you alive with Christ. He forgave us all our sins, having canceled the charge of our legal indebtedness, which stood against us and condemned us; he has taken it away, nailing it to the cross. And having disarmed the powers and authorities, he made a public spectacle of them, triumphing over them by the cross.
>> COLOSSIANS 2:13–15

4. *Goal:* The climax of this story is still to come (which means, in narrative terms, we are still living within the time of tension). It will end when the King returns to restore his kingdom—or rather, the even greater story will only just be starting:

> Just as people are destined to die once, and after that to face judgment, so Christ was sacrificed once to take away the sins of many; and he will appear a second time, not to bear sin, but to bring salvation to those who are waiting for him.
>
> HEBREWS 9:27–28

5. *Outcome*: Eternity is a reality, as are heaven and hell (despite the impossibility of imagining them). However, Reinhold Niebuhr was prudent: "It is unwise for Christians to claim any knowledge of either the furniture of heaven or the temperature of hell."[32] What is coming is the long-awaited and perfect experience of God's unassailable justice and exquisite grace. Sin, death, and fear are forever banished in Christ's earthly, tangible, blissful kingdom:

> No longer will there be any curse. The throne of God and of the Lamb will be in the city, and his servants will serve him. They will see his face, and his name will be on their foreheads. There will be no more night. They will not need the light of a lamp or the light of the sun, for the Lord God will give them light. And they will reign for ever and ever.
>
> REVELATION 22:3–5

This is the secure home we've been searching for all our lives.

So much more needs saying about each of this story's iceberg tips, especially for the skeptic or incredulous. But as soon as the ceiling is lifted off the closed universe, it is surely no less intrinsically unbelievable than other worldviews — and in contrast to many, there are surprisingly many more evidences and grounds for its plausibility than might at first have appeared.

The crucial issue is the differences it makes to the period of tension in which we currently find ourselves. There are many we could touch on, but we will focus on just three. This means there are aspects of Christ's authority clearly seen and available now, but there is still much to come. This is why theologians frequently refer to "the already ... and the not yet." It is precisely this tension that gives the Christian view plausibility in a confusing and cynical world. It never claims everything is yet as it should be; instead, it robustly confronts injustice and wrong while offering grace to all who would accept it. And it holds out hope for full restoration when the foot-washing King's reign is fulfilled.

It is a kingdom of power, of course. How can it not be? But this power is always subservient to the demands of love and justice, and always creative, not destructive.

A Kingdom of Justice

In his letter to the Romans, Paul writes these words:

> God presented Christ as a sacrifice of atonement, through the shedding of his blood—to be received by faith. He did this to demonstrate his righteousness, because in his forbearance he had left the sins committed beforehand unpunished—*he did it to demonstrate his righteousness at the present time*, so as to be just and the one who justifies those who have faith in Jesus.
>
> ROMANS 3:25–26, emphasis mine

Paul weaves a tight argument in these short lines in Romans. In essence, he acknowledges there is a delay in divine justice, an element of the "already ... and not yet" to it. But it must be like this, and for my friends M. and D., grasping this was essential. The fact that Christ died on the cross for sin proves the seriousness with which God views sin. But how have so many of the most appalling power abusers escaped scot-free? In a play on words ("justice," "righteousness," and "justify" share the same root in Greek), Paul explains the genius of the atonement, God's means by which we and ultimately the world are made "at one" with him. Sin is condemned as it must be—God really is as morally righteous as we need him to be. But simultaneously, there is hope for the guilty. As we saw in chapter 8, Christ's death offers forgiveness or, in Paul's words, the chance to be justified through trusting him. The "not yet" is realized at Christ's return, bringing the closure of ultimate justice. If this seems a fearful thing, it is because it is. But consider this: If justice is something desperately needed in an unjust world, who else would you rather have administer it than the foot-washing Son of Man?

The error many have made, and indeed exploited, is to imagine that the delay for ultimate justice means the absence of ultimate justice. After all, the return of Jesus seems as laughable today as it has always seemed. Peter had to remind his readers that "scoffers will come, scoffing" (2 Peter 3:3) about such an absurdity. If Jesus did indeed rise, an event consistently proclaimed in the New Testament, the implications are vast. As Paul told a skeptical audience in Athens nearly two thousand years ago, "[God] has set a day when he will judge the world with justice by the man he has appointed. He has given proof of this to everyone by raising him from the dead" (Acts 17:31). Peter Berger rightly notes, "Religious hope offers a theodicy [a vindication of God's moral authority in the face of evil] and therefore consolation to the victims of inhumanity. But it is equally significant that religion provides damnation for the perpetrators of inhumanity."[33] But that is not all. If it were, Jesus' return would be too dreadful to contemplate.

A Kingdom of Love

The attempt to pit divine love and divine justice against each other, as some are inclined to do, will always lead to error. There is no conflict within God. So within just a few paragraphs of describing God's justice demonstration, Paul insists that the cross is simultaneously a love demonstration:

> You see, at just the right time, when we were still powerless, Christ died for the ungodly. Very rarely will anyone die for a righteous person, though for a good person someone might possibly dare to die. *But God demonstrates his own love for us in this*: While we were still sinners, Christ died for us.
>
> ROMANS 5:6–8, emphasis mine

This is the epicenter of divine grace, the greatest demonstration of *agapē* that the world has ever known. The cross offers the bedrock of a believer's confidence. It is an immovable historical event and so assures the follower that divine love is both sure and personal, even in the face of life's (and others') inconstancy.

The kingdom inaugurated at Christ's first coming and consummated at his second will be characterized by this love. For eternity. This may sound like a recipe for interminable boredom. Aldous Huxley, for one, mocked the notion of an afterlife, jesting that he could not imagine anything worse than living with Aldous Huxley forever.[34] This is primarily because human language and imagination falter whenever we attempt to puncture the fringes of the finite. But because *agapē* lies at its heart, this eternal existence will never (in Peter's words) "perish, spoil or fade" (1 Peter 1:4).

It will truly be living because we will love and will be loved eternally. That may sound like the hyperbole of a limp pop ballad, but it is nothing of the sort. This love was proven at the cross.

A Kingdom of Life

When the apostle John was granted his privileged peek behind the curtains of eternity, he noticed something especially exciting in the new Jerusalem that has descended to the earth: The "water of life" flows from God's throne through the middle of the city (Revelation 22:1). Then, "on each side of the river stood the tree of life, bearing twelve crops of fruit, yielding its fruit every month. And the leaves of the tree are for the healing of the nations. No longer will there be any curse" (Revelation 22:2–3).

The language is symbolic, but the point is obvious. Humanity can now live for eternity—just as we were created to enjoy. So for those with the humility to accept Christ's grace, death is not a terminus but a gateway. Death is not really a death; this life is not the totality of life; historical events can only be "penultimate," as Dietrich Bonhoeffer put it.[35] Death is no longer to be feared because Christ's resurrection has wonderfully demystified it. This changes the fundamental nature of grief, even if it does not eliminate grief's agony in this life. As one pastor put it, "For the Christian, nothing is ultimately fatal."[36]

It is impossible to overstate the implications of this. In fact, this future reality has already begun. In his sublime high priestly prayer, Jesus gives a surprising definition of eternal life: "Now this is eternal life: that they know you, the only true God, and Jesus Christ, whom you have sent" (John 17:3). In other words, the *very act* of putting trust in Christ, and thus being united to him by his Spirit, means eternal life has already started. We are subjects of this eternal kingdom now, despite also being citizens of many nations, as well as victims and culprits of *LiGWaiM.*

This means we are to live out the values of this eternal kingdom in the complexity and shambling disorder of this world. That is the essence of the Sermon on the Mount (Matthew 5–7). Jesus never intended these teachings to be a kind of celestial entrance requirement—we would all be doomed if he had. Instead, it is the most concise and penetrating ethical document ever conceived—designed for God's forgiven people. This is the *agapē* life we are to live together. Now. And forever. This is true virtue; it is true altruism. For we never love God and love others to gain spiritual bartering currency—to do so would be self-centered blackmail. We love because we are loved; we serve because we have been served. We are freed to do good for its own sake, not for what we can get out of it.

To be sure, the church has occasionally been guilty as charged for pacifying the oppressed with opiates. But never Jesus. For if we are living according to our calling as his people, the future reality is our greatest incentive to change the present. Jesus' kingdom has been inaugurated. It does not need us to shore it up or to revive it. It simply *is.* But we do have the challenge to live it out in every aspect of our lives.

Our confidence in future justice cannot become a justification for not seeking justice, however flawed and provisional, in this life. We would never allow that for our biological family; why should our grace-won family be different? We must not allow the hope of future shalom and wholeness to be a justification for showing little concern for those things in this life. We are to seek justice, show love, and live life to the full as much as we can in the present, precisely *because* of our confidence that abundant justice, love, and life will come in the future.

There is nothing new in this. The prophet Zechariah said this to God's people almost two and half millennia ago: "This is what the LORD Almighty said: 'Administer true justice; show mercy and compassion to one another. Do not oppress the widow or the fatherless, the foreigner or the poor. Do not plot evil against each other'" (Zechariah 7:9–10).

Could it not be that because God's people have historically failed to do this, our saving message of ultimate justice, love, and life through faith in Christ has rung so hollow?

The Grandest Story of Them All

T. S. Eliot concluded what was arguably his last great work, *Little Gidding* (No. 4 of *Four Quartets*) with some of his most beautiful language. He was one of English literature's most acute observers of the effect of modernity on humanity, and this final poem is avowedly theological in its themes (much to the dismay of some contemporaries). It is particularly loved for these words:

> We shall not cease from exploration
> And the end of all our exploring
> Will be to arrive where we started
> And know the place for the first time.[37]

However, one of the poem's central themes (the result of Eliot's lifetime of spiritual exploration) is a stark choice between two doves, which bring two types of fire and water, and two roses. One is the dark dove of the bombs raining down on London during the Second World War Blitz, which Eliot witnessed firsthand. These brought rose-colored fire onto the "rose" of England, only extinguished by the force of firefighters' water. In contrast, there is the dove that can only be identified as God's Holy Spirit because of the emphatic imagery of Pentecost, the moment in Acts 2 when the Spirit comes down on God's people:

> The dove descending breaks the air
> With flame of incandescent terror
> Of which the tongues declare
> The one discharge from sin and error.
> The only hope, or else despair
>> Lies in the choice of pyre or pyre —
>> To be redeemed from fire by fire.

The Spirit is fire — the refiner's fire — and he purifies and cleanses because of the rose-colored blood of divine love shed at the cross. So Eliot is saying ultimately there is no escape from fire — either the destruction of human fire (with the Blitz an expression of *LiGWaiM* at its most extreme) or the refinement of Spirit fire.

But the poem's climax (following verse after verse that confronts the realities of pain, despair, and death) is one of the most wonderful statements of confident faith in the English language, echoing the words of the medieval mystic, Mother Julian of Norwich:

> Quick now, here, now, always —
> A condition of complete simplicity
> (Costing not less than everything)
> And all shall be well and
> All manner of thing shall be well
> When the tongues of flame are in-folded
> Into the crowned knot of fire
> And the fire and the rose are one.

"All shall be well, and all shall be well, and all manner of thing shall be well"![38] This is the refrain of the grandest story there is: *All shall be well!* This really *is* a story with a "happily ever after." Not because of a demagogue's rhetoric or a dictator's jackboot or a utopian vision, or any other human endeavor. All shall be well because of the foot-washing Master who stooped as a slave, the divine King who was crowned on a cross. All shall be well because love shall conquer all. All shall be well because love *has* conquered all. This was the apostle John's confidence, and it can be our confidence as well:

> I saw the Holy City, the new Jerusalem, coming down out of heaven from
> God, prepared as a bride beautifully dressed for her husband. And I heard
> a loud voice from the throne saying, "Look! God's dwelling place is now

among the people, and he will dwell with them. They will be his people, and God himself will be with them and be their God. 'He will wipe every tear from their eyes. There will be no more death' or mourning or crying or pain, for the old order of things has passed away."

REVELATION 21:2–4

In Summary

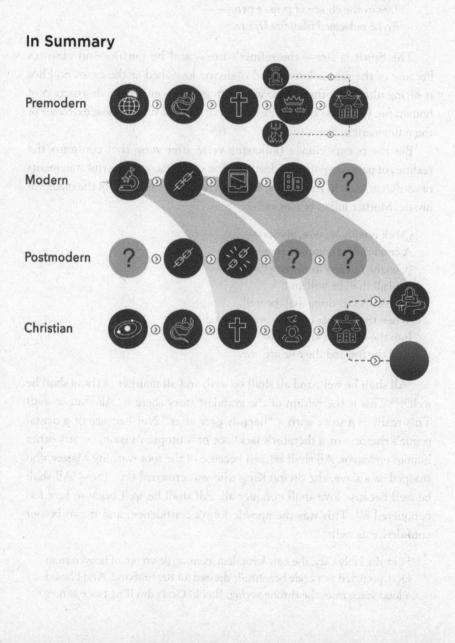

ACKNOWLEDGMENTS

If I have been able to see any distance at all in this cursory glance across huge plains, it is only the result of standing on giants' shoulders. I am not a scholar of history, psychology, or literature, but I have learned from many who are. I am immensely grateful to them for the stimulation of conversations and insights. Of course, I take full responsibility for the end product, but if it has any quality at all, it is because of the contributions of many generous friends.

I have especially appreciated the valuable time given to me by the following:

In the UK: Professor Timothy Garton Ash, Edward Lucas, David Cornwell, Martin Packard, Gordon Corera, Charles Cumming, Dr. Simon Willmetts, Dr. Tess Rosalie, Andrew Bunnell, Ziya Meral, and Dr. Brennan Jacoby. It was especially good to interact with my great uncle in his ninetieth year, Rt. Hon. James Ramsden. He could still draw on his fascinating recollections of his time as junior minister in the Ministry of War under John Profumo, only to succeed him after his ignominious fall to become the last ever Minister of War (the department was subsumed into the new Ministry of Defence).

Elsewhere I have appreciated interactions and conversations with Pfarrer Sebastian Führer in Leipzig; John Goering and Jay Eastman in Berlin; Andrew Macdonald Exum and Thomas Auld in Washington, DC; Rabbi Michael Shevack in Pennsylvania; Ted Turnau in Prague; Pastor Slavko Hadzic in Sarajevo; and Dr. Kosta Milkov in Skopje.

I'm grateful for the opportunities I have had to explore some of these topics through giving talks in various places—as diverse as Athens; Skopje; the European Leadership Forum in Eger, Hungary; All Souls Church, Langham Place; English L'Abri in Greatham, and the Word Alive event in a blustery

202 A Wilderness of Mirrors

North Wales. I have been greatly helped by a cohort of faithful friends who have willingly read and commented on various parts of this book as it has developed: Graham Carr, Gordon Corera, Jonny Dyer, Francesca Elston, Andrew Fellows, John Goering, Anthony Haden-West, Professor Glynn Harrison, Martin Helgesson, Melinda and Ross Hendry, Marcus Honeysett, Jem and Lucy Hovil, Gavin McGrath, Ellie Mitchell, Anna and Lauri Moyle, Marsh Moyle, Chris Oldfield, Ian Paul, Jennie Pollock, Louise Prideaux, Andrew Tate, Gareth Wroe, and (last but definitely not least) Christopher and Elizabeth Meynell. Giles Walker saved me hours of work by transforming the footnotes into a more appropriate form. Alex Webb-Peploe has done a superb job in deciphering my illegible scribbles in order to craft the graphics. I am especially grateful to Andy Flannagan for enthusiasm and creativity in the final furlong as we have considered how to take this project further.

This project has been on my mind for nearly four years. It would never have been possible to complete it without the many sacrifices made by Hugh Palmer and my other colleagues at All Souls, stepping into the breach when I was distracted and detained. I am very grateful to you all.

Mark Hunt very kindly supported this project at a time when there was little to show for it; in particular, he introduced me to Madison Trammel at Zondervan, who has been a superb editor—encouraging, insightful, and wise. Then through him, it has been a real privilege to be supported by such a friendly and professional team at Zondervan.

Finally, I owe so much to my family. Joshua, Zanna, and Rachel have shown superhuman patience, endurance, and love—to each, words are woefully insufficient to express my deepest indebtedness, love, and gratitude.

The book is dedicated to two dear friends, Gavin and Andrew, who in their different ways have inspired, supported, and aided me in my thinking and writing.

S.D.G.

Mark Meynell, London,
September 2014

NOTES

PART 1

INTRODUCTION: THE STATE WE'RE IN

1. Ipsos MORI, "Politicians Trusted Less Than Estate Agents, Bankers and Journalists," poll conducted February 9–11, 2013, www.ipsos-mori.com/researchpublications/researcharchive/3133/Politicians-trusted-less-than-estate-agents-bankers-and-journalists.aspx (accessed November 7, 2013).

2. Gallup, Inc., "Confidence in Institutions, 2014," poll conducted June 5–8, 2014, www.gallup.com/poll/1597/confidence-institutions.aspx? (accessed October 2, 2014).

3. Onora O'Neill, A Question of Trust: The BBC Reith Lectures 2002 (Cambridge: Cambridge University Press, 2002), 18.

4. Ibid., 99.

5. Quoted in Chris Mullin, "Dalai Lama Seeks Peking Accord," Guardian, March 27, 1980.

6. Arthur Ponsonby, Falsehood in War-Time (London: George Allen and Unwin, 1928), 11.

7. As in Jean-François Lyotard's oft-quoted (to the point of becoming a commonplace) definition of the postmodern as "an incredulity toward metanarratives" (The Postmodern Condition: A Report on Knowledge [Minneapolis: University of Minnesota Press, 1984], xxiv).

CHAPTER 1: WHERE THE BUCK STOPS!
Rulers Have Failed Us

1. Quoted in Andrew Rawnsley, The End of the Party (London: Penguin, 2010), 185.

2. To be fair, Jonathan Powell later recalled a conversation with Blair (while his chief of staff) when he said his biggest regret was to have studied law instead of history at university (see Jonathan Powell, The New Machiavelli: How to Wield Power in the Modern World [London: Bodley Head, 2010], 53).

3. See, for instance, Charles Townshend, *When God Made Hell: The British Invasion of Mesopotamia and the Creation of Iraq, 1914–1921* (London: Faber and Faber, 2011), or James Barr, *A Line in the Sand: Britain, France, and the Struggle That Created the Middle East* (London: Simon and Schuster, 2012).

4. Graham Greene, *Our Man in Havana* (London: Vintage, 2001), 6.

5. Walker Percy, *Signposts in a Strange Land*, ed. Patrick Samway (New York: Farrar, Straus and Giroux, 1991), 309.

6. Wikipedia, "Charles Holland Duell," http://en.wikipedia.org/wiki/Charles_Holland_Duell (accessed October 3, 2014).

7. Frederick Taylor, *The Berlin Wall: A World Divided, 1961–1989* (New York: HarperCollins, 2007), 22.

8. Barbara Wertheim Tuchman, *The Guns of August* (1962; repr., New York: Random House, 1994), 439.

9. Ibid., 174.

10. National Archives, "The First World War: The Battle of the Somme," www.nationalarchives.gov.uk/pathways/firstworldwar/battles/somme.htm (accessed October 3, 2014).

11. See Gary Sheffield, *Forgotten Victory: The First World War; Myths and Realities* (London: Headline Review, 2002), 180.

12. See John Lewis Gaddis, *The Cold War* (London: Penguin, 2007), 9.

13. "Lions led by donkeys" is a phrase popularly used to contrast the courage of ordinary British soldiers in World War I with that of their commanding officers.

14. George Orwell, *Orwell's England: The Road to Wigan Pier in the Context of Essays, Reviews, Letters and Poems Selected from the Complete Works of George Orwell*, ed. Peter Davison (London: Penguin, 2001), 151.

15. Quoted in Tuchman, *Guns of August*, 440.

16. Siegfried Sassoon, *The War Poems* (London: Faber and Faber, 2006), 67.

17. Nancy Gibbs and Michael Duffy, *The President's Club: Inside the World's Most Exclusive Fraternity* (New York: Simon and Schuster, 2012), 8.

18. Laurent Binet, *HHhH* (New York: Farrar, Straus and Giroux, 2012), 103.

19. Tuchman, *Guns of August*, 226.

20. Ibid., 233 (emphasis mine).

21. Ibid.

22. National Archives, "First World War."

23. Miranda Carter, *George, Nicholas, and Wilhelm: Three Royal Cousins and the Road to World War I* (New York: Vintage, 2011), 382.

24. Tuchman, *Guns of August*, 169.

25. Tony Blair, *A Journey* (London: Hutchinson, 2010), 517.

26. Terry Deary, *Horrible Histories: Frightful First World War* (London: Scholastic, 2007), 8, 11.

27. Woodrow Wilson, "Address Delivered at the First Annual Assemblage of the

League to Enforce Peace," May 27, 1916, www.presidency.ucsb.edu/ws/?pid=65391 (accessed October 3, 2014).

28. Woodrow Wilson, "Address to a Joint Session of Congress on the Conditions of Peace," January 8, 1918, www.presidency.ucsb.edu/ws/?pid=65405 (accessed October 3, 2014).

29. Ibid.

30. See Jill Lepore, "The Prism: Privacy in an Age of Publicity," New Yorker, June 24, 2013, www.newyorker.com/magazine/2013/06/24/the-prism (accessed October 3, 2014).

31. Ibid.

32. U.S. Department of State Office of the Historian, "Foreign Relations of the United States, 1945–1950," https://history.state.gov/historicaldocuments/frus1945-50Intel/d292 (accessed October 3, 2014).

33. Timothy Melley, The Covert Sphere: Secrecy, Fiction, and the National Security State (Ithaca, NY: Cornell University Press, 2012), 3.

34. Winston Churchill, "The Sinews of Peace" (Iron Curtain Speech), March 5, 1946, www.nationalchurchillmuseum.org/sinews-of-peace-history.html (accessed October 3, 2014).

35. See Michael D. Haydock, City under Siege: The Berlin Blockade and Airlift, 1948–1949 (Washington, DC: Brassey's, 2000), back cover copy.

36. Matthew J. Bruccoli and Judith S. Baughman, eds., Conversations with John le Carré (Jackson: University Press of Mississippi, 2005), 58.

37. Taylor, Berlin Wall, vi.

38. Speech to the House of Commons, March 1, 1848, in Hansard's Parliamentary Debates, 3rd series, vol. 97 (London: Cornelius Buck, 1848), col. 122.

39. See also, for example, Joseph Fitchett, "What about the Taliban's Stingers?" New York Times, September 26, 2001, www.nytimes.com/2001/09/26/news/26iht-stinger_ed3_.html (accessed October 3, 2014).

40. See Gordon Corera, The Art of Betrayal: Life and Death in the British Secret Service (London: Widenfeld & Nicolson, 2011), 307.

41. See Dominic Tierney, "Bashar al-Assad and the Devil's Gambit," Atlantic, July 16, 2014, www.theatlantic.com/international/archive/2014/07/assad-and-the-art-of-the-devils-gambit/374501/ (accessed October 3, 2014).

42. See, for example, Corera, Art of Betrayal, 286–87.

43. See Giles Whittell, Bridge of Spies (London: Simon and Schuster, 2011), 173.

44. Michael R. Beschloss, Mayday: Eisenhower, Khrushchev, and the U-2 Affair (London: Faber and Faber, 1986), 17.

45. Ibid., 39.

46. Gaddis, Cold War, 168.

47. See Beschloss, Mayday, 9.

48. Gaddis, Cold War, 168.

49. Ibid., 73.

50. Kennedy used this issue many times in his campaign; see Christopher A. Preble, "Who Ever Believed in the 'Missile Gap'?" *Presidential Studies Quarterly*, 33.4 (December 2003): 801–26, www.jstor.org/discover/10.2307/27552538?uid=2129&uid=2&uid=70&uid=4&sid=21102291940827 (accessed October 3, 2014); Dwayne A. Day, "Of Myths and Missiles: The Truth about John F. Kennedy and the Missile Gap," *Space Review*, January 3, 2006, www.thespacereview.com/article/523/1 (accessed October 3, 2014). See also online archives at the John F. Kennedy Presidential Library website, www.jfklibrary.org/ (accessed October 3, 2014).

51. See David Leip, "1960 Presidential General Election Results," http://uselectionatlas.org/RESULTS/national.php?year=1960 (accessed October 3, 2014).

52. Whittell, *Bridge of Spies*, 198.

53. See BBC News, "Timeline: The 45-Minute Claim," October 13, 2004, http://news.bbc.co.uk/1/hi/uk_politics/3466005.stm (accessed October 3, 2014).

54. Statement by Prime Minister Tony Blair to the House of Commons, "Iraq and Weapons of Mass Destruction," September 24, 2002, in *Hansard's Parliamentary Debates*, www.publications.parliament.uk/pa/cm200102/cmhansrd/vo020924/debtext/20924-01.htm (accessed October 3, 2014).

55. As the Hutton inquiry heard in September 2003; see Matthew Tempest, "Memo Reveals High-Level Dossier Concern," *Guardian*, September 5, 2003, www.theguardian.com/media/2003/sep/15/huttoninquiry.politicsandiraq (accessed October 3, 2014).

56. Steven Garber, *Visions of Vocation* (Downers Grove, IL: InterVarsity, 2014), 20.

57. See former United Nations secretary-general Kofi Annan's interesting reflection on the differences between Zimbabwe's Robert Mugabe and Nelson Mandela (Kofi Annan, *Interventions: A Life in War and Peace* [London: Allen Lane, 2012], 169).

58. Timothy Garton Ash, *The File: A Personal History* (London: HarperCollins, 1997), 225.

59. Václav Havel, *Summer Meditations* (New York: Knopf, 1993), 6.

60. Duffy and Gibbs, *President's Club*, 526.

61. Michael Dobbs, *One Minute to Midnight: Kennedy, Khrushchev, and Castro on the Brink of Nuclear War* (London: Arrow, 2009), 226.

62. Ibid.

63. Ibid., 350.

64. Gaddis, *Cold War*, 52–53.

65. Graham Greene, *The Quiet American* (London: Vintage, 2007), 52.

CHAPTER 2: LEND ME YOUR EARS!
Informers Have Failed Us

1. Greg Clarke, "Taking the 'Con' Out of Deconstruction," *Kategoria* (Autumn 1996), 61.

2. For example, Oxford University's Latin motto is a translation of Psalm 27:1: "The LORD is my light."

3. F. S. Michaels, *Monoculture: How One Story Is Changing Everything* (Kamloops, BC: Red Clover, 2011), 67.

4. Edward L. Bernays, *Propaganda* (Brooklyn, NY: Ig Publishing, 2004), 13.

5. Ibid., 76.

6. Ibid., 77.

7. See Michaels, *Monoculture*, 73.

8. Daniele Fanelli, "How Many Scientists Fabricate and Falsify Research? A Systematic Review and Meta-Analysis of Survey Data," *PLoS ONE* 4(5), May 29, 2009, http://journals.plos.org/plosone/article?id=10.1371/journal.pone.0005738 (accessed October 3, 2014).

9. Quoted in Anthony Seldon, *Trust: How We Lost It and How to Get It Back* (London: Biteback, 2009), 161.

10. See S. L. Titus, J. A. Wells, and L. J. Rhoades, "Repairing Research Integrity," *Nature* 453 (June 19, 2008): 980–82.

11. David Mamet, "Wag the Dog" (movie script), October 14, 1996, www.imsdb.com/scripts/Wag-the-Dog.html (accessed October 3, 2014).

12. See Daniel J. Boorstin, *The Image: A Guide to Pseudo-Events in America* (London: Vintage, 1997).

13. Mamet, "Wag the Dog."

14. Jean Baudrillard, *The Gulf War Did Not Take Place* (Bloomington: Indiana University Press, 2002), 10.

15. Andrew Sparrow, "September 11: 'A Good Day to Bury Bad News,'" *Daily Telegraph*, October 10, 2001, www.telegraph.co.uk/news/uknews/1358985/Sept-11-a-good-day-to-bury-bad-news.html (accessed October 3, 2014).

16. See Frederick Taylor, *The Berlin Wall* (New York: HarperCollins, 2007), 262.

17. Despite the fact that House of Commons clerks are usually very strict about not allowing bills to have politically slanted titles.

18. George Orwell, "Politics and the English Language," in *The English Language: Essays by Linguistics and Men of Letters, 1858–1964*, ed. W. F. Bolton and D. Crystal (Cambridge: Cambridge University Press, 1969), 225.

19. Ibid.

20. Ibid., 226.

21. Jeremy Paxman, "The 2007 James MacTaggart Memorial Lecture," August 24, 2007, www.bbc.co.uk/blogs/legacy/newsnight/2007/08/the_james_mactaggart_memorial_lecture.html (accessed October 3, 2014).

22. See Andrew Roberts, *Napoleon and Wellington: The Long Duel* (London: Orion, 2003), 81.

23. Quoted in Richard Davenport-Hines, *An English Affair: Sex, Class and Power in the Age of Profumo* (London: HarperPress, 2013), 202.

24. Andrew Rawnsley, *The End of the Party* (London: Penguin, 2010), 120, emphasis mine.

25. Marilyn Chandler McEntyre, *Caring for Words in a Culture of Lies* (Grand Rapids: Eerdmans, 2009), 57–58.

26. Quoted in Joshua Levine, *Operation Fortitude: The Story of the Spy Operation That Saved D-Day* (London: Collins, 2011), 197.

27. See ibid., 286.

28. Clay Shirky, *Here Comes Everybody: How Change Happens When People Come Together* (London: Penguin, 2009), 60.

29. Eliane Glaser, *Get Real: How to Tell It Like It Is in a World of Illusions* (London: Fourth Estate, 2012), 46.

30. Thomas Merton, *Conjectures of a Guilty Bystander* (New York: Doubleday, 2009), 238, original emphasis.

31. Ibid. (original emphasis).

32. Ibid.

33. Glaser, *Get Real*, 51.

34. Ibid., 90.

35. Neil Postman, *Amusing Ourselves to Death: Public Discourse in the Age of Show Business* (London: Methuen, 1987), 103.

36. Jacques Ellul, *Propaganda: The Formation of Men's Attitudes* (New York: Knopf, 1973), vi.

37. Steven Swinford, "Osama bin Laden Dead: Blackout during Raid on bin Laden Compound," *Telegraph*, May 4, 2011, www.telegraph.co.uk/news/worldnews/al-qaeda/8493391/Osama-bin-Laden-dead-Blackout-during-raid-on-bin-Laden-compound.html (accessed October 3, 2014).

38. Bernays, *Propaganda*, 21.

39. Quoted in Ellul, *Propaganda: The Formation of Men's Attitudes*, x.

40. Peter Oborne, *The Rise of Political Lying* (London: Free Press, 2005), 6.

41. Ian Kershaw, *The "Hitler Myth": Image and Reality in the Third Reich* (Oxford: Oxford University Press, 1987), 189.

42. Ibid., 214.

CHAPTER 3: SHOULDERS TO CRY ON?
Professional Caregivers Have Failed Us

1. Victoria Ward and Nick Britten, "Music School Abuse Scandal Alleged to Involve Five Top Schools," *Telegraph*, May 8, 2013, www.telegraph.co.uk/news/

uknews/10045117/Music-school-abuse-scandal-alleged-to-involve-five-top-schools.html (accessed October 3, 2014).

2. Ted Gregory, "$10 Million Award in Psychiatry Suit New Blot on Therapy," *Chicago Tribune*, November 7, 1997, http://articles.chicagotribune.com/1997-11-07/news/9711070136_1_false-memories-recovered-memory-therapy-rush (accessed October 3, 2014).

3. David Batty, "Q & A: Harold Shipman," *Guardian*, August 25, 2005, www.theguardian.com/society/2005/aug/25/health.shipman (accessed October 3, 2014).

4. Joseph P. Chinnici, *When Values Collide: The Catholic Church, Sexual Abuse, and the Challenges of Leadership* (Maryknoll, NY: Orbis, 2010), 86.

5. Quoted in Anthony Seldon, *Trust: How We Lost It and How to Get It Back* (London: Biteback, 2009), 138.

6. World Medical Assembly, "Declaration of Geneva," www.wma.net/en/30publications/10policies/g1/ (accessed October 3, 2014).

7. Paul Tournier, *The Violence Within* (New York: Harper, 1978), 134.

8. Ibid., 137.

9. Archive footage and research on the experiment can be found at www.prisonexp.org (accessed October 3, 2014).

10. Philip Zimbardo, *The Lucifer Effect: Understanding How Good People Turn Evil* (New York: Random House, 2008), 173.

11. Ibid., 277.

12. Ibid., 21.

13. Thomas S. Kuhn, *The Structure of Scientific Revolutions*, 3rd ed. (Chicago: University of Chicago Press, 1996).

14. Adolf Guggenbühl-Craig, *Power in the Helping Professions* (Dallas, TX: Spring Publications, 1971), 5.

15. See Orlando Figes, *Just Send Me Word: A True Story of Love and Survival in the Gulag* (London: Allen Lane, 2012), 119.

16. Brendan O'Neill, "Homosexuals Were Once Branded as Mentally Disordered. Now Homophobes Are Treated the Same Way," *Telegraph*, March 4, 2013, http://blogs.telegraph.co.uk/news/brendanoneill2/100205210/homosexuals-were-once-branded-as-mentally-disordered-now-homophobes-are-treated-the-same-way/ (accessed October 3, 2014).

17. See Simon de Bruxelles, "Science 'May One Day Cure Islamic Radicals,'" *The Times*, May 30, 2013, www.thetimes.co.uk/tto/news/uk/article3778053.ece (accessed October 3, 2014).

18. For more information, visit the official Centers for Disease Control and Prevention report at www.cdc.gov/tuskegee/ (accessed October 3, 2014).

19. Peter Knight, *Conspiracy Culture: From Kennedy to The X-Files* (London: Routledge, 2000), 25.

20. See Matthew Goodman, *The Sun and the Moon* (New York: Basic Books, 2008), 98.

21. Ibid., 103.

22. Jürgen Moltmann, *Theology Today* (London: SCM, 1988), 93.

23. Quoted in Steve Wookey, *When a Church Becomes a Cult: The Marks of a New Religious Movement* (London: Hodder & Stoughton, 1996), 35.

24. Quoted in Ronald Enroth, *Recovering from Churches That Abuse* (Grand Rapids: Zondervan, 1994), 17.

25. Herbert L. Rosedale and Michael D. Langone, "On Using the Term 'Cult,'" www.icsahome.com/articles/onusingtermcult (accessed October 3, 2014).

26. See Wookey, *When a Church Becomes a Cult*, 16–17.

27. Candace R. Benyei, *Understanding Clergy Misconduct in Religious Systems: Scapegoating, Family Secrets, and the Abuse of Power* (Binghamton, NY: Haworth, 1998), 59–72.

28. Ibid., 64.

29. Quoted in Enroth, *Recovering from Churches That Abuse*, 33.

30. David R. Miller, *Breaking Free! Rescuing Families from the Clutches of Legalism* (Grand Rapids: Baker, 1992), 34–35.

31. See the helpful, balanced statement from the Lausanne Theology Working Group, www.lausanne.org/content/a-statement-on-the-prosperity-gospel (accessed October 3, 2014).

32. Investigative Staff of *The Boston Globe*, *Betrayal: The Crisis in the Catholic Church* (New York: Little, Brown, 2003), 6.

33. Heather Saul, "Church of England Issues 'Unreserved' Apologies to Victims of Chichester Child Abuse after Investigation Reveals Extent of Failures," *The Independent*, July 8, 2013, www.independent.co.uk/news/uk/church-of-england-issues-unreserved-apologies-to-victims-of-chichester-child-abuse-after-investigation-reveals-extent-of-failures-8695416.html (accessed October 3, 2014).

34. Benyei, *Understanding Clergy Misconduct*, 59.

35. See the website dedicated to the investigation at www.boston.com/globe/spotlight/abuse/ (accessed October 3, 2014).

36. Investigative Staff of *The Boston Globe*, *Betrayal*, 165.

37. Ibid., vii.

38. Ibid., 6.

39. Ibid., 14.

40. Chinnici, *When Values Collide*, 15.

41. See Investigative Staff of *The Boston Globe*, *Betrayal*, 40.

42. Ibid., 96.

43. Ibid., 97.

44. Ibid., 57.

45. For more details, visit Voice of the Faithful's website at www.votf.org (accessed October 3, 2014).

46. Clay Shirky, *Here Comes Everybody: How Change Happens When People Come Together* (London: Penguin, 2009), 159.

PART 2

INTRODUCTION: DISORIENTED FURY:
A Personal Coda

1. Nick Duffell, *The Making of Them: The British Attitude to Children and the Boarding School System* (Bridport, UK: Lone Arrow, 2000), 35.

2. C. S. Lewis, *A Grief Observed* (1961; repr., New York: HarperCollins, 1989), 18–19.

CHAPTER 4: LONELY IN A CROWD:
Alienated and Adrift

1. Anna Funder, *Stasiland: Stories from behind the Berlin Wall* (Cambridge: Granta, 2004), 28.

2. Timothy Garton Ash, *The File* (London: HarperCollins, 1997), 72.

3. Nick Duffell, *The Making of Them* (Bridport, UK: Lone Arrow, 2000), 35.

4. Quoted in George Weigel, *The Cube and the Cathedral: Europe, America, and Politics without God* (New York: Basic Books, 2005), 33.

5. Václav Havel, *The Power of the Powerless* (New York: Routledge, 2009), 56.

6. Václav Haval, "Politics and Conscience," www.dadychery.org/2012/03/25/politics-and-conscience-an-essay-by-vaclav-havel/ (accessed October 3, 2014).

7. Luc Ferry, *A Brief History of Thought* (New York: HarperCollins, 2011); from a confessional position, see Norman L. Geisler and Paul D. Feinberg, *Introduction to Philosophy: A Christian Perspective* (Grand Rapids: Baker, 1987), or at a more popular level, James W. Sire, *The Universe Next Door: A Basic Worldview Catalog* (Downers Grove, IL: InterVarsity, 2009).

8. These summaries are adapted from Dick Keyes, *True Heroism in a World of Counterfeit Celebrities* (Colorado Springs: NavPress, 1995), 39.

9. Keyes, *True Heroism*, 35.

10. See, for example, Ben Macintyre, *Forgotten Fatherland: The Search for Elisabeth Nietzsche* (London: Bloomsbury, 2013).

11. Friedrich Nietzsche, *Beyond Good and Evil: Prelude to a Philosophy of the Future* (Cambridge: Cambridge University Press, 2002), 173, emphasis added.

12. Luc Ferry, *Learning to Live: A User's Manual* (London: Canongate, 2010), 144.

13. Quoted in Peter Knight, *Conspiracy Culture* (London: Routledge, 2000), 99.

14. Quoted in Os Guinness, *Time for Truth: Living Free in a World of Lies, Hype, and Spin* (Grand Rapids: Baker, 2002), 97.

15. Will Self, "Why I Hate Easter," *The Independent*, April 2, 1999, www.independent.co.uk/arts-entertainment/why-i-hate-easter-1084509.html (accessed October 22, 2014).

16. Michel Houellebecq, *Atomised* (London: Vintage, 2001), 354.

17. Joyce Carol Oates, "Adventures in Abandonment," *New York Times*, August 28, 1988, www.nytimes.com/1988/08/28/books/adventures-in-abandonment.html (accessed October 22, 2014).

18. Keyes, *True Heroism*, 40.

19. David Aaronovitch, *Voodoo Histories: How Conspiracy Theory Has Shaped Modern Thought* (London: Vintage, 2010), 102.

20. See Jeffrey N. Wasserstrom, *China in the 21st Century: What Everyone Needs to Know* (Oxford: Oxford University Press, 2013), 52.

21. Garton Ash, *File*, 96.

22. Funder, *Stasiland*, 233.

23. Duffell, *Making of Them*, 35.

24. Timothy Garton Ash, "The Optimists of Davos Past Now Face a World Whose Script Has Gone Awry," *Guardian*, January 26, 2011, www.theguardian.com/commentisfree/2011/jan/26/davos-optimists-face-world-script-awry (accessed October 29, 2014).

25. Quoted in David Lyon, *Karl Marx: An Assessment of His Life and Thought* (Tring: Lion, 1988), 163.

26. John Lewis Gaddis, *The Cold War* (London: Penguin, 2007), 117.

27. Sir Thomas More famously coined the word *utopia* as a Greek play on words: *topos* means "place"; *ou* means "no/not"; and *eu* means "good." Thus a good place is actually no place, a mirage.

28. Quoted in Gaddis, *Cold War*, 186.

29. Eliane Glaser, *Get Real* (London: Fourth Estate, 2012), xii.

30. Havel, *Power of the Powerless*, 25.

31. Anthony Giddens, *Modernity and Self-Identity* (Cambridge: Polity, 1991), 99.

32. Quoted in Marie-Françoise Allain, *The Other Man: Conversations with Graham Greene* (London: Penguin, 1984), 17.

33. David Lyon, *Jesus in Disneyland: Religion in Postmodern Times* (Cambridge: Polity, 2000), 42–43.

34. Quoted in Thurston Clarke, *JFK's Last Hundred Days: An Intimate Portrait of a Great President* (London: Allen Lane, 2013), xi.

35. George Monbiot, "It's Business That Really Rules Us Now," *Guardian*, November 11, 2013, www.theguardian.com/commentisfree/2013/nov/11/business-rules-lobbying-corporate-interests (accessed October 22, 2014).

36. Timothy Egan, "Tapes Show Enron Arranged Plant Shutdown," *New York Times*, February 4, 2005, www.nytimes.com/2005/02/04/national/04energy.html?_r=0 (accessed October 22, 2014).

37. James Kirkup, "Occupy Protesters Were Right, Says Bank of England Official," *Telegraph*, October 29, 2012, www.telegraph.co.uk/finance/newsbysector/banksandfinance/9641806/Occupy-protesters-were-right-says-Bank-of-England-official.html (accessed October 29, 2014).

38. World Bank, "Poverty Overview," April 2014, www.worldbank.org/en/topic/poverty/overview (accessed October 22, 2014).

39. Quoted in George Packer, *The Unwinding: An Inner History of the New America* (New York: Farrar, Straus and Giroux, 2013), 373.

40. Studs Terkel, *Working* (New York: New Press, 1974), 49–50.

41. Naomi Klein, *No Logo: Taking Aim at the Brand Bullies* (London: Flamingo, 2000), 261.

42. Quoted in Rob Parsons, *The Heart of Success: Making It in Business without Losing in Life* (London: Hodder and Stoughton, 2009), 22.

43. F. S. Michaels, *Monoculture* (Kamloops, BC: Red Clover, 2011).

44. Zygmunt Bauman, *Work, Consumerism, and the New Poor* (Buckingham: Open University Press, 1998), 38.

45. Henri J. M. Nouwen, *Lifesigns: Intimacy, Fecundity, and Ecstasy in Christian Perspective* (New York: Doubleday, 1989), 12.

46. Carne Ross, *The Leadership Revolution: How Ordinary People Will Take Power and Change Politics in the 21st Century* (London: Penguin, 2013), 16.

47. Packer, *Unwinding*, 4.

48. Michaels, *Monoculture*, 17.

49. Ibid., 33.

50. Peter Sloterdijk, *Critique of Cynical Reason* (Minneapolis: University of Minnesota Press, 1987), 5.

51. "I Am a Rock," lyrics by Paul Simon (1965).

52. Nicholas Negroponte, *Being Digital* (New York: Vintage, 1995), 151.

53. Funder, *Stasiland*, 267.

54. Garton Ash, *File*, 223–24.

CHAPTER 5: LOST IN THE WILDERNESS OF MIRRORS:
Betrayal and Paranoia

1. Glenn Greenwald, *No Place to Hide: Edward Snowden, the NSA, and the U.S. Surveillance State* (New York: Metropolitan, 2014), 3.

2. C. S. Lewis, *Mere Christianity* (New York: Macmillan, 1943), 104.

3. Christopher Bigsby, ed., *The Portable Arthur Miller* (London: Penguin, 2003), 325.

4. Cited in Frederic Spotts, *Hitler and the Power of the New Aesthetic*, rev. ed. (London: Pimlico, 2003), 36.

5. Stuart Sim, *Irony and Crisis: A Critical History of Postmodern Culture* (Cambridge: Icon, 2002), 7.

6. Peter Knight, *Conspiracy Culture* (London: Routledge, 2000), 3, emphasis mine.

7. Matthew J. Bruccoli and Judith S. Baughman, eds., *Conversations with John le Carré* (Jackson: University Press of Mississippi, 2005), 36.

8. Ibid., 43.

9. Francis Wheen, *Strange Days Indeed: The 1970s; The Golden Age of Paranoia* (New York: PublicAffairs, 2010).

10. Timothy Melley, *The Covert Sphere* (Ithaca, NY: Cornell University Press, 2012), 34.

11. See Ronald Kessler, "James Angleton's Dangerous CIA Legacy," *Newsmax*, March 28, 2012, www.newsmax.com/Newsfront/James-Angleton-CIA-spies/2012/03/28/id/434109 (accessed October 29, 2014).

12. Flannery O'Connor, *Mystery and Manners: Occasional Prose* (New York: Farrar, Straus and Giroux, 1969), 77–78.

13. See Ben Macintyre, *For Your Eyes Only: Ian Fleming and James Bond* (London: Bloomsbury, 2009), 5.

14. Frederick P. Hitz, "The Reality Is Stranger Than Fiction: Anglo-American Intelligence Cooperation from World War II through the Cold War," in *Intelligence Studies in Britain and the US*, ed. Christopher R. Moran and Christopher J. Murphy (Edinburgh: Edinburgh University Press, 2013), 179.

15. Macintyre, *For Your Eyes Only*, 197.

16. Kim Philby, *My Silent War* (New York: Modern Library, 2002).

17. Macintyre, *For Your Eyes Only*, x.

18. Walter Lippman, *Liberty and the News* (New York: Harcourt, Brace and Howe, 1920), 64.

19. Jacques Barzun, "Findings: Meditations on the Literature of Spying," *American Scholar* (Spring 1965), http://theamericanscholar.org/meditations-on-the-literature-of-spying/#.VFJvGITD-70 (accessed October 29, 2014).

20. Melley, *Covert Sphere*, 26 (original emphasis).

21. Ibid., 25.

22. Ibid., 111.

23. Quoted in Knight, *Conspiracy Culture*, 1.

24. Quoted in Wheen, *Strange Days Indeed*, 11.

25. Quoted in Knight, *Conspiracy Culture*, 14 (original emphasis).

26. Andrew Rawnsley, *The End of the Party* (London: Penguin, 2010), 338.

27. Carne Ross, *The Leadership Revolution* (London: Penguin, 2013), 15.

28. Wheen, *Strange Days Indeed*, 166.

29. Frank Gardner, "MI5 Chief Andrew Parker Warns of Islamist Threat to UK," *BBC News* online, October 9, 2013, www.bbc.com/news/uk-24424596 (accessed October 29, 2014).

30. Greenwald, *No Place to Hide*, 209.

31. Ian Traynor and Paul Lewis, "Merkel Compared NSA to Stasi in Heated Encounter with Obama," *Guardian*, December 17, 2013, www.theguardian.com/world/2013/dec/17/merkel-compares-nsa-stasi-obama (accessed October 29, 2014).

32. Cited in Greenwald, *No Place to Hide*, 176.

33. Melley, *Covert Sphere*, 28.

34. See Laura Bergquist, *A Very Special President* (New York: McGraw-Hill, 1965), 15.

35. Melley, *Covert Sphere*, 29.

36. Thurston Clarke, *JFK's Last Hundred Days* (London: Allen Lane, 2013), 96–97.

37. John Lewis Gaddis, *The Cold War* (London: Penguin, 2007), 104.

38. Cited in Wheen, *Strange Days Indeed*, 152.

39. Ibid., 98.

40. Ibid., 260.

41. Ibid., 71.

42. Andrew Marantz, "Unreality Star: The Paranoid Used to Fear the CIA. Now Their Delusions Mirror 'The Truman Show,'" *New Yorker* (September 16, 2013), 33, www.newyorker.com/magazine/2013/09/16/unreality-star (accessed October 29, 2014).

43. Ibid., 34.

44. John le Carré, *The Honourable Schoolboy* (New York: Scribner, 2002), 588.

45. Mark Roseman, *The Villa, the Lake, the Meeting: Wannsee and the Final Solution* (London: Penguin, 2003), 19.

46. Hannah Arendt, *The Origins of Totalitarianism* (New York: Harcourt, 1973), 7.

47. Don DeLillo, *Running Dog* (New York: Vintage, 1989), 111.

48. Bruccoli and Baughman, *Conversations with John le Carré*, 48.

49. David Aaronovitch, *Voodoo Histories* (London: Vintage, 2010), 10–14.

50. U.S. Department of Defense, "News Transcript: Secretary Rumsfeld Press Conference at NATO Headquarters, Brussels, Belgium," June 6, 2002, www.defense.gov/transcripts/transcript.aspx?transcriptid=3490 (accessed October 29, 2014).

51. Marrs has self-published the protocols and written an introduction to them ("The Man Who Gave the World the Protocols of Zion"), www.texemarrs.com/122011/man_who_gave_protocols.htm (accessed October 29, 2014).

52. Quoted in Gregory S. Camp, *Selling Fear: Conspiracy Theories and End-Times Paranoia* (Grand Rapids: Revell, 1997), 176.

53. Aaronovitch, *Voodoo Histories*, 326.

54. See Camp, *Selling Fear*, 13.

55. Hanging chads hit the headlines in the notorious Bush versus Gore election of 2000, as a result of disputes over Florida's recount of ballots.

56. See Knight, *Conspiracy Culture*, 147.

57. Jawanza Kunjufu, *Countering the Conspiracy to Destroy Black Boys* (Chicago: African American Images, 1995), 1–2.

58. Quoted in Gaddis, *Cold War*, 192.

59. Peter L. Berger, *A Rumor of Angels: Modern Society and the Rediscovery of the Supernatural* (New York: Anchor, 1970), 16.

60. Barbara Tuchman, *Stilwell and the American Experience in China, 1911–45* (New York: Macmillan, 1971), 132.

PART 3

INTRODUCTION: FLEEING OR YIELDING TO THE MATRIX

1. Alister McGrath, "Address to CCCU [Council for Christian Colleges and Universities] International Forum," Grapevine, TX, April 1, 2006.

CHAPTER 6: TRUST NO ONE?
An Ancient Hermeneutic of Suspicion

1. Graham Greene, *The Honorary Consul* (London: Vintage, 2004), 34.

2. H. G. Wells, *A Short History of the World* (London: Penguin, 2007), 344.

3. Quoted in Timothy J. Keller, *The Reason for God: Belief in an Age of Skepticism* (New York: Dutton, 2008), 159.

4. Quoted in Os Guinness, *Time for Truth* (Grand Rapids: Baker, 2002), 109.

5. Quoted in Ross Gregory Douthat, *Bad Religion: How We Became a Nation of Heretics* (New York: Free Press, 2012), 20.

6. W. H. Auden, "As I Walked Out One Evening," in *Collected Poems: W. H. Auden*, ed. Edward Mendelson (New York: Modern Library, 2007), 135.

7. Quoted in Timothy J. Keller, *King's Cross: The Story of the World in the Life of Jesus* (London: Hodder and Stoughton, 2012), 77.

8. Alister E. McGrath, *The Twilight of Atheism: The Rise and Fall of Disbelief in the Modern World* (London: Random House, 2005), 230.

9. These have been unpacked with trenchant skill by Glynn Harrison in *The Big Ego Trip* (Nottingham: Inter-Varsity, 2013) and Ross Douthat in chapter 7 of *Bad Religion*.

10. Arthur Schlesinger Jr., foreword to *Niebuhr and His Age*, by Charles C. Brown (Harrisburg, PA: Trinity Press, 2002), viii–ix.

11. Rowan Williams, *The Lion's World: A Journey into the Heart of Narnia* (London: SPCK, 2012), 22.

12. C. S. Lewis, *Prince Caspian* (London: Collins, 1998), 212.

13. G. K. Chesterton, *The Scandal of Father Brown* (London: Penguin, 2013), 34.

14. Christopher J. H. Wright, *Old Testament Ethics for the People of God* (Downers Grove, IL: InterVarsity, 2004), 118.

15. The global ministry of A Rocha ("the rock," in Portuguese), whose tagline is "Caring for God's Earth," is an inspiring antidote to these attitudes; for more, visit www.arocha.org.

16. Wright, *Old Testament Ethics*, 123.

17. Victor Lee Austin, *Up with Authority: Why We Need Authority to Flourish as Human Beings* (New York: T&T Clark, 2010), 149.

18. Marci Shore, *The Taste of Ashes: The Afterlife of Totalitarianism in Eastern Europe* (New York: Broadway Books, 2013), 101.

19. Blaise Pascal, *Pensées* (Mineola, NY: Dover, 2003), 108.

20. Dick Keyes, *True Heroism in a World of Counterfeit Celebrities* (Colorado Springs: NavPress, 1995), 26.

21. The Hebrew text here literally means, "Eating you may eat," in parallel with Genesis 2:17, "Dying you will die." This is an idiomatic way of emphasizing the certainty of the statement. So freedom is a perfectly legitimate inference from this, which is why it is commonly used in translation.

22. Francis Spufford, *Unapologetic: Why, Despite Everything, Christianity Can Still Make Surprising Emotional Sense* (London: Faber and Faber, 2012), 27–28.

23. Keyes, *True Heroism*, 122.

24. Pascal, *Pensées*, 115.

25. John le Carré, private conversation, May 2013.

26. John le Carré, private conversation.

27. Pascal, *Pensées*, 121.

28. G. K. Chesterton, *Orthodoxy* (Chicago: Moody, 2009), 28.

29. John Bennett, "Christian Realism: A Symposium," *Christianity and Crisis* 28.14 (August 5, 1968): 176.

30. See Alan Jacobs, *Original Sin: A Cultural History* (New York: HarperCollins, 2008), 150.

31. Graham Greene, *The Quiet American* (London: Vintage, 2007), vii.

32. Quoted in Marie-Françoise Allain, *The Other Man* (London: Penguin, 1984), 163.

33. Andy Crouch, *Playing God* (Downers Grove, IL: InterVarsity, 2013), 167.

34. See Jacobs, *Original Sin*, 236.

35. *New Yorker*, March 3, 2014, 40.

36. See Glenn Greenwald, *No Place to Hide* (New York: Metropolitan, 2014), 97.

37. Quoted in Charles Milner Atkinson, *Jeremy Bentham: His Life and Work* (London: Methuen, 1905), 84–85.

38. David Lyon, *Surveillance Studies: An Overview* (Cambridge: Polity, 2007), 57.

39. J. Robert Oppenheimer, "The Atom Bomb and College Education," in *The General Magazine and Historical Chronicle* (1946), 265.

40. See James A. Hijiya, "The *Gita* of J. Robert Oppenheimer," *Proceedings of the American Philosophical Society* 144.2 (June 2000): 123–24.

41. Norman Stone, *World War Two: A Short History* (London: Penguin, 2014), 160.

42. P. J. O'Rourke, *All the Trouble in the World* (New York: Atlantic Monthly Press, 1994), 2.

43. See J. Richard Middleton and Brian Walsh, *Truth Is Stranger Than It Used to Be: Biblical Faith in a Postmodern Age* (Downers Grove, IL: InterVarsity, 1995), 9.

44. See "Obituary: Saparmurat Niyazov," *Telegraph*, December 22, 2006, www.telegraph.co.uk/news/obituaries/1537565/Saparmurat-Niyazov.html (accessed October 29, 2014).

45. Richard Keyes, *Chameleon or Tribe? Recovering Authentic Christian Community* (Leicester: Inter-Varsity, 1999), 72.

46. Gene E. Veith, *Guide to Contemporary Culture* (Wheaton, IL: Crossway, 1994), 63.

47. Aldous Huxley, *Ends and Means* (London: Chatto and Windus, 1937), 270.

48. Timothy Garton Ash, *The File* (London: HarperCollins, 1997), 172.

49. Harry Emerson Fosdick, *On Being a Real Person* (New York: Harper, 1943), 83.

50. Quoted in Ian Morgan Cron, *Jesus, My Father, the CIA, and Me* (Nashville: Nelson, 2011), 15.

51. A beautiful expression of this reality can be found in Miriam Jones's haunting song "I Am One" on her 2007 album, *Being Here*.

52. Veith, *Guide to Contemporary Culture*, 57.

53. Otto Dov Kulka, *Landscapes of the Metropolis of Death* (London: Allen Lane, 2013), 9.

54. Crouch, *Playing God*, 134.

55. Ibid., 54.

56. Quoted in David Remnick, "Putin and the Exile," *New Yorker*, April 26, 2014, www.newyorker.com/magazine/2014/04/28/putin-and-the-exile (accessed October 29, 2014).

57. Quoted in Cron, *Jesus, My Father, the CIA, and Me*, 136.

58. Václav Havel, *The Power of the Powerless* (New York: Routledge, 2009), 20.

59. Marci Shore, *The Taste of Ashes* (New York: Broadway Books, 2013), 357.

60. Aleksandr I. Solzhenitsyn, *The Gulag Archipelago* (London: Harvill, 2003), 312.

61. Quoted in Franklin H. Littell, "First They Came for the Jews," *Christian Ethics Today* 9 (February 1997): 29, http://christianethicstoday.com/cetart/index.cfm?fuseaction=Articles.main&ArtID=155 (accessed October 29, 2014).

62. Kofi Annan, *Interventions* (London: Allen Lane, 2012), 299.

63. Quoted in Gene D. Phillips, ed., *Stanley Kubrick Interviews* (Jackson: University Press of Mississippi, 2001), 73.

64. Miroslav Volf, *Exclusion and Embrace* (Nashville: Abingdon, 1996), 304.

65. Mary Eberstadt, *The Loser Letters: A Comic Tale of Life, Death, and Atheism* (San Francisco: Ignatius, 2010), 43.

CHAPTER 7: TRUST THIS ONE!
Dominion in Safe Hands

1. Quoted in Marci Shore, *The Taste of Ashes* (New York: Broadway Books, 2013), 13.

2. Tony Benn, *Letters to My Grandchildren: Thoughts on the Future* (London: Random House, 2009), 49.

3. N. Thomas Wright, "Jesus and the Identity of God," *Ex Auditu* 14 (1998): 42–56, http://ntwrightpage.com/Wright_JIG.htm#_edn20 (accessed October 29, 2014).

4. David B. Capes, "Carmen Christi—Hymn to Christ," http://davidbcapes.com/2013/06/21/carmen-christi-hymn-to-christ/ (accessed October 29, 2014).

5. Andreas Köstenburger and Michael Kruger, *The Heresy of Orthodoxy* (Wheaton, IL: Crossway, 2010), 81.

6. Robin Griffith-Jones, *The Da Vinci Code and the Secrets of the Temple* (Norwich, UK: Canterbury, 2006), 9.

7. N. T. Wright, *Creation, Power, and Truth: The Gospel in a World of Cultural Confusion* (London: SPCK, 2013), 43.

8. H. Richard Niebuhr, *The Meaning of Revelation* (New York: Macmillan, 1941), 154.

9. Václav Havel, *The Power of the Powerless* (New York: Routledge, 2009), 17.

10. Ibid., 12.

11. Quoted in Augustus Granville Stapleton, *George Canning and His Time* (London: Parker, 1859), 67.

12. Rowan Williams, *The Lion's World: A Journey into the Heart of Narnia* (London: SPCK, 2012), 50.

13. George Packer, *The Unwinding* (New York: Farrar, Straus and Giroux, 2013), 115.

14. Alain de Botton, *Status Anxiety* (London: Penguin, 2005), 3–4.

15. D. A. Carson, *The Gospel According to John* (Leicester: Inter-Varsity, 1991), 461.

16. Cited in Francis Wheen, *Strange Days Indeed* (New York: PublicAffairs, 2010), 77.

17. Havel, *Power of the Powerless*, 21–28.

18. G. K. Chesterton, *The Collected Works of G. K. Chesterton*, vol. 7 (San Francisco: Ignatius, 1986), 152.

19. Timothy J. Keller, *King's Cross* (London: Hodder and Stoughton, 2012), 191.

20. D. A. Carson, *Scandalous: The Cross and Resurrection of Jesus* (Wheaton, IL: Crossway, 2010), 21.

21. Andy Crouch, *Playing God* (Downers Grove, IL: InterVarsity, 2013), 287.

22. Quoted in David Lyon, *Jesus in Disneyland* (Cambridge: Polity, 2000), 136.

23. Graham Tomlin, *The Power of the Cross: Theology and the Death of Christ in Paul, Luther, and Pascal* (Carlisle: Paternoster, 1999), 279.

24. For a much fuller treatment, see my own *Cross-Examined* (Leicester: Inter-Varsity, 2005).

25. Octavius Winslow, *No Condemnation in Christ Jesus* (Edinburgh: Banner of Truth, 1991), 358.

26. When sociologist Rodney Stark wrote his account of early Christianity, he completely ducked the question of the resurrection's historicity. He merely said that "on the morning of the third day *something happened* that turned the Christian sect into a cult movement" (*The Rise of Christianity* [San Francisco: HarperSanFrancisco, 1997], 44, emphasis mine). That is hardly enough to go on, though! Many books tackle this fundamental question well: Paul Copan and Ronald K. Tacelli, eds., *Jesus' Resurrection: Fact or Figment?* (Downers Grove, IL: InterVarsity, 2000); Frank Morrison, *Who Moved the Stone?* (Milton Keynes, UK: Authentic Media, 2006); John Wenham, *Easter Enigma* (Eugene, OR: Wipf & Stock, 2005).

27. Philip H. Kern, "'The Word of the Cross': The Language of the Cross in 1 Corinthians," in *The Wisdom of the Cross: Exploring 1 Corinthians*, ed. Brian S. Rosner (Nottingham: Inter-Varsity, 2011), 94.

28. Ian Morgan Cron, *Jesus, My Father, the CIA, and Me* (Nashville: Nelson, 2011), 174.

29. Crouch, *Playing God*, 293.

30. Friedrich Nietzsche, *The Gay Science* (New York: Vintage, 1974), 228.

31. Tomlin, *Power of the Cross*, 304.

32. Crouch, *Playing God*, 45.

CHAPTER 8: THE SAFEST PLACE ON EARTH?
A Community with Integrity

1. Steven Gish, *Desmond Tutu: A Biography* (Westport, CT: Greenwood, 2004), 101.

2. See Lamin O. Sanneh, *Translating the Message: The Missionary Impact on Culture* (Maryknoll, NY: Orbis, 2009).

3. Nelson Mandela, *Long Walk to Freedom* (Boston: Little, Brown, 1994), 38.

4. Ross Douthat, *Bad Religion* (New York: Free Press, 2012), 132.

5. Quoted in Margot Patterson, "At Kansas L'Arche Community, Love Is the Not-So-Secret Ingredient," *National Catholic Reporter* online, November 1, 2002, www.natcath.org/NCR_Online/archives/110102/110102m.htm (accessed October 29, 2014).

6. Fernando Flores and Robert C. Solomon, "Creating Trust," *Business Ethics Quarterly* 8.2 (April 1988): 225.

7. This theme was affectingly explored by John Stott in the penultimate chapter of his final book, *The Radical Disciple* (Nottingham: Inter-Varsity, 2010), 103–13.

8. Quoted in David W. Smith, *The Kindness of God: Christian Witness in Our Troubled World* (Nottingham: Inter-Varsity, 2013), 147.

9. See Chris Green, *The Message of the Church* (Nottingham: Inter-Varsity, 2013), 35.

10. Christopher Ash's *Remaking a Broken World* (Milton Keynes: Authentic Media, 2010) is a superb survey of the Bible's story from Genesis to Revelation through the lens of God's gathering of a scattered humanity.

11. Rodney Stark, *The Rise of Christianity* (San Francisco: HarperSanFrancisco, 1997), 7.

12. Francis Schaeffer, *The Mark of the Christian* (Downers Grove, IL: InterVarsity, 2006), 26.

13. Lesslie Newbigin, *The Gospel in a Pluralist Society* (Grand Rapids: Eerdmans, 1989), 227.

14. Larry Crabb, *The Safest Place on Earth: Where People Connect and Are Forever Changed* (Nashville: Nelson, 1999), 35.

15. N. T. Wright, *After You Believe: Why Christian Character Matters* (San Francisco: HarperOne, 2012), 184.

16. Dietrich Bonhoeffer, *Life Together* (London: SCM, 2008), 25.

17. Crabb, *Safest Place on Earth*, 34.

18. C. S. Lewis, *The Weight of Glory, and Other Addresses* (New York: HarperCollins, 2001), 182.

19. Smith, *Kindness of God*, 147.

20. C. S. Lewis, *The Four Loves* (New York: Houghton Mifflin Harcourt, 1971), 78.

21. Bonhoeffer, *Life Together*, 86.

22. Crabb, *Safest Place on Earth*, xiii.

23. Dietrich Bonhoeffer, *The Cost of Discipleship* (London: SCM, 2001), 45.

24. Jean Vanier, *From Brokenness to Community* (Mahwah, NJ: Paulist, 1992), 40.

25. Eugene Peterson, foreword to *The Safest Place on Earth*, by Larry Crabb (Nashville: Nelson, 1999), viii.

26. Lewis, *Weight of Glory*, 141–57.

27. Quoted in Richard N. Longenecker, *Galatians* (Waco, TX: Word, 1990), 157.

28. World Vision International, "Hope for the Girl Child: A Briefing Paper to the United Nations Commission on the Status of Women at Its 51st Session" (2007), 8, www.essex.ac.uk/armedcon/story_id/000769.pdf (accessed October 29, 2014).

29. Alan Jacobs, *Original Sin* (New York: HarperCollins, 2008), 53.

30. Quoted in Stark, *Rise of Christianity*, 83.

31. Roy Hattersley, "Faith Does Breed Charity: We Atheists Have to Accept That Most Believers Are Better Human Beings," *Guardian*, September 12, 2005, www. theguardian.com/world/2005/sep/12/religion.uk (accessed October 29, 2014).

32. Richard Keyes, *Chameleon or Tribe?* (Leicester: Inter-Varsity, 1999), 51.

33. Ibid., 111–12.

34. D. A. Carson offers a fuller treatment of forgiveness and reconciliation in *Love in Hard Places* (Wheaton, IL: Crossway, 2002), 71–85.

35. Onora O'Neill, *A Question of Trust* (Cambridge: Cambridge University Press, 2002), 25.

36. Peter L. Berger, *A Rumor of Angels* (New York: Anchor, 1970), 32.

37. See David Lyon, *Jesus in Disneyland* (Cambridge: Polity, 2000), 34.

38. Andy Crouch, *Playing God* (Downers Grove, IL: InterVarsity, 2013), 226.

39. Victor Lee Austin, *Up with Authority* (New York: T&T Clark, 2010), 31.

40. Bonhoeffer, *Life Together*, 85.

41. Graham Tomlin, *The Power of the Cross* (Carlisle: Paternoster, 1999), 280.

42. Stephen Arterburn and Jack Felton, *Toxic Faith: Experiencing Healing from Painful Spiritual Abuse* (Colorado Springs: WaterBrook, 2001), 155.

43. Sir Charles P. Snow, "Either-Or," *Progressive* 25 (February 1961): 24.

44. See Stark, *Rise of Christianity*, 11.

45. Tomlin, *Power of the Cross*, 31.

46. Quoted in Roger Haydon Mitchell, *Church, Gospel, and Empire: How the Politics of Sovereignty Impregnated the West* (Eugene, OR: Wipf and Stock, 2011), 183.

47. Tomlin, *Power of the Cross*, 312.

48. Andy Crouch, "A Community of Foes," *Re:generation Quarterly* 7 (Winter 2001): 3.

49. John R. W. Stott, *Christian Mission in the Modern World* (Downers Grove, IL: InterVarsity, 2008), 17.

CHAPTER 9: EVERYTHING *IS* CONNECTED!
Relishing the True Story

1. Walter Brueggemann, *Theology of the Old Testament* (Minneapolis: Fortress, 2005), 206.

2. Roger Scruton, *Modern Culture*, 2nd ed. (London: Continuum, 2007), 63.

3. Marilyn Chandler McEntyre, *Caring for Words in a Culture of Lies* (Grand Rapids: Eerdmans, 2009), 132.

4. Luc Ferry, *A Brief History of Thought* (New York: HarperCollins, 2011), 72.

5. Vishal Mangawaldi, *The Book That Made Your World: How the Bible Created the Soul of Western Civilization* (Nashville: Nelson, 2012), 181.

6. Peter J. Leithart, *Solomon among the Postmoderns* (Grand Rapids: Baker, 2008), 33.

7. John Gray, *Straw Dogs: Thoughts on Humans and Other Animals* (London: Granta, 2002), 173.

8. Quoted in Francis Spufford, *Red Plenty* (London: Faber and Faber, 2010), 4.

9. Ben Lewis, *Hammer & Tickle: The History of Communism Told through Communist Jokes* (London: Phoenix, 2009), 306.

10. Scruton, *Modern Culture*, 68.

11. Ibid., 80.

12. Ibid., 18.

13. Julian Barnes, *Nothing to Be Frightened Of* (London: Vintage, 2009), 1.

14. Ibid., 118.

15. Frederick Taylor, *The Berlin Wall* (New York: HarperCollins, 2007), 363.

16. Julian Barnes, *Levels of Life* (London: Vintage, 2014), 86.

17. Ibid.

18. Václav Havel, *Open Letters: Selected Writings, 1965–1990* (London: Faber and Faber, 1991), 95.

19. Cited in Steven Garber, *Visions of Vocation* (Downers Grove, IL: InterVarsity, 2014), 97.

20. Sonia Orwell and Ian Angus, eds., *The Collected Essays: Essays, Journalism, and Letters of George Orwell*, vol. 2 (London: Secker and Warburg, 1968), 15–16.

21. David Mamet, *Three Uses of the Knife: On the Nature and Purpose of Drama* (New York: Vintage, 2000), 3.

22. Quoted in Leslie Garis, "Susan Sontag Finds Romance," *New York Times*, August 2, 1992, www.nytimes.com/books/00/03/12/specials/sontag-magromance.html (accessed October 29, 2014).

23. Douglas Coupland, *Player One: What Is to Become of Us; A Novel in Five Hours* (London: Windmill, 2011), 5.

24. Richard Hofstadter, *The Paranoid Style in American Politics* (Cambridge, MA: Harvard University Press, 1996), 36–37.

25. William Manchester, "No Evidence for a Conspiracy to Kill Kennedy," *New York Times*, February 5, 1992, www.nytimes.com/1992/02/05/opinion/l-no-evidence-for-a-conspiracy-to-kill-kennedy-809692.html (accessed October 29, 2014).

26. Quoted in Marie-Françoise Allain, *The Other Man* (London: Penguin, 1984), 131.

27. Donna Tartt, "Spirit and Writer in a Secular World," in *The Novel, Spirituality, and Modern Culture*, ed. Paul Fiddes (Cardiff: University of Wales Press, 2000), 38.

28. Dan B. Allender, *To Be Told: God Invites You to Coauthor Your Future* (Colorado Springs: WaterBrook, 2006), 60.

29. Quoted in Alex Ross, "Bach and Belief," *New Yorker*, October 10, 2009, www.newyorker.com/culture/alex-ross/bach-and-belief (accessed October 29, 2014).

30. C. S. Lewis, *Mere Christianity* (New York: Macmillan, 1960), 120.

31. Ted Turnau, *Popologetics: Popular Culture in a Christian Perspective* (Phillipsburg, NJ: P & R, 2012), 256–57.

32. Reinhold Niebuhr, *The Nature and Destiny of Man: A Christian Interpretation*, vol. 2 (New York: Scribner, 1964), 294.

33. Peter L. Berger, *A Rumor of Angels* (New York: Anchor, 1970), 88.

34. Cited in Dick Keyes, *True Heroism in a World of Counterfeit Celebrities* (Colorado Springs: NavPress, 1995), 116.

35. Dietrich Bonhoeffer, *Ethics* (New York: Touchstone, 1995), 125–32.

36. Quoted in Turnau, *Popologetics*, 267.

37. T. S. Eliot, *Four Quartets* (London: Faber and Faber, 2001), 43.

38. Julian of Norwich, *Revelations of Divine Love*, chapter 27, *Christian Classics Ethereal Library* online, www.ccel.org/ccel/julian/revelations.xiv.i.html (accessed October 29, 2014).